SHE TURNED HER HEAD AWAY

An Adoption Memoir

SHE TURNED HER HEAD AWAY

An Adoption Memoir

PATRICIA MOFFAT

CROWSNEST BOOKS

Crowsnest Books

www.crowsnestbooks.com

Distributed by the University of Toronto Press

Edited by Allister Thompson

Proofreader: Britanie Wilson

Cataloguing data available from Library and Archives Canada

ISBN 978-0921332-64-0 (paperback)

ISBN 978-0921332-65-7 (ebook)

Printed and bound in Canada

CONTENTS

For my grandchildren,

biological and step,

with love:

Nico, Tara,

Jasper, Nathan,

Clara, Lucas,

Georgia Grace

INTRODUCTION

Being adopted is not the worst thing that can happen to a child. It's not like being born in a war zone or with a severe disability. But it is a bit like having your whole family die on you. It's like discovering that you were actually sort of an orphan taken in by strangers who then became the only family you know. Some of us are lucky and fit right in with our adoptive families. Others rebel and act out.

But orphans usually know who and where they came from and can seek connections through photographs and conversations with people who knew their parents. Those millions of us from the institution of closed adoption have no such options. The door to the past was firmly locked, with only a few pieces of information rationed out. And everyone pretends that this is fine, this is normal, aren't you lucky to have such a clean slate to write your life upon and to be part of such a nice family now?

I have found that most people who are not adopted tend to trivialize the feelings that many adopted children and adults struggle with. If you are not adopted, for example, it is difficult to imagine what it must be like not to know anyone in the entire world to whom you are related by blood. Most people take family heritage and genetic relationships so much for granted that they sometimes joke they'd feel relieved not to be related to their families. And so they may react with surprise or disapproval when hearing that an adult adoptee wishes to search for her biological family. They may wonder how she could be so ungrateful, so hurtful to her adoptive parents.

Most people who aren't adopted can't imagine what it's like never to have heard the story of your own birth (how your parents woke suddenly in the middle of the night, it was in a snowstorm/it was in the hottest July on record, how you were almost born in the taxi/in the elevator) but to have, instead, an uncomfortable, even painful sense of being unwanted, given away, being not good enough to keep. The story of our adoption day, pleasant though it may be from the viewpoint of our adoptive parents, often just opens up more questions.

Of course times are changing in adoption today. Open adoption — where birth parents keep in contact with their relinquished children and their adoptive parents in varying degrees through life — was virtually unheard of when I was adopted in the mid-1940s, but is increasingly common today. Adoptees from open adoptions have no need to search for birth parents and grow up without most of the questions that plague adoptees from the closed system.

Sealed adoption records are opening up in many North American jurisdictions, making it much easier for birth relatives to connect. Often, now, a connection can be made simply by putting one's name and basic information on a registry. However, the emotional questions around reunions, the worries about hurting adoptive parents, and the unknowns about what sorts of relationships will develop with birth relatives are similar to the emotions and questions that arose in me in the 1970s, an adoptee searching from within the closed adoption system.

This is my personal story of adoption, reunion, and reconciliation. I hope it will speak to you, whether you are an adoptee, a birth parent, or an adoptive parent, or even if you have no personal connection to adoption but have other challenges in your life and other quests to pursue. For I feel that all personal quests share a similar goal: to find the key that will unlock the heart.

PATRICIA MOFFAT

Parents (adoptive) Kate & George on their honeymoon in Banff, early 1940s

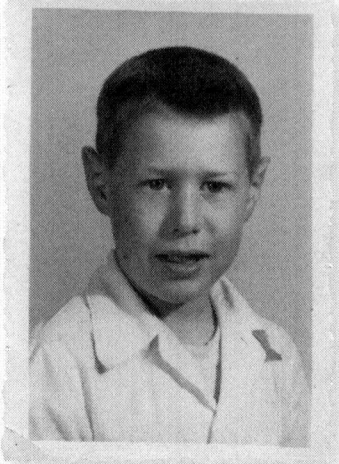

Adoptive brother Rick, Age 7

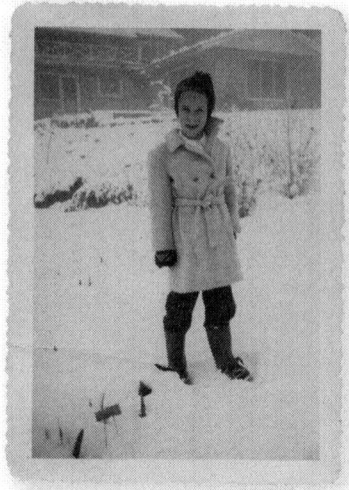

Me with a rare snowfall at our Ukiah home

Mom's parents, Grandma & Grandpa Boyd (Wilhemina and Jack)

PART I:
CURTAINS PARTING

The earliest photo of me, Ukiah

CHAPTER 1

On a warm June evening in Toronto in 1976, I'm kneading bread dough in the kitchen. The kids are asleep upstairs — Derek has just turned two, and Tessa is four months old — while Harald is watching TV in the living room. I just let my thoughts wander as I push the dough, turn, fold, and push again; push, turn, fold, and push again.

Going on sabbatical this December, nine months long. I'm so glad we've decided on California! It'll be wonderful to be near Mom, Dad, and Rick again. They can get to know Derek and Tessa better, not just a rushed trip at Christmas or Easter. And how lucky to miss a whole Canadian winter! We'll rent this house out then find a place to rent on the Monterey Peninsula....

"Hey, are you finished in there?" Harald switches off the TV and strolls out to the kitchen. As I cover the loaf pans with damp tea towels, I glance over to see him leaning against the doorframe, his muscular body clad in shorts and T-shirt, his wavy, prematurely graying hair backlit by the hall light. "There's something I want to talk to you about," he continues.

When we've settled into our usual places in the living room — Harald on the wide orange couch and me cross-legged on the floor at the round coffee table — he launches the missile that will change our lives.

"I've been wondering, since we're going to be in California next year," he begins matter-of-factly, "whether you've thought about looking for your natural parents while we're out there."

"What? Oh no, Harald, no!" I respond immediately, shocked. "Of course I haven't thought about that! I couldn't possibly do that. Why are you bringing this up?" I reach quickly for the pack of cigarettes on the table and light up.

"Well, I know you've been thinking about your birth parents quite a lot lately. You've said so. I'm just wondering whether it might be a good idea to do something about it. We probably won't have the chance again to be out there for such a long time. That's where you were born and adopted. That's where all your records would be."

I can't even look at this. My mind is numb, and my hands have begun to tremble. "Harald, just think of what you're suggesting! Mom and Dad! No, this is out of the question, it really is."

"You think they couldn't take it?" he continues, pushing. "Your parents are reasonable, understanding people."

"About most things yes, but about this? No, no, it would be like a slap in the face to them. I'm their daughter! Can't you imagine how they would feel?"

"Why is it, then, that you've been thinking so much about your birth parents lately, especially your mother?"

"Isn't that obvious? I can't help it now, with the kids — having my own children. But it's like ... she's miles and miles away from my real life. She's just in my imagination. Maybe I'll stop thinking about her as the kids get older."

"Maybe, maybe not. But what about you? Do you think it might be good for you if you knew who your mother was?"

The trembling increases as I shift my focus from Mom and Dad to myself — and to that darkness at the beginning of my life, to that void from which I sprang into the waiting arms of my adoptive parents, to that shadow mother who has accompanied me through my life, her presence, her absence, sometimes benevolent, other times threatening.

The psychic nerve that Harald has exposed throbs now. A wave of sadness and longing washes through me, bringing tears. Harald moves down from the couch to the floor beside me and puts his arm around my shoulder. "I'm not sure whether it would be good for me to know who my mother is or not," I finally reply. "Maybe it's best to just go on wondering about her than to really find out."

"Are you afraid of her?" Harald's questions reveal his many years of undergoing psychotherapy.

"Yeah, sure, I'm a bit afraid of her. She could be a terrible person, someone I wouldn't want to be connected with...."

"Why are you assuming she would be a terrible person?" Harald continues. "Do you think you might be projecting your worst fears about yourself out onto her?"

Oh boy, here he goes again, I think as I suck in the low-tar, low-nicotine smoke, trying hard to keep that wave of fear under control. Now that my tears are abating, Harald taps a cigarette out of the pack on the table, lights up, and returns to his place on the couch.

"It's not that I'm assuming she'd be a terrible person, Harald. That's just the worst-case scenario, I guess. I don't know about projecting fears about myself onto her, but yeah, she could be a cold, insensitive, superficial person. She might not even want to see me."

"She might reject you again? Just the way she did when you were born?"

"Yes." I feel cold now on this warm evening. The only warmth I feel is the sharp smoke in the back of my throat as I inhale. I take a final drag and stub the thing out in the glass ashtray.

"You know," I sigh, "she's probably a very ordinary lady, married, with grown-up children, involved in her own activities. It would probably throw her off-balance if I were to suddenly appear."

"And you wouldn't want to upset her, right? Just like you wouldn't want to upset your mom."

He's pursuing this relentlessly now, poking at it, like our cat Nemo playing with a mouse. He's implying that I'm passive, a wimp, caught between two mothers, not willing to rock anybody's boat. Actually, I feel like I'm just treading water in these moments, trying to grasp this new possibility and stay afloat psychologically. I have never before thought seriously about finding my birth mother.

"Look Harald, it scares me — maybe finding a mother I wouldn't even like, or her saying she didn't want anything to do with me. But mostly it's Mom. I just can't hurt her."

"Well, I think that finding your birth mother could be a very good thing for you," Harald says, as if he's winding up a successful therapy session. "No matter what sort of person she might turn out to be, you'd be forced to examine yourself and to try to define who you are."

* * *

We talked so long that evening that the bread dough, forgotten in the warm kitchen, tripled in size and overflowed its pans. Once Harald had cracked through my armor, I began tentatively to think about finding my birth mother. For my entire life I'd known that my past was blocked. All my life I had tried to accept the ambiguity of never knowing who and where I had come from. I'd tried to keep my yearnings to know about my birth parents within the safe boundaries of fantasy. Now, it felt like a dammed-up river was being released. Pent-up yearnings, memories, fears, and hopes began flooding into my consciousness.

For the rest of that summer and fall before we went to California, I couldn't help reviewing my life, dwelling especially on those times when my adoption had loomed large. I remembered how often I had thought about my birth mother as I was growing up, and how important she had been to me in my imagination. I tried to stare down my double-barreled fear: the fear of hurting my adoptive mother by searching for my birth mother, perhaps risking damage to our life-long close relationship, and the fear of finding a birth mother who could be uncaring, disappointing, even hostile or frightening.

But regardless of what I might find, did I have a *right* to know where I came from? I dared to ask myself toward the end of that summer. Did

I have the right, for my own sake, and for my children too? And if so, did my right, my need, my curiosity, and yearning override any pain that Mom might feel or any disruption in her life that my birth mother might experience? They had both been willing and active partners in the closed adoption contract signed thirty years before, while I, of course, had not been consulted. But now I was an adult and a mother myself. Whose need was more important? Mine to know or theirs to keep the past hidden?

Post-war parents, 1946–47

Me, age 2

Gypsy & me, 1948

CHAPTER 2

My younger brother Rick and I grew up in the postwar years in Ukiah, the small-town county seat of Mendocino County in Northern California. Our closest friends in the neighborhood, Faith and Fred, were also adopted. So were our two cousins in faraway Washington, D.C. Ricky and I were adopted with silver spoons in our mouths, transported from that blank, dark place where faceless mothers had given us away into a home where we had been wanted for years, waited for patiently.

From the beginning of their marriage, my parents knew they would not have their own children. When she was only twenty-five, Mom had had a hysterectomy. As she often said, she "cried a roomful of tears" when she came out of the anesthesia and the surgeon told her that she would be unable to bear children. She felt that no one would want to marry her, that her life would be very different from what she had always imagined, and she fell into a depression. Not long after her surgery, she got to know my father, since both of them were county welfare workers in the San Francisco Bay area. When things became serious, one evening my mother held her breath and asked, "Is it important to you to have children?"

My father replied, "Of course. But it isn't necessary for them to be mine biologically."

In the late 1940s and 1950s, many babies were available for adoption in North America. The pill was decades in the future, abortion was practically unheard of, and the stigma for young women attempting to raise children "out of wedlock" was severe. Adoption agencies played God and were able to place babies in adoptive homes with great care. Social workers interviewed and tested both the pregnant woman and the prospective adoptive parents extensively — and of course separately. A major aim was to "match" the child as closely as possible to the adoptive family in looks, probable talents and interests, probable intelligence, and religious and ethnic backgrounds.

The purpose of matching was to camouflage the fact of the adoption in order to make life easier for the child and to present the adoptive parents with children who could pass as their own natural offspring. In our case, the adoption agency did such a good job of matching that Mom and I were amused as time and time again over the years people commented on the strong family resemblance between us. This made it much easier for me to "pass as natural."

* * *

During World War II, while Dad was on a Navy transport ship in the Pacific, Mom bought two hilly acres of pear orchard with a creek running along one side of it in the heart of Ukiah. When he returned home after the war, they transformed that patch of land into an idyllic place to raise a family. We grew most of our own fruit and vegetables, which Mom canned or froze for the winter. We had a beautiful, mischievous bay mare that lived in the big green barn and corral at the edge of the pasture. I can't remember learning to ride and may have actually ridden Gypsy before I could walk. In late summer we baled hay in the dry pasture, and in the fall we collected the English and black walnuts that we shook down from the tall trees at the front of the property and then burned the fragrant piles of fallen leaves. My parents nurtured a rock garden spilling over with pastel succulent plants, a formal rose garden, a whole sweeping hillside of brilliant, subtly scented varieties of iris, and an upper and lower lawn where Ricky and I and the neighborhood children turned cartwheels, played "Mother May I?", ran in the sprinkler, and played croquet. The creek, with its small fish, crawdads, frogs, and tall, overhanging trees, was my favorite place to explore.

We weren't rich, but we were comfortable. Dad was a high school history teacher, later a school administrator, while Mom gave up her position as head of the Mendocino county welfare department to become a full-time mother, earning "pin money," as she called it, as a self-taught landscape designer. My parents were both respected leaders in our community. Both had Masters' degrees, Mom's in psychology, Dad's in education. Daddy was an elder in the Presbyterian Church and active in the local Lion's Club and Masonic Lodge. Mom started the town's popular Garden Club, and because she was such a good public speaker, she was often asked to emcee local fashion shows or to give lectures on such wide-ranging topics as the history of African violets or the biography of American folk composer Stephen Foster, talks that she researched thoroughly at the Ukiah Public Library.

Both sets of grandparents moved to Ukiah from the San Joaquin Valley and from Berkeley soon after Daddy returned from Okinawa and I, the first grandchild, arrived on the scene. Sunday dinners and holidays were always spent with the extended family. I loved visiting my grandparents. Grandma and Grandpa Boyd had a chicken coop in the backyard and a cat that produced litters of kittens. Grandpa Dietterle pounded out ragtime tunes on the upright piano with his slender, liver-spotted hands. On my seventh birthday, his present to me was his piano; he said his fingers were too arthritic to play much any more.

Mom and Dad nurtured the talents Rick and I had come to them with. We both had swimming lessons, and Rick became a fish in the water, a good competitive swimmer. There were daily bedtime stories, which lit my passion for reading, and Dad quizzed me on spelling and arithmetic while he washed and I dried the dishes at night. I took piano lessons and by my early teens was playing in contests, talent shows, and recitals.

I loved school and always did well. We had a happy if uneventful family life. My parents never fought, never even argued in our presence. Could anyone have asked for a happier childhood?

During my childhood, my adoption was a melody in a minor key, always playing in my head but only occasionally insistent enough to create real discord. I can't remember the first time I learned that I was adopted. My parents had followed the wisdom of the time (and still today) in discussing my adoption early, openly, and casually. For me there was no trauma of first finding out. Being adopted was just a fact of my life, a mysterious beginning to my childhood, which made my life a little more puzzling, my step a little less sure than it might have been otherwise. For some woman out there, my original mother, my "real mother," the most important person in my life in fact, had not wanted me when I was born. She had given me away.

* * *

In elementary school and junior high, I had always done well and had enjoyed school. When we moved to Monterey the year I started high school, I became a perfectionist and an over-the-top achiever. I strove academically, and I strove to be the ideal well-rounded student.

My goal throughout high school was "Getting into Stanford," which was Dad's alma mater. I grew up convinced it was the best college around; on the West Coast, Harvard was jokingly referred to as the "Stanford of the East." In the early 1960s, it was harder for women to get into Stanford than it was for men, for the admissions committee adhered to an infamous "ratio": only one woman was accepted for every three men.

So in order to get into the best, I set about to be the best. I earned straight As in every course I took in high school. Once, in my junior year, I was worried that I might get a B in an advanced algebra course, so midyear I switched into a lower-powered math course and earned my A easily. I graduated first in a class of four hundred and gave the valedictory speech. I was the piano accompanist for the music department and singing clubs. I was president of my freshman class within a few weeks after we had moved to Monterey, and in my senior year I was student body president. As if all this wasn't enough, in the spring of my senior year I was voted Queen of the Prom. Along with feeling on top of the world that night, I experienced a little stab of regret that it was too late to include this distinction in my Stanford application.

At the time, I didn't connect my overwhelming drive to succeed with my fear of that void at the beginning of my life. I didn't connect my desire to be best with that shadow mother who must have felt I wasn't good enough to keep. But privately I was often afraid of failure, worried that if I made one slip-up, got one B, lost one election, or botched one recital, the entire house of cards I was constructing would collapse. I would never "Get into Stanford." I would be exposed as the unextraordinary girl that I was.

I tried to convince myself that my life began when Mom and Dad adopted me, when I entered a home of well-educated parents, people who were respected and liked by all who knew them. I had to meet that standard and exceed it. I had to make them proud of me, to keep on securing their love. Yet they never pushed me. During high school their constant refrain was, "Slow down, Pat, don't push yourself so hard," as I stayed after school for extracurricular activities, practiced the piano, and set my alarm clock for 4:00 or 5:00 a.m. to study before breakfast. During my childhood and teens, I was prone to stomachaches. I polished my fingernails but chewed my cuticles raw.

I had no idea, really, what lurked in my blank past before I came to Mom and Dad, but I suspected the worst. Perhaps my intelligence and talents were only part of the house of cards, carefully nurtured, even created over the years by my parents, but not innate, not really mine. I had been given love and security since I was six weeks old, and yet my life still had no foundation. It floated over a gaping emptiness. In high school, with my goal set, I tried especially hard not to look into it. I had to keep on pushing, keep on excelling, moving forward.

As I grew up, I never managed to forget about my adoption. My shadow mother was always present. I wondered and fantasized about her with varying intensity, but I also managed to keep her at bay. During my four years at Stanford and two years in Uganda with the Peace Corps, when it seemed to me that I was well on my way in life, I rarely looked back. She was simply gone. She had given me away.

That attitude of resolution and acceptance all changed, however, when I had my own children.

PATRICIA MOFFAT

Derek & Rick
in Monterey,
Christmas 1976

Me pregnant with
Tessa and playing
with Derek on
Carmel Beach,
Winter 1976

Dad & Derek, Monterey 1976

CHAPTER 3

After Harald and I were married in June of 1972, he completed his dissertation and was granted tenure. I got a job teaching high school English and English to New Canadians the fall after we were married. I taught for two years, and in June of 1974 our son was born. In the first few days of Derek's life, my thoughts returned repeatedly to that unknown mother who had given birth to me.

After Derek's birth, I had to remain in the hospital for six days. That was more the practice in the early 1970s than it is today. Besides, I had had preeclampsia late in the pregnancy and a rapid childbirth, and my doctor wanted to monitor my blood pressure and other conditions as my body returned to normal. During the hospital stay, my emotions were very close to the surface. I was, as Mom — who had flown in from California for two weeks to welcome her first grandchild — put it, "fiercely maternal" toward my bald, red, perfect son. I felt that I constantly had to fight for his rights and mine in the hospital. I was upset all out of proportion when I discovered that for one feeding, instead of bringing Derek to me, the nurses had fed him glucose water in the nursery and he had fallen asleep. It made me furious to see those tiny babies made subservient to the hospital routine when it should have been the other way around. I wanted Derek with me all the time, but "rooming-in" hadn't been established at that hospital yet; it was a special concession to me and to one other mother on the floor that for a few days a student nurse brought us our babies and left them for the mornings in our rooms.

But for me this "privilege" ceased, and I wasn't even able to feed Derek or hold him at all on the third and fourth days of his life, because I began running a high fever. My milk had "come in" about 2:00 a.m. the night before. Instead of bringing the baby to me and letting him nurse, he was fed glucose water as usual in the nursery because it wasn't "hospital policy" to bring babies out to their mothers during the night. At first my doctor thought I had the flu; next he thought I had a blood infection. So Derek and I were kept apart, and I wept bitterly as I expressed my milk into the bathroom sink.

During my fever, I spent a lot of time with my nose pressed against the nursery window. When Derek cried, screwing up his little red face and shaking his tiny fists, the nurses often took a long time before attending to him. As I watched him, alone and miserable both of us, I felt as if something were physically squeezing my heart.

Gradually and gaining force hour by hour as I stand watching him through the nursery window, a recognition rises in my consciousness, bringing with it wonder, pain, sadness, joy: this baby behind this glass is the first blood relative I have ever seen! In the entire world, this small, bald human being is my only known relative. My blood is mixed with Harald's in his tiny blue veins. Half the genes in every cell of Derek's little body come from me. I gave my baby blood, I gave him genes, but who gave them to me? Can I glimpse my unknown parents in my newborn son?

In the days after Derek's birth, I often imagined my birth mother lying in a similar hospital bed twenty-eight years earlier, to be separated from her baby not for the duration of a milk fever but for forever. I felt close to her then. My heart went out to her, whoever and wherever she was. In my feverish state, I felt an urge to comfort her if she had suffered. I wanted to somehow let her know that I was all right, that I had had a happy childhood and a good life, and now I could understand how difficult my birth must have been for her.

My thoughts were like waves of love reaching out to her. It was a familiar sense of inner, spiritual communion that I had experienced as a child and had almost forgotten, when many times I would sense my "real mother" as a benevolent presence looking in on my life, sometimes singing me softly to sleep from far away or wordlessly sending me warm waves of love and encouragement. Those almost-forgotten sensations returned to me now, except that I was the one reaching out.

* * *

My roommate in the hospital was a young Italian woman who had just given birth to her third child, a much-wanted baby girl after two little boys. On the third day, after a feeding (the Southern European women in the hospital were all happily bottle-feeding their babies, while the two WASPs were happily breast-feeding), Maria was talking to her baby and fondling her, which made me feel worse than ever because my fever still raged and Derek was still being kept in the nursery.

Suddenly I heard her gasp, and in her broken English she managed to ask me why the baby had a strange name on her anklet. I climbed out of bed to have a look, and indeed, the name of the baby was different from Maria's name. Hardly believing our eyes, we realized that the hospital staff must have switched two babies. Maria and another woman must have given birth at the same time in adjacent delivery rooms. For three days, another woman had been feeding Maria's baby and cooing to her, while Maria had been bonding to this infant. Maria hurriedly rang the bell, and within minutes half a dozen horrified nurses grouped themselves around Maria's bed. The babies were immediately sorted out.

As Maria held her own daughter for the first time, she ruminated, "My husband, he said something not right with that baby. Too brown and hadda big nose." I, looking on, was feeling for the very first time extremely lucky to be in this small hospital in Toronto's Italian-Portuguese community, because Derek was the only blond, blue-eyed baby in the nursery. Even though I wasn't allowed to hold him or feed him, at least it would have been impossible to have mixed him up.

Yet why was I, along with Maria, so shocked by the switching of the babies? Hadn't I been a changeling too? I had been substituted for the child Mom and Dad couldn't have. What would have happened to Maria's child and the brown, big-nosed baby if the exchange hadn't been discovered? They would have grown up in families of roughly the same ethnic background, just as I had. They surely would have been loved as members of the family, as I had been. And yet, without anyone realizing it, they would have grown up like adopted children. I, the adopted daughter, tried to shrug the whole thing off. But like Maria, I, the birth mother, was appalled.

* * *

Tessa's birth twenty months later brought on even more thoughts about my first mother and myself as a baby, for the obvious reason that she was a girl. We had changed hospitals this time, and the staff at the Toronto General were more in tune with their patients and more flexible in nursery routines. Instead of whisking Tessa away right after the cord was cut, as had been done with Derek, and instead of commanding me not to touch the baby as he lay howling and thrashing on my stomach, this time the doctor picked the baby up and handed her to me to nurse, with the umbilical cord still connecting us.

Tessa was a plump and rosy newborn with bright blue eyes. She was a quiet, satisfied little person right from the beginning. During the few days after her birth, she was with me in my room all the time, so I was able to get to know her quickly. I appreciated her as a unique personality even during those early days and couldn't help comparing her with the little baby I had once been. I wondered whether I had been as alert, aware, and self-possessed as a newborn. While Tessa lay sleeping beside me during our stay in the hospital, I wondered where I had spent my first six weeks before Mom and Dad had gotten me. I doubted that I had lain peacefully sleeping beside my mother. I wondered whose hands had held me, had bathed and changed me, had given me my bottle (for surely I hadn't been breastfed?). Had anybody talked to me as I talked to Tessa? Had anybody lovingly traced the lines of my body and my features with her fingers? Had anybody sung to me? Perhaps a nurse or a temporary foster mother? Had my real mother seen me or held me, even once?

I felt that same physical pain in my chest that I'd felt watching Derek through the nursery window, when I imagined never seeing Tessa again, imagined turning her over to nurses and social workers, casting her out upon the world totally dependent upon the goodwill of strangers for all her needs for her whole life. My baby! How could my mother have done such a thing? It was inconceivable to me that I could abandon my babies! To give up a real, fully formed infant with her own distinct personality already evident was so terrible, I had trouble really envisioning it. How long had I been her baby? A few days or only an instant?

With Tessa's birth, I began pondering another aspect of the void at the beginning of my life. When Harald and I were in the labor room about an hour before Tessa was born, a medical clerk came around with a form to be filled out for the hospital records. He was a warm, friendly fellow with a job to do, and during the interview he seemed genuinely interested in us.

When he came to the list of questions on medical history, he began, "Are your parents still alive?" Of course I said yes.

"Are they in good health?" Again, yes.

Soon it dawned on me what he was asking. "Is there any history of hereditary diseases in your family?" he continued.

I had to tell him then that if there were any hereditary diseases, I wouldn't be affected by them because I had been adopted.

"Oh!" he said. "Then it really doesn't matter, those questions about your parents.... Well, what medical history *do* you know about your biological parents? Are they living?"

I said he'd have to leave that whole section blank because I didn't know a thing. Whether his distress sprang from genuine concern for me, about to go into childbirth without any medical knowledge that may have helped in an emergency, or whether it sprang from his dissatisfaction at having to turn in an incomplete form, I don't know for sure. But for the first time, I saw my situation through someone else's eyes, and I felt uneasy. Throughout my life I had almost convinced myself that being adopted was normal; it was just a slightly different way of becoming part of a family. But now a stranger, a medical professional, was obviously unsettled by it. Maybe there were indeed medical facts about my biological parents that I should know, both for my sake and for the sake of my children. Perhaps there were hereditary diseases I might be passing on to my children, and if I knew what they were, I could be more easily clued in to symptoms in my children. There was no sudden urge in me at that point to do anything about my ignorance. I was much too occupied with the birth in progress — but I did feel a little rush of fear about my blank background. I wished that I had been able to answer the clerk's questions for the sake of Derek and the child about to be born.

* * *

Derek and Tessa were incredibly, surprisingly, sensuous beings. I loved the feel of their warm little bodies, loved the sensations of nursing. My children! Although they were no longer physically part of me, something of me was in them, would be in them always, and would be passed on to their children. Continuity: a chain of invisible umbilical cords connecting generation after generation, a hint of physical immortality.

Yet in my case, that continuum rolled on only into the future. It originated with me. Behind me was a severing. Suddenly I wanted to look back as well as forward. Previously the void that constituted my heredity and family history had applied only to me. But now I saw Derek and Tessa as enigmas, like myself, bereft of half their heritage.

Then there were Derek's eyes. When Derek was born, everyone thought he was the image of Harald, except for the dimple on his chin, which came from me. Then as he grew, he began to show signs of having my long,

34

slender build. Only one feature was a mystery to us. Harald and I both have blue eyes with rather short, light brown lashes. Derek's eyes are also blue but look large and vibrant because they are fringed with long black lashes. No one in Harald's family has eyes like that. We guessed that either my biological mother or father must have. A tiny detail, a few millimeters of dark hair, and yet, studying the face of your first-born — and the first human being to whom you are related — all details are magnified, every feature of the small body is engrossing. We wondered whether aspects of his character might emerge, which, like his eyelashes, may have been passed on from his unknown grandparents.

Harald was right. I had been thinking about my birth mother a great deal since the kids were born. As Derek took his first steps, said his first words, and proudly learned to use his potty, and as Tessa began to laugh, turn over, and reach for objects, I often found myself wondering whether my mother had missed me, had thought about what I looked like and how old I was when I hit my milestones as a baby and a toddler, or had wished she could have peeked into my life and seen me now and then for just a few moments. I sometimes felt a powerful rush of love for my children and wondered what that feeling would do, where it would go, if a child died or was taken away. I had had an abortion in 1970, and when my children were small, I often thought about that lost child my first love, Paul, and I chose not to have. I imagined him as a bright, sandy-haired, sturdy little boy three years older than Derek. I grieved for him all over again as I watched my children growing, but I was sure the sadness would have been magnified a thousand-fold if I had had him and had then given him up for adoption.

What had my mother felt about me, if she had had other children later? What would she say now, if she knew she had two grandchildren?

Mom & Derek,
Georgian Bay, 1975

Adoptive parents George
& Kate, 1960s

Dad & Derek, 1976

CHAPTER 4

Today, searching for birth parents is so common and is considered so psychologically healthy that adoptees who are not "in search" are often judged to be "in denial." Birth parents and birth siblings are also now searching successfully for grown-up children relinquished years ago through adoption. Adoption registries in most states and provinces can make it much easier to locate lost relatives than it used to be. And the masses of information instantly available on the Internet sometimes can short-circuit a long and difficult search entirely. With companies like Ancestry.com and 23andMe, which use DNA technology to determine ethnic heritage and even identify relatives, we are into a new era of searching and finding. Sometimes relatively little detective work is needed to find parents, children, siblings, and other relatives, given the information revealed by DNA data. We are used to seeing reunited birth families on TV or reading their stories in magazines, newspapers, and online. Search-and-reunion is becoming an accepted part of our social fabric.

But in 1976, "searching" was just beginning to be in the air. Few books were available at that time on adoptees searching for roots, and self-help groups were just starting to form across the continent. Searching was not viewed as the positive process that it is today. Perhaps today, just as in the 1970s, many adoptive parents are hurt and angry when a beloved child goes off in search of other parents. Perhaps many adoptees are both scared of what they might find and burdened with guilt about their adoptive parents. Perhaps many birth parents feel threatened by the reappearance of a relinquished child and the reawakening of the pain and shame that was part of the birth and relinquishment. The difference is that today resources are available to help everyone work through their feelings and to know they are not alone. There are books that explore the phenomenon of search-and-reunion, and self-help support groups, and therapists who understand and even specialize in the issues of the adoption community.

But in the 1970s, there weren't even search manuals, or reliable suggestions for successful reunions, or easily available resources for integrating whatever one found at the end of the search into one's life. What there was, however, perhaps even more than today, was a secrecy about searching that was in keeping with the secrecy of the whole enterprise of closed adoption. There was often hostility toward searching from adoptive parents, as well as negative, judgmental attitudes from members of society who had little familiarity with adoption. We inched forward in the dark in the seventies, leaning on other seekers for information and support, making it up as we went along, with only a few experienced guides to help light the way: Jean Paton of Orphan Voyage, Florence Fisher of Adoptees' Liberty Movement Association (ALMA), and Betty Jean Lifton, whose *Twice Born* was inspiration and encouragement to so many of us.

I don't think I ran across any media treatment of searching until the summer of 1976. Surely there must have been items in newspapers, magazines, on TV programs and radio call-in shows before then, but if there were, I wasn't aware of them until I was ready. That summer, a local Toronto magazine carried a long article on successful reunions between birth mothers and adult adoptees, which I read twice, slowly, shedding tears both times. I also saw a short TV interview with a young man who had found his birth mother. I hardly moved during the program, comparing his every statement to my own experiences of being adopted, and my own doubts and hopes.

It gave me tremendous hope to learn that other people had gone through the decision-making process that I was now struggling with, had overcome the bureaucratic obstacles involved in the search, and had succeeded. Even though I personally didn't know anyone else who was searching or even thinking about it, just knowing that an underground movement was beginning to form of adoptees searching for their birth parents gave me some sense of community and confidence. It was a real shift in my thinking to consider that yes, some adult daughters and sons do feel they have the right to uncover their own pasts.

However, neither the TV interview nor the long magazine article made any mention of adoptive parents at all. The focus was on the search, the excitement of finding the birth parent, and the new relationship that usually developed. There was complete silence about the parents these people had grown up with. It was almost as if they didn't exist. I wondered whether perhaps these driven adoptees had come from backgrounds less fortunate than mine, whether they had been neglected or abused, and therefore experienced far fewer mixed feelings about searching for their original parents than I was struggling with.

For despite the happy daydreams I began indulging in about my natural mother, and my tentative plans as to how I might start looking for her, I was still very concerned about Mom and Dad. In my most realistic (or most fearful) moments, that small, new opening Harald had made in my armor would close up again, and I would view the whole idea of finding my birth mother as a wild tangent. I would never have the nerve to actually do it. It was selfish and damaging, and the best thing would be to forget about it. It might have been different if I had had an unhappy childhood or cold, uncaring parents. But I had been blessed. Why was I considering tempting my luck and hurting my family?

The more I thought about it, the more I realized that I wasn't looking for another mother, in the everyday sense of the word. I was hoping for a friend in my birth mother and a chance to mend the painful rent with which my life began, to bring the course of my life to a sense of completion and fresh beginning now that I was an adult and had my own children. I wanted to know her, both out of sheer curiosity and in order to develop a more grounded sense of self. I wanted to hear from her the stories of how I was conceived and born, and why she gave me up for adoption. I yearned to let her know that all was well with me, to still any feelings of guilt or regret that she may have carried all these years. But as for finding other parents, in the sense that Mom and Dad are my parents, I just didn't have that need. I envisioned almost a spiritual relationship — like that inner communion I'd experienced or imagined as a child, and in the aftermath of Derek's birth — not another mother to depend upon, to struggle with, to be so close to in day-to-day living. If I could somehow get this across to Mom and Dad, then maybe they could understand, maybe I could search for my birth mother without being dragged down by guilt.

But what if I found my birth mother and she had other ideas? What if she didn't want to meet me at all? In that case, there wouldn't be that sense of peace and completion that I wanted so much, but I felt I could deal with that in time. At least I might be able to satisfy my curiosity about what sort of person she was, and perhaps she would consent to talk to me about my birth and why she had given me up for adoption.

It was the other side of the coin that I actually thought about more. My older and wiser artist friend Mary Hecht said to me near the end of that summer, "You will feel a sense of personal responsibility for her when you find her. If she needs to depend upon you, financially or emotionally, you will respond. You will care for her." Instinctively, I felt this to be true. If my mother needed mothering, I would mother her, and she would become a part of our lives.

Or, pushing it further, what if she wanted to become my *mother* as much as is possible after thirty years? I felt that that would be very tricky, for I would feel a sense of betrayal toward Mom, and I wouldn't be able to play along with my birth mother without being deeply disturbed by our roles. I sincerely felt that my biological mother couldn't become my real mother now that my childhood was over, now that I so definitely had another mother and was even a mother myself.

These were hypothetical twists and turns that might lie far down the road. Most likely they would never come up. But just thinking about what sort of relationship, if any, might develop if I contacted her made the contacting seem that much more possible.

I considered and rejected the idea of keeping a search secret from my family. This would be akin to my parents never having told me I was adopted. It would be like living a lie. And yet I thought of the one secret I was aware of in our family: my abortion. Perhaps Mom would be more comfortable not knowing about my search, if indeed I started one. Perhaps her attitude toward my abortion — her decision to keep it from Dad and Rick because she felt the knowledge might hurt them — actually indicated a need to protect herself from hurt.

Eventually, I realized that I was tying myself in knots, attempting to think out every possibility and make decisions based on what others might or might not feel. In the end, I decided that if I did search, I would not keep a search from my parents in order to spare their feelings; rather, I would invite them to share it with me.

Wrestling with my guilt and worries about my parents absorbed much of my energy over the summer. Yet I spent even more time giving in to thoughts about my birth mother. She began to obsess me. Turning these thoughts off would have been like trying to stuff a big, grinning genie back into a tiny, tight bottle of forgetting. It was as if Harald tearing a hole, just for a few minutes, in the curtain of fear and guilt that surrounded my adoption meant that the way through, the path through to my birth mother, was permanently there if I would just decide to step out and follow it.

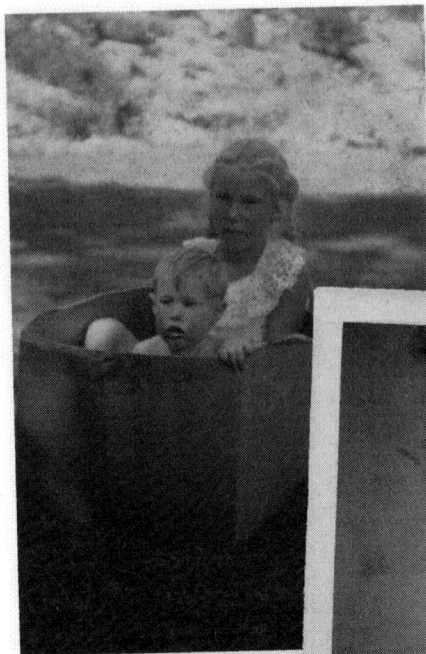

RICK (18 months) &
me (6 years),
ukiah summer, 1952

Me with our
Big Tom

Childhood home: 711 Willow Ave, ukiah, California

CHAPTER 5

Daydreaming about my birth mother was nothing new. She had accompanied me throughout my life, donning different disguises as I grew. I can pinpoint the day when she first walked into my imagination. It was the day I learned there might be something shameful in being adopted.

August morning, already hot. I can smell the dry dust. It's nice on Mrs. Church's shady porch. Carol and I sit on the top step, leaning against the wooden pillars. In my seersucker sun shorts and top, the dry wood and peeling paint feel rough against my skin.

"Shall we read some comics?" I ask. At ten years old, three years older than me, Carol reads better than I do. I love lying on our stomachs on the wide porch bed and reading Archie and Veronica, Casper the Friendly Ghost, and especially Mary Jane, the little girl who like Alice in Wonderland can make herself very small, almost invisible. Carol reads aloud, and I follow the words carefully.

"Nah, I don't have any new comics," Carol says.

Carol stares out across the road to our place. The heat is rising off our new black asphalt driveway, slithering up like invisible fire. I like Carol's page-boy haircut. Her hair is dark brown and glossy, much finer than my thick blond braids. Her eyes are big and light brown and look ever larger behind her glasses.

"Do you want to come over and play the piano?" It's cool in our den, and I always like listening to Carol play Grandpa's piano. I am learning classical, but Carol plays pop and show tunes with her big hands from memory.

"Maybe later," she replies. Carol isn't usually so quiet. I scratch a day-old mosquito bite on my ankle.

"You shouldn't do that, you know," she says. "It could get infected and they might have to cut off your foot."

"That's stupid," I protest. But I stop scratching. If I had an older sister, would she be like Carol?

Carol turns to me suddenly, her shining hair swinging. "You know, your parents aren't your real parents. You were just adopted."

I stare at her. "Yeah, I know I'm adopted. So what?"

"Well, you didn't come out of your mama's tummy like most people did," Carol continues.

Now I can hardly breathe. "I know."

"Well, that means your parents aren't your real parents. They're just taking care of you because your real parents didn't want you. Your real mother got rid of you. You don't even know who she is."

Carol's words punch me in the stomach. My eyes start to sting and my throat feels tight.

"You shouldn't say that," I tell this girl I look up to, the city girl who comes from San Francisco every summer to visit her grandmother, my favorite babysitter. Carol knows so much more than I do. I look forward to her visits every year. Now I just want to go home. I'm going to cry, and I don't want her to watch.

"I'll see you later, I have to go now," I say, and I try to walk away across the road like everything's fine, though my tears begin to fall and the August morning blurs. After a few steps, I run. I run across the dusty road and up the hot, black asphalt of our driveway, sobbing, gulping for air.

Mama's in the kitchen working at the counter, stripping corn off the cobs. The familiar sweet smell makes me cry even harder.

"Whatever in the world is the matter, Patty?" Mama kneels down, inspecting me for skinned knees or elbows.

I can't look at her. I say to the cool green linoleum, "Carol... Carol said..."

"There, there." Mama strokes my back. "You can't talk while you're crying like that."

She acts just like my Mama who loves me, but could she be only pretending?

"Carol said you and Daddy aren't my real parents because I was just adopted." I say through my sobs. "She, she said...my real mother...got rid of me."

Now I'm shocked to see Mama start to cry too. She hugs me tightly then straightens up. "We're going over there right now to have a little talk with Carol," Mama says.

"Oh, no, I don't want to do that," I say. I wipe my tears away quickly with my hands.

"No, I want you to come along, I want you to hear every word I have to say," Mama says, briskly untying her apron.

Mama and I march back to Mrs. Church's front porch. She holds me by the hand down the hot driveway and out across the dirt road. I feel like a five-year-old. Mama doesn't usually hold my hand like this any more. I look up and see her face streaked with tears. Carol is sitting right where I left her, on the steps in the shade. Now she seems small, a hunched figure in her white sundress and sandals, watching us approach. Oh, I've been bad, I'm a tattle-tale, Carol's going to get in trouble, she won't ever like me again.

"Hello, Carol," Mama begins and settles herself down on the porch steps. "I understand you've been talking to Patty about adoption." Carol doesn't say anything. She looks up at my Mama for a moment, then folds her arms around her chest and leans in tight against the wooden pillar. "Come, Patty, you sit down here." Mama motions to me. Reluctantly, I sit behind Mama by the other pillar. Now we're in for it. I wish I was far away.

"Carol, I'm sure you didn't mean any harm in what you said to Patty," Mama says. "I think you just don't understand what adoption is. I'm going to tell you about it, and how Patty became our daughter."

Carol is looking scared, and I am squirming. Now I know that Mama is going to tell Carol the Story of My Adoption Day. It's my private story; no one else has ever heard it. I'm always the star in this story, and I like to hear Mama and Daddy tell it. But how will it sound to somebody else?

"You see, Carol, adopted children are always wanted. Their parents choose them specially to love. Sometimes mothers who have their children by giving birth to them really want their children too. Sometimes they don't want them so much, but they have them anyway. But adopted children are never accidents. Their parents always want them very, very much.

"Mr. Dietterle and I asked for a baby at the adoption agency a long time before Patty came to us. We waited for years before we were able to get her. The woman who gave birth to Patty wasn't able to keep her. The circumstances of her life were too difficult. So she went to the adoption agency and asked them to find the very best home for Patty that they could. When the agency finally phoned us and said our baby had arrived, we were so excited. We drove down to San Francisco the very next day to bring her home.

"There were a lot of babies at the agency, and we walked up and down the rows of bassinets, looking at each one. When we saw Patty, we said to the social worker, 'Oh, this baby is so pretty! Could we have her, please?' And the social worker said, 'Well, aren't you lucky? This is the baby we've picked out for you!' Patty was just six weeks old when we brought her home."

I shoot a glance at Carol, who is examining the peeling wooden steps in front of her.

"Most parents have many months to get things ready for their baby," Mama continues, "but we weren't prepared at all. We took Patty home in a wicker laundry basket, and she spent her first night sleeping in her Daddy's padded dresser drawer. But from that very first day, she was our baby, she was our little daughter." Mama's confident words are starting to tremble again. "I want to make sure you understand this, Carol. Look at me."

Carol raises her head slowly to look at my Mama. Her shoulders beneath her white sundress are shaking, and tears roll out from under her round glasses. Mama reaches over and takes her hand.

"Mr. Dietterle and I are Patty's real parents. Don't you ever think we're not. I want you to promise me you will never, ever, say again that Patty isn't our real daughter and we aren't her real parents."

"No, I won't," Carol whispers.

"I hope you understand now what adoption means. It's a very special way of becoming part of a family."

I feel empty. The story I love to hear sounds like a fairy tale now, like something Mrs. Courtland would read aloud at Saturday Story Hour down at the library, stopping between the pages to show us the pictures. I know that by telling Carol this story, Mama is telling me again — even more so because someone else is listening — that she and Daddy love me, that maybe they even love me more than most parents do because they couldn't have children "the normal way," and because they wanted me so much. She's trying to erase Carol's words — "They're not your real parents, you were just adopted" — and make me feel good again.

But now I see that there's more to this story. Most people, like Carol, must think there's something bad about being adopted, something to be ashamed of. How come I didn't know that before? Also, for the first time I see another person, a very important person hidden in my story, almost invisible behind the bright rows of bassinets and Mama and Daddy's happiness. I let myself wonder about her for the first time. Why did she give me away? What was she like? I am the daughter Mama and Daddy wanted so much, but I was the daughter she did not want. She had me, she carried me in her tummy just like Carol's mommy did with her, and then she gave me away. My life didn't start on the day of my adoption after all.

* * *

Somewhere out there, unless she had died, was my "real mother," I concluded when I was seven. By talking about her, even sneeringly, Carol had called this mother into being. Although Mama and Daddy loved me, I truly did come from somewhere and someone else. I began feeling oddly out of kilter with the only family I had known and fantasized about the mother who had given me life and then given me away. I felt sad, for surely I would never know who she was or where I came from.

I remember two different occasions, probably separated in time by years, but merged in my memory, of standing and watching, mesmerized, while a friend's mother breastfed her baby. Pam's mother and Christine's mother lay drowsily in darkened rooms with their infants nestled close, nursing, tiny hands kneading the breast. Standing in the doorway, holding the frame for support, I knew I might be intruding but was unable to move away. I listened to the soft suckings, absorbing the physical intimacy of the mother and child. Mama had never fed me that way. I had taken my milk from a bottle. I had come out of my first mother's body, I had known her body's sounds, textures, and smells. I wondered whether she might have fed me like that even once before she gave me away. But if she had, how could she have given me away?

In fact, I asked myself as a child, what sort of woman would have a baby and then give that little baby away? Had my real mother been a loose woman? Had she been cold and unfeeling, since she had rejected her own child? Since I came from her, was I harboring these capacities within myself? Was it inevitable that someday I would disappoint my parents?

There were fears enough in my childhood. There was the amorphous, pulsating thing that lived under my bed, so that I never let my feet dangle over the side. There was the hairy thing with claws that hid behind my dresses in the dark closet, so I had to be extremely careful when I slid open the doors, even in the daytime. There was the Pacific Northwest mask, shiny black, with straw hair, evil eyes, and a bright red mouth that stared at me malevolently from a map showing Native American crafts that hung on the stairwell. Were fears about my unknown past stoking these monsters that lurked in the dark places of our house?

I asked Mom and Dad questions about my "other parents." Who were they? Why had they given me away? The Story of My Real Parents floats in my memory over my childhood. I don't know whether it was told to me in one sitting, whether I built it up into one story in my mind as my questions were answered over the years, or whether I misinterpreted the

48

answers and constructed a story that made sense to me. But this is all I knew about them as a child, these are all the "facts" my imagination fed upon:

"Your parents were in their early twenties when you were born. They were married, but your father was away during most of the war. When he returned, your mother discovered she had fallen out of love with him. She was pregnant with you and decided she couldn't keep you since she didn't love your father any more.

"The people at the adoption agency told us that your mother was one of the prettiest women who had ever walked into their office. She had gone to college and was a singer. Your father was of German background and was a Merchant Marine during the war."

These thin facts suggest that my birth mother was something of a cold fish. It doesn't necessarily follow that because she didn't love her husband she would therefore give his — and her — child away. The possibility exists within the story that my father had continued to love my mother and that he might have loved me too. Yet he is outside of the picture in my mind. He has no force, no choice, no ability to affect her decision. It was my mother who became a figure in my imagination as a child, not my father. Despite the fact that she might have acted coldly toward me, it was my mother with whom I felt a deep kinship, because I had grown inside of her for nine months, because presumably she had suffered during my birth, because she may have seen me, touched me, perhaps even nursed me, and because she made the decision that determined the course of my life. It was she who put my future into the hands of social workers who passed me on to Mom and Dad.

This knowledge that I came from someone and somewhere else, felt at a deep emotional level, often made me feel like an alien within our family. I couldn't understand why Ricky seemed to have so much curiosity about family history. He loved to ask questions about where our adoptive grandparents had come from, what their parents had been like, and on into the mists of history. I heard the stories many times: how Grandma Dietterle's Jewish parents had emigrated from Germany in the mid-19th century and had moved out west on a long and difficult journey; how she had been born in Virginia City, Nevada, when it was a booming silver town, and that's why her name was Rose Virginia; about Grandpa Boyd's adventures as a young man of eighteen in the Klondike Gold Rush, and the nuggets he had brought back; about Grandpa Dietterle's imposing mother, the matriarch Mom had been so timorous about meeting. (It always surprised me to hear that my mother could have been cowed by anyone.)

I absorbed it all, but the stories made me uncomfortable. I was an imposter in this history. I was a twig from elsewhere, grafted onto the family tree. It amazed me that no one else could see this or admit it — neither my parents nor my aunts and uncles or whoever else was recounting the stories. This was not my real family history at all — or Ricky's — yet everyone pretended it was. In truth, I had other family stories, other histories, other relatives I would never know.

Where was my mother? Who and where were the people I had come from? Knowing that I had been born and adopted in San Francisco meant that visiting "The City" was always emotionally charged for me, because my mother possibly still lived there. San Francisco was a two-and-a-half-hour drive south of Ukiah, and when we went there, we stayed for a few days, either in a hotel or with a favorite great-aunt and uncle. I loved going to The City. We were tourists: we rode the cable cars, had lunch on Fisherman's Wharf, shopped for trinkets in Chinatown, visited Golden Gate Park. We often visited The City before Christmas and went shopping at I. Magnin's, City of Paris, and Macy's — small-towners gawking at the glittering Christmas decorations.

While the family, myself included, enjoyed all the things we did in San Francisco, I also enjoyed the torture of another, internal sort of tourism. Being in The City was an opportunity for me to search faces in crowds, looking for Her. I have since learned that most adopted people do this. It's a spontaneous, uncontrollable impulse. Wherever we were in The City, I would search out and watch older women — tall, blond, blue-eyed, pretty women about Mom's age. I would stare at noses that looked a little like mine, with a bump in the middle. I would feel the thrill of goose bumps if a woman who looked like Her would also look at me for longer than a moment. Like watching a movie of someone else's life, I would wonder whether my real mother and I had passed each other on a busy street without even knowing it, whether we had exchanged glances in a restaurant, whether we had even bumped into each other and said "Excuse me" in a crowded department store, a moment filled with meaning that we would never recognize, a moment that would not be remembered by either of us, ever.

In my lively imagination as a child and teenager, I was with my "real mother" most often in music. The adoption agency had told Mom and Dad that she had been "musical" and a "singer," so when I practiced the piano I would often play to her, for her, imagining a spiritual connection with her.

I visualized my mother as a real person most often when I played the piano before an audience — when I was up on stage by myself in school performances, recitals, and contests. I would imagine her sitting at the back of the auditorium, having stolen in silently as I played the opening chords. Always alone, she would sit nervously in the folding metal chair, her eyes never leaving me, her hands clasped tightly to the handbag in her lap, listening intently. During my piece I was able to project my nervousness out upon her and concentrate on playing the music to her, to my parents, my piano teacher, and the rest of the audience. During the applause, she would slip out of her chair and leave as unobtrusively as she had entered, invisible to everyone but me.

This mother I could never know became a more sympathetic figure to me than the "facts" of my adoption suggest. Even though she may have coldly fallen out of love with my father and given me away, in my inner life she often assumed the role of a detached and benevolent spirit. Except for the mother hunts in The City and my piano performances, most of the time my birth mother's form was hazy. I sometimes sensed her presence at a distance as I fell asleep at night, watching me, looking in on my life from time to time, and sending out feelings of love, encouragement, and optimism toward me. If the hairy, scary monsters that lurked in the house were my personal devils, this imaginary mother was my guardian angel.

Her essence was warm, gentle, understanding, embracing. She was my ideal mother who loved me unconditionally, never spanked me or yelled at me, never sent me to my room if I misbehaved.

Many children go through a period of imagining that they were adopted. Unhappy with their parents, they fantasize about other, better, kinder, more interesting, more attractive, richer parents who might someday come and rescue them. But for me, as for all adopted children, this common fantasy had a deep twist, for we actually did have other parents somewhere. We were the prince left in the basket on the doorstep, the princess left in the cabbage patch.

Sometimes, knowing that I came from someone and somewhere else was liberating to me as a child: I was not hemmed in by any limits that my adoptive parents might have set or represented. I could imagine that my heritage and my potential were limitless, that I could be anything or do anything that I wanted. Less often, my birth mother scared me a little. I sometimes worried that her apparent coldness in giving birth to me and then giving me away might be part of my future too. But mostly I believed that her act had been forced upon her, and I felt buoyed by the vibrations of love that I imagined my guardian angel-mother was sending my way.

This element in my life, the intermittent and deeply felt interior communion with my imaginary "real mother," I kept hidden from my parents. Amid all my outpourings about school, friends, aspirations, reflections, worries, this was too private to share. I felt they wouldn't be able to understand it. I felt they would be hurt if they knew I thought about her. Besides, I would have been embarrassed to let them know how vulnerable I was, how affected I was by something, someone, they had probably forgotten.

PATRICIA MOFFAT

My stanford graduation photo, 1967

CHAPTER 6

The questions and daydreams about my "real mother" floated through my mind less often as I grew older and left home. But then, abruptly — after four years at Stanford and two years teaching in East Africa — my shadow mother erupted from her closet and assumed nightmarish forms. The reason was that I found myself in a situation that must have been strikingly similar to hers: I was twenty-four years old, unmarried, and pregnant.

Paul had been my boyfriend at Stanford for our final three years, and I loved him with all the mad passion of first sexual love. When we graduated in 1967, we joined the Peace Corps together, hoping to receive teaching posts in the same town in Uganda, during what would turn out to be two of its last three years as a sleepy, peaceful little country before General Idi Amin took over. But before the end of our three months of training in New York, Paul was "deselected" from the program, the State Department's euphemism for "rejected." We were shattered. In the end we decided that he should return to California and take premed courses, while I would carry on to Uganda. We would both grow, we told ourselves and each other; we would write often and see how we felt after the two years.

That decision was the hardest I had had to make in my twenty-two years. I finished the rest of the training program in a numbed, grieving state. In December 1969, as soon as I returned home from Uganda, Paul and I made love in total disregard for the consequences, and I became pregnant.

In February, when the pregnancy test results came in, I was still experiencing culture shock, which was more intense and disorienting than what I had felt upon first arriving in East Africa. My head felt dizzy and my nerves were raw from the traffic on the California freeways, the overabundance of food and non-necessities on display in the supermarkets, the millions of kilowatt hours of electricity wasted every night in the Bay Area, and the superficial conversations among my friends and family. I was enrolled in a full-time master's program in linguistics at San Francisco State College. I was working, also full-time, at the San Francisco Peace Corps recruiting office to pay for my classes. And I had taken a cheap room in a stultifying household with a bookkeeper landlady and another female graduate student.

When I learned the results of the pregnancy test, my first reaction was elation. Our problems had been solved for us! For the first time since leaving Uganda, I felt that I had finally come home again. Everything was going to be wonderful now. I wanted Paul's baby, and I wanted to live my whole life with him.

But deep down I knew this was a false hope. I wasn't surprised when Paul told me that he loved me but he just couldn't imagine marrying me or anyone yet, and perhaps never. He seemed genuinely afraid of such a commitment and even said he was sure I would come to hate him someday if we did marry. I tried for several weeks to change Paul's mind. It was obvious that he felt and hurt deeply through the experience. It was always *our* predicament, never mine alone. But he stood fast in his decision.

I had three options. I considered having the baby and keeping it. I felt overwhelmed by the difficulties this would cause in my life, but I wanted the child and felt that I loved it already. The second option, an abortion, made me feel sterile and empty. I knew it would be the simplest solution, despite the emotional stress in carrying through with it, the danger to my health if we went to Mexico, or the degrading bureaucratic hassles if it were done legally in California. I also sensed that an abortion — killing our child — would create a turning point in my relationship with Paul, and that made the decision even more difficult.

The option I recoiled from even more than an abortion was the idea of bearing the child and giving it up for adoption. I ruled that out almost immediately. I knew I would be haunted by the child forever, would be unable to lead a normal life, always regretting the decision, always searching for the child. Hadn't I spent enough time in my life searching faces in crowds for my own mother? Selfishly, I knew it would be healthier for me to abort the baby than to become obsessed by its absence.

So we decided to try for a legal abortion at the Stanford hospital. Having made the decision, every morning I woke up physically aching, for I slept with my body in a tight ball, my teeth clenched and my fingernails digging into my palms. Then I would get up and go through the motions of each long day, at the office, on streetcars or in my little blue Volkswagen Beetle, in classes in the late afternoons and evenings, though I seemed unable to forget about the baby for even a few minutes. My breasts were swollen and painful, and I couldn't bear to look at food until the afternoon. I felt deadened, as if I existed at a great distance from my body, forcing it, like a mechanical puppet, to move through its daily routines. Nobody I lived with, went to school with, or worked with knew I was pregnant. Paul and I saw each other or talked on the phone every day, but he was in Palo Alto and I was in San Francisco. I had told one close girlfriend in Palo Alto that I was pregnant, and I had told Mom.

I had dreaded telling Mom, because as usual I didn't want to admit to anything I had done that would disappoint her, and I could think of few things that would upset her as much as this. But I needed her emotional support, and so after a week of agonizing, my need overcame my worries. The pregnancy was almost as painful for Mom as it was for me. She knew how deeply I loved Paul and how much I wanted to have the baby. She was also very aware of the more existential reason that this pregnancy was so difficult to me, for at one point I cried out to her, "And what if my biological mother had had an abortion?"

Although Mom never said she was disappointed in me or that the pregnancy was a disgrace, her determination to keep this between the two of us was proof enough that she was shocked. She asked me not to tell Daddy or Rick that I was pregnant. She said Dad would be deeply hurt if he knew, and also since there was still the possibility that someday Paul and I might get married (which I seriously doubted), she didn't want Dad to develop any negative feelings toward him. As far as Rick was concerned, Mom said she felt he would have great difficulty handling the news, since he looked up to me; I was his big sister and his example. I would have preferred that my whole family could have helped me through the worst crisis in my life to date, not just Mom. I felt sad and awkward on the two weekends I spent in Monterey before the abortion, when Mom and I could talk about "it" only when Dad and Rick were out of earshot. I felt depressed that at age twenty-four, I was still polishing that image of the perfect daughter. Only this time it was Mom who was doing most of the polishing.

Several months after the abortion, when Mom must have decided for some reason that the time was right, she told Rick about it. He was concerned that I had had to go through such a difficult experience but was not overly shaken by it. Daddy didn't learn about my abortion until many years later, by accident, and he and I never discussed it at all.

* * *

In order to have a legal abortion in California in 1970, three years before Roe v. Wade, two medical doctors and a psychiatrist had to sign papers stating that termination of the pregnancy was necessary for the physical and/or mental health of the mother. In my case, the two medical doctors would take their cue from the psychiatrist, because there were no obvious physical dangers for me in bearing this child.

As I parked my car at the Stanford Medical Center on the day of my appointment with Dr. Davis, I was shaking, afraid both that he would refuse to sign the paper and that he *would* sign it. I felt small and powerless, for my personal situation had become the property of others who were probably overworked and didn't know me at all. As I sat facing him in his office, I was terribly nervous but essentially so normal that I didn't see how he would find anything to warrant my having an abortion.

For half an hour he asked me questions about how the pregnancy was affecting my work and my studies. He probed into my relationship with Paul and asked whether I had thought about keeping the child and how this might affect my life. He probed into the past, into my relationship with my parents, asked questions about my childhood, obviously hunting for some childhood trauma and finding none. His manner was desultory, almost bored.

Finally, Dr. Davis pushed his pencil aside, folded his hands on his desk, leaned forward and asked, "Isn't there anything else you can tell me?" I took that to mean, "There's nothing I can put my signature on so far." Throughout the interview, I had *forgotten* about it, and now suddenly the words sprang from me: "Well, I was adopted."

He looked up sharply. "You were *adopted*? Why didn't you say so in the first place?"

For the rest of the session, his pencil scratched rapidly on his yellow pad as he returned to the past, asking me how I had found out I had been adopted, what I knew about my natural parents, what I had thought about them as a child, how I felt about being adopted now. As his questions hit me, one after another like bits of shrapnel, I felt invaded. I tried to push thoughts of my birth mother away, and I tried not to cry.

Finally, Dr. Davis said, "In my opinion it would be damaging to you psychologically to relive your mother's experience." At that moment I knew I would have the abortion, and I was stunned by the irony of the reason: Because my mother did not have an abortion, I was allowed to have one.

* * *

The weekend before the surgery, Paul and I went home to the Monterey Peninsula. I was with Mom and Dad in Monterey, and he was with his mother in Carmel Valley. On Saturday night we went out to Zapeda's in Monterey, since we were both Mexican food addicts. The restaurant was crowded, and we sat at the candle-lit table and talked while we waited. I was basking in the love flowing between us, powerful and electric as always.

Maybe just because for once we weren't talking about "it," because for a while things seemed easy again, my throat unexpectedly tightened, and tears filled my eyes. Paul's comforting words, his hands enclosing mine, only made my tears begin to fall. Embarrassed to be making a scene in a busy restaurant, I hurriedly left the table to have a cry in the ladies' room.

I push open the heavy door, and a woman moves toward me slowly as if in a dream. She is weeping, whimpering audibly. Her eyes are swollen and red, her cheeks streaked with tears and mascara. Her limp posture spells hopelessness, yet she confronts me with defiance in her eyes. Who is this mad woman? Please go away!

She stares right back, her gaze boring into me, now pleading — for what? What does she want from me?

Who are you? Do I know you? Your face looks so familiar.

You know very well who I am, she replies hollowly from inside my head. I am you and you are me. Your predicament was my predicament. Feel the pain — feel my pain too!

Go away! Stop staring at me like that! My mother, it's you, isn't it? Yes, I know it's you. Why did you follow me? There isn't room for us both in here, it's so cramped and hot, I'm afraid I'll scream. Please leave me alone!

Panicking, I reached out to push the crazy woman away. But my fingers encountered a cool mirror covering the entire wall. The breath I'd been holding in escaped in a rush from my lungs. Shakily, I bent over the small sink, splashing her/my puffy face with cold water, grateful that no one else had entered the bathroom during my lapse. *This must really be getting to me*, I thought as I dabbed my face dry with a rough paper towel and smoothed my hair back into a ponytail. *I hope I'm not going crazy.*

There had been neither comfort nor accusation in that long moment I'd spent with the apparition of my birth mother, simply the knowledge of being in the same place together. So this was how it was, this was my beginning: this pain, fear, and desperation. This was my mother, this suffering double. And this was my fate, playing itself out as if written in my genes: I would repeat her act, hurt my family, and lose my child. In those few mad moments of staring into the mirror, I had been my mother, trapped inside her body and her predicament.

My pregnancy would be over in a few days. While I knew that a scar would remain, I would go on living without the responsibility of raising my child alone and without the obsession that would have taken over my life if I'd chosen adoption. But for my mother, the suffering must have continued. Had she loved my father even half as much as I loved Paul? After all these years, did she still think about the baby she had given up? Did she remember my birthday? Did she, too, search faces in crowds? For the first time, because of the fetus I was carrying, I thought about my birth and adoption from my mother's perspective. I experienced a sharp double sadness, with her aloneness a mirror image of my own.

Back at the table, I tried to explain to Paul the trick my mind had played on me. "Patty, I'm so sorry, this is a whole lot harder on you than it is on me," he said, taking my hand in both of his and stroking it near the warmth of the candle flame. Our dinners had arrived while I was gone, the plates heaped high with steaming refried beans and enchiladas. We sipped our wine a while longer, talked quietly, and then left Zapeda's, unable to touch our food.

* * *

Saturday morning was abortion time at the Stanford Hospital. I was one of half a dozen young women waiting, all of us lying on narrow gurneys lining the corridor outside the operating room, dressed in white hospital gowns and paper caps. Paul was with me as long as he was allowed in the beginning, and as soon as I came out of the anesthetic he was beside me. When my doctor came in to check on me after I had woken up, I asked her whether the fetus had been a boy or a girl. She looked at me strangely and said I was being morbid. She said brusquely that "the tissue" had been destroyed and she hadn't noticed the sex.

Though I still loved Paul dearly, after the abortion our relationship became different, as I had suspected it would. Without understanding what I was doing at the time, I began running away from him. I plunged back into my job and master's program. I had a couple of brief affairs. And in February of 1971, exactly a year after the abortion, I moved all the way across the continent. I went to Toronto, where I continued my studies and began a relationship with Harald, who had been Paul's and my older friend at Stanford.

* * *

Throughout the rest of that last year in San Francisco after the abortion, my birth mother continued to haunt me. As always, I searched for her face on city streets and in stores and museums, but now with some faint sense of purpose. Also, commuting from work to school in my little blue vw, four times each day I had to pass the Shriners' Hospital, where Mom and Dad had long ago told me I had been born. It was unavoidable, right on 19th Avenue, between San Francisco State College and the Steinhart Aquarium, where I now worked in a science program for gifted children.

I rarely passed the hospital without being reminded of my birth, my mother, and my abortion. Sometimes I challenged myself to turn the car into the hospital driveway, walk right in, and ask to see my birth records. But I never had the nerve. I was still afraid of her, too close to my double.

I had a recurring daydream during that time, which would spring into my mind at odd times when I was driving. In my daydream, or more accurately "daymare," I was driving around San Francisco clutching my birth mother's address in my hand, hunting for her house. Finally, I located it, a decrepit Victorian midway up one of the city's steep hills. I parked my VW, remembering to turn the wheels into the curb, and with a sense of personal mission, openness to her, and great nervousness, I walked up the steps and rang the bell.

Soon the door was opened halfway by a hostile, slovenly woman in her late fifties, who peered out at me suspiciously. The details of her appearance never varied. She wore a soiled pink bathrobe with a button missing. Old, furry, blue-green slippers stuck out below swollen, purplish ankles. Her hair was in curlers, with grayish blond ends bristling out everywhere. Not bothering to remove the cigarette sticking to her lower lip, this witch-like person asked me what I wanted. I asked, "Are you Mrs. So-and-so?" and when she replied yes, I told her that I believed she was my mother who had given me up for adoption in 1945. She looked at me coldly for a moment and then said, "I didn't want you then, and I don't want anything to do with you now. They told me I wouldn't ever have to see you again. Go away and don't bother me again." With that, she slammed the door in my face.

* * *

Six years later, as I spent the summer of 1976 with my children, with Harald, with my friends, and with my intense, internal pro-and-con arguments about whether or not to search for my birth mother, she returned to my daydreams. But now the frightening apparitions from the time of my abortion had disappeared. The nightmares had become pleasant dreams, fear had become hope, and the witch had become the guardian angel again. These new, optimistic daydreams fueled my growing desire to try to find her, no matter what the consequences.

My birth mother would be into music, I fantasized that summer, she would be into charities, and literature, and we would spend occasional quiet afternoons together. She would tell me all about my father, the love affair she had had in her youth, and we would share many common interests. There would be a peaceful sense of completion in both of us, meeting at last.

Or she would be dying and would have been hoping for me to find her before the end. She would find release in being able to unburden herself after so many years, and we would share her last days.

Or she would be happily married, with teenaged children still at home. We would secretly meet a few times and begin to know each other, though she would have difficulties revealing my presence in her life to her family.

In these simple scenarios, my mother was a person worthy of respect — intelligent, talented, independent, sensitive — and she responded to me with warmth. Our relationship was outside the stream of our normal, daily lives, something valuable for both of us. I feel that this surfacing of positive fantasies was a healthy thing. It helped to balance out the years of sensing something dark, mysterious, and threatening in my blank background, something to make up for. Perhaps also, as Harald had suggested when he mentioned "projecting" my thoughts about myself out onto my birth mother, it was a surfacing of more positive feelings about myself as I began thinking seriously for the first time about embarking upon a difficult search. If I did undertake that search, I would need all the optimism and self-confidence I could muster, for finding her would not be easy.

One summer afternoon, sitting alone in the backyard while the children napped, writing in my journal, I experienced a powerful feeling that *she* wanted me to find her. It felt like a loving request, tugging at me, coming from somewhere completely outside of myself. She wanted to see me. She wanted to say something to me. In those days before adoption records were opened up and state adoption registries were established, my birth mother was powerless to find me, so I would have to do the work. In the shady garden that hot afternoon, I pushed my adult skepticism aside and surrendered to the inner communion I had experienced as a child. My mother was calling to me — she wanted to be found!

PATRICIA MOFFAT

Me with our sheltie, Dandy

CHAPTER 7

Perhaps I was able to feel my birth mother tugging at me that afternoon because still inside of me, perhaps even closer to the surface now that I shared every day with my two young children, was my own child-self. That child had needed time to be alone, lived in close touch with nature, was tuned into a spiritual realm glimpsed just beyond the everyday, and inhabited an imaginative life that felt very real.

My favorite place as a child was "the Big Tree," a large, gnarled old oak that arched over the creek at the bottom of our property behind the barn. Halfway out the trunk and almost directly over the creek was an ideal place to sit, with a natural backrest and footrest. I would often go there just to be alone. I would lie back and watch the clouds moving above the filigree of leaves, or I would lie on my stomach and lose myself in the eddies of the water and the clear bright stones on the creek bottom.

My curiosity about religion began when I was four and asked my parents whether I could go to Sunday school with my neighborhood friend Faith, who like her brother Fred, was also adopted. I had heard all about Sunday school from Faith and felt that I was missing out on something.

Mom and Daddy didn't attend church at the time, but they sent me off to the Baptist church Sunday school with Faith and her family every week after I'd asked. I wasn't disappointed. There were child-sized chairs and tables in a bright room with tall windows. There was a colorful wooden ark and all the pairs of animals to play with. Mysterious pictures were tacked onto the walls, which I soon learned represented scenes from the Bible, such as Jesus with the children, Joseph in his coat of many colors, and poor little baby Moses floating all alone down the Nile in his woven reed basket. We sang "Jesus loves me, this I know," and I learned to pray "Now I lay me down to sleep."

I don't recall how long I went to the Baptist church with Faith, but at some point my parents announced that we all would be going together to a different church, the big, white Presbyterian church on Mason Street.

I became a religious child, a fact that surprises me now, stalwart agnostic that I have been for most of my life. As a child, I read in my Bible every night, memorizing verses. I prayed earnestly, kneeling on my bed, clasping my hands together on the windowsill while taking in the view of the town and the moonlit clouds and the stars above. I prayed to God to help me be a better person (it was so hard to remember all the things our minister said we needed to do or not do in order to get into Heaven), and I asked God to use my life for His purposes.

I was not above praying for specific things. For several weeks when I was eight or nine, I prayed that I would find a kitten. Mom had said we didn't need another animal, what with the horse, Gypsy, and Dandy, our toy Collie, Sparky the parakeet, and a tank full of goldfish — but I badly wanted a cat. These prayers ceased when one morning while walking down to the barn I heard an insistent mewing. A small, scrawny, black-and-tan tabby kitten sat crying all alone near the compost heap. Controlling my excitement so as not to scare the kitten, I walked slowly over and picked him up. He grew up into our beloved Big Tom, who always slept on my bed at night.

I have often wondered where my strong pull toward religion came from, without any prompting from my parents. I found comfort in the idea of being "a child of God," comfort in knowing that no matter what, there was a "Heavenly Father" who would always love and protect me. I remember feeling jealous when I learned from a Catholic friend that they actually prayed to Mary, the Mother of Jesus, for She would have brought something softer and motherly into our masculine Protestant trinity.

My religious faith as a child was in part another facet of my need to be alone, for as I grew up, I discovered that prayer often fulfilled the same purpose as my Big Tree. Today I still find that inner state of peacefulness and focus when alone in nature, and also in meditation. Daydreaming, being close to nature, being alone, playing the piano, and praying were all bound up together in my childhood. It was within this private, meditative space, this emotional core of my life that I kept hidden, that my communion with my birth mother also took place. It was the inner space where she sang me to sleep or sent me waves of love and encouragement.

* * *

I had an active fantasy life as a child. My dolls and stuffed animals all "talked" with me, of course, and with each other. Of all of them, one toy stands out.

At my eleventh birthday party, a school friend gave me a pair of bright red china donkeys, a mother donkey and a baby, which were bound together with a little brass chain. They became Mrs. Donkey and Danny, and soon the three of us began having long conversations. Danny was a funny, witty, sometimes obstreperous little fellow. Mrs. Donkey was long-suffering and devoted to him. Mrs. Donkey and Danny stood on my high dresser so that they could survey everything in my bedroom and we could speak face to face.

Ricky was a trusting little boy, and I once tested his devotion to me with the help of the donkeys. He loved them almost as much as I did; he was in awe of them. Mrs. Donkey and Danny often talked with Ricky, using my vocal cords. One time Mrs. Donkey was complaining of the cold nights and how nice it would be if Danny could have a blanket. Ricky had recently been given a crisp dollar bill, which he was proudly hoarding. Mrs. Donkey asked him for it very movingly, convinced that the dollar would keep Danny warm on these cold winter nights. Ricky made several alternative suggestions for blankets, but Mrs. Donkey was pityingly insistent on having the dollar bill. And so, with great selfless love, my little brother padded into his bedroom and returned tearfully with his cherished dollar bill, laying it carefully over Danny to keep him warm.

I am quite certain I never intended to keep the dollar for myself. In fact, Mrs. Donkey may even have surprised me with her unusual request. But I did want to know how much Ricky believed in the donkeys, how much he loved them, and by extension how much he loved and trusted me. My experiment was cut short, however, when Mom intervened, scolding me and returning the dollar to Ricky.

Yet there was no deceit involved in my convincing Ricky of the reality of the china donkeys' personalities. They were so real to me that I once even fell to physical blows defending them. One afternoon my friend Faith stood with me in front of the donkeys, listening to my involved conversation with them with a smirk. "You're silly!" she said. "They're just little toy donkeys. They aren't real! They can't talk!" Whereupon I punched her in the mouth, damaging her expensive braces.

Later, sitting at the bottom of the stairs, I felt woeful and ashamed as I listened to Mom talking on the phone in the front hall, apologizing to Faith's mother and offering to pay for the visit to the orthodontist and the repair of the braces. I wondered myself what had come over me, why I had hit my best friend, and why at age eleven when most children had outgrown such things, those little toy donkeys were so important to me.

Of the dozens of animated toys that inhabited my imagination, carrying on conversations and adventures, these two just had to be real. Perhaps it was because they were the only toys I had that were mother and child. Mrs. Donkey loved her child unconditionally. She would never, ever, leave him or give him away. The two of them were bound together by a golden chain. Surely my mother would have stayed with me like that too if the circumstances had been different. But the chain between us had been broken.

* * *

It seemed to me as a child that the line between what was real and what was unreal, even between what was visible and what was invisible, was a thin and arbitrary one. One afternoon when I was five — I know I was five because Ricky hadn't come to us yet and Mom's mother, Grandma Boyd, was still alive — I saw three angels in the sky. We were taking a Sunday drive, Mama and Daddy and I and Grandma and Grandpa Boyd. We stopped to explore a construction site, a new residential development in what was then the outskirts of Ukiah. This was one of my parents' favorite activities at the time because they were about to start construction to expand our small house. As we all stood in front of a partly-built new home, its walls open and still without a roof, I looked up, and there, in full daylight in the afternoon, against a background of wispy clouds and the pure, pale blue sky, were three angels hovering quite close, looking down at us. They looked like pretty teenage girls whispering together, their hair flowing loose, their feet bare under their long pastel robes, except that they each had a pair of large, iridescent, graceful, shimmering, feathered wings.

"Look! Look at the angels!" I cried excitedly to my parents and grandparents, pointing up to the sky.

"What? Where?"

"Lordy, the imagination that child has!" Grandma said to Mama, shaking her head, and they chuckled companionably together. I looked back up at the sky, and the angels were still there. Now they had noticed me and were smiling at me, chuckling together like Mama and Grandma but sharing the joke with me.

It was confusing, learning to tell what was real and what was not, and drawing distinctions between what was invisible and real, and what was invisible but not real. Mrs. Donkey and Danny were visible but supposedly not real. Santa Claus, the Easter Bunny, and the Tooth Fairy were real but invisible, but they stopped being real when you grew up. God and Jesus and the Holy Ghost were invisible but real. You were supposed to believe in them your whole life, not just when you were little. My birth mother was invisible and more real to me than Jesus. As for angels, you were supposed to believe in them, because they were in the Bible, but you weren't supposed to actually see any. Like my birth mother, they were real but invisible.

PATRICIA MOFFAT

CHAPTER 8

At the end of my decision-making summer, in early September of 1976, I telephoned Pat Richardson, the head of Parent Finders in Toronto, an organization of adult adoptees searching for birth parents, which had been mentioned in the magazine article I'd read. Pat gave me the address of a woman she felt might be able to help me with a California search: Jean Paton, the founder of Orphan Voyage, a self-help organization for adoptees in Colorado. She also suggested I come to the September meeting of Parent Finders.

I went to the meeting not with the intention of beginning a search right away, but rather to get an idea of what the experience was like in order to help myself make the decision before we left for California at Christmas. The people in the small discussion group I sat in on were several steps ahead of me, already having dealt with the emotional pros and cons leading up to the decision to search. They were involved in the practical and extremely frustrating process of worming bits of information out of a tangled bureaucracy dedicated to the principle of secrecy in adoption and then fitting those small clues into a mental jigsaw puzzle. I learned that in most cases the best way of gaining information was not to tell the truth, not to indicate why you want the information, but to lie. It seemed so ironic to me that our social system makes it necessary to lie in order to learn the truth about oneself. It also bothered me in a more practical way: I am a terrible liar, so it was possible that I wouldn't be able to gather many clues about my background.

For two hours, the hall buzzed with excitement, frustration, and an intense feeling of shared purpose. I sensed a gambler's obsession in some of the people I listened to: just three more steps, two more steps, one more step, if I can manage it somehow, and I'll win! I'll find her! This was clearly the most important challenge these people had ever assigned themselves. I knew myself well enough to know that once I made the decision to start a search, I would become equally obsessed, not letting it rest until I had reached the end.

There was one woman in the group I joined that night who became a symbol to me, giving me the impetus to begin more than anyone else I met or anything that was said. She was gray-haired and in her late sixties, accompanied by her husband who was encouraging and supportive. After all those years, she was trying to find her birth mother when it was very likely that her mother was dead. It was more difficult for this woman to get information, simply because the records were older and many had been destroyed. After many attempts, she had not even been able to find out her mother's maiden name. She didn't have one specific piece of information to go on, yet her dedication to her search was unflagging.

I thought about that woman often after the Parent Finders meeting. I saw myself in her many years later, if I didn't find the courage to begin when we were in California. To spare her adoptive parents' feelings, she had waited until they had died to look for her birth parents. Feelings of love and guilt very similar to mine had kept her from searching years ago, when she might have had a much better chance of finding her birth parents.

My thoughts about my first mother, my family heritage, and my genetic background weren't going to diminish as the children grew older and as my life stretched out further in time from its blank beginning. I felt sure that the questions would continue to haunt me, perhaps even increase in intensity, as each profound experience in my life would throw me back again to my origins. For the first time, I began feeling an urgency to begin. This was not a project I could put on hold indefinitely, occasionally toying with the idea as I grew older, waiting until events in my life were perfect for beginning the search. No, it was possible I'd already waited too long. That ESP-like experience in the garden was probably just my imagination: she might already be dead!

* * *

During that pivotal conversation with Harald in June, I had not considered the logistics of searching for my birth mother at all. We discussed, and I tried to face only the emotional issues. It never occurred to me that it might be extremely difficult or even impossible to find my mother. The important point was just to decide whether or not I wanted to do it. But now, for the rest of the fall before we went to California, my mind turned to more practical questions.

I began acting. I riffled through boxes of old papers and files, looking for anything that would help. I found three things.

One was my "amended birth certificate." I'd had that little black embossed document since 1965, when I'd needed it to apply for my first passport, to go to Stanford-in-Germany. But I had never studied it carefully. It gave Mom and Dad's names as my parents and listed all the information relevant to them: occupations, dates of birth, and addresses at the time. In effect, this "amended" birth certificate, possessed by all adoptees from the closed system, was a curtain hiding my true identity from view. Holding the document and studying it, I was reminded of those black-and-white illustrations in my old high school biology textbook where in a chapter on diseases, the eyes and genitals of the subjects were covered with black strips to create the illusion of anonymity. Similarly, blanks had been pasted over my genetic heritage and my life prior to my adoption to ensure secrecy. The hospital where I had been born, other children born to my mother, and the details of her pregnancy and labor were all left blank. And yet there were a few bleed-throughs from my original birth certificate, a few clues peeking out from under that curtain of secrecy, specifics that were no doubt required by law to be there: my date of birth, and the time, and most important, the attending physician's signature, which was clearly legible: Jeanne M. Thompson, M.D.

The second thing I found was a recipe for a feeding formula from the adoption agency, which Mom had pasted in my baby book. The heading on the stationery read "The Babies Aid, 740 31st Avenue, San Francisco." I doubted whether this agency still existed but felt it was worth a try. Perhaps there was a way to gain access to old agency records through files in City Hall, in the State Capitol, or wherever such documents were kept.

The third item I discovered astounded me. Had Mom realized what she was pasting into my baby book? It was a pink carbon sheet entitled "Medical Information Exchange Blank," and must have been the medical form that discharged me from the Babies Aid the day Mom and Dad took me home. It summarized my state of health, gave my date of admission as December 13, 1945 (by which time I was almost one month old), and the date of the medical examination as January 9, 1946. Someone had written "ok for adopting" at the bottom of the form, and the doctor's signature was completely illegible, but the space after "Child's Name" was FILLED IN!

In a rush, a childhood memory returned to me. At nine or ten years of age, I'm taking this same pink sheet of paper into the kitchen to ask Mom about it, to ask her to help me decipher this name, my name. Together we puzzle over it for a while and decide that it looks like "Melcoty." What an odd name. I later looked in the Ukiah phone book and found no name even vaguely similar to Melcoty. But Mom had said that this was just the name I had been given at the agency. They never would have put down any real name on those papers, she'd said. But Melcoty, I thought — why give a little baby such a weird name? Why not Linda or Susan?

But now I studied the loopy handwriting very closely. Harald helped me, and we went over each hastily written letter, comparing each stroke with all the other handwritten words on the pink carbon sheet. The tentative name we came up with was "Metcalf." Several evenings later, I asked my friend Mary to try to decipher it too, without telling her our conclusion. She studied it carefully under a strong light for a few minutes while I held my breath. Finally she looked up and said, "It must be Metcalf."

Metcalf! Not a very unusual name, but not so common as to fill me with immediate discouragement like Jones or Smith. The day after we deciphered the name, I was sitting in the University of Toronto library reference room poring over the current San Francisco telephone book. There were about a dozen Metcalfs listed and quite a few women's names. I thought it most likely that my mother had married and her name would be different now, but nevertheless I was strongly tempted to send off short notes to all those Metcalfs asking for information.

But I also realized, gazing out the tall library windows with the phone book open on the table in front of me and Tessa dozing in her yellow stroller at my side, that I just might hit bull's eye and scare her off, or alert a relative who might be able to cut off possible sources of information for me. My mother had the right to refuse to see me, but I also wanted to be absolutely sure of who and where she was before she exercised that right. I had no idea what sort of person my mother was and what sort of reception I would have whenever I first contacted her, so I felt I had to curb my enthusiasm and never act rashly. I had to be sure of myself every step of the way and plan my moves carefully.

Metcalf! "Child's Name." My mother's name. My original name. It became more familiar as I said it over and over again, as I told my friends what I was hoping to do during our upcoming sabbatical, and that I knew that my original name was "Metcalf." It was the most vital piece of information I needed in order to find her — the very piece of information that gray-haired woman at the Parent Finders meeting was still seeking after years of effort — and already I had it, by a slip, a fluke, a mistake!

At the end of September I wrote to Jean Paton in Colorado, as Pat Richardson had suggested, telling her of my plans to search for my birth mother, briefly outlining the information I had so far, and asking for any practical advice she might be able to give me about searching for birth parents in California. In those days before the Internet and email, this letter was the beginning of a long, slow process. Within a week or so, I received a warm, helpful reply, referring me on to an acquaintance in the Bay Area who could help me better once we were in California, Mary Ramos of ALMA (Adoptees' Liberty Movement Association), in Menlo Park.

* * *

After Harald had planted the seed, the decision to search for my mother grew within me over the summer and fall. I became aware that I had in fact made the decision only after the wheels were already in motion, as I was jotting down notes in the library or sticking copies of letters into a new file folder labeled "SEARCH." Before the meeting of Parent Finders, I had reached an impasse because of my worries about Mom and Dad and my fears about what I might find. I needed to start acting, to see how it felt to finally begin looking for my mother. It felt absolutely right.

PATRICIA MOFFAT

ADOPTEE BACKGROUND INFORMATION

MOTHER	FATHER
Nationality/Race English	German
Religion Protestant	Protestant
Age at Birth of Child 24	23
State of Birth Washington	Washington
Physical Description 5'5" tall, blue eyes, medium brown golden hair, very pretty, poised, charming. Above-average intelligence according to psychological report of Wechsler-Bellevue IQ Test.	6 foot tall, reddish, blonde wavy hair, blue eyes, fair, well built.
Education 2 years university.	High School
Occupation waitress	Merchant Marines.
Special Interests dramatics; singing; dancing.	Singing, very good singing voice. Radio work, studying singing
Health (Include Any Evidence of Hereditary Diseases) Health good. No known history of hereditary disease or abnormality.	Good
Mother's Health at Birth of Child Good. "RH neg - no titer" per physician's report. No complications of pregnancy. Breech delivery.	
Extended Family Parents are living and in good health. Had two sisters and two brothers. An uncle died from tuberculosis.	Parents living.
Military Service None	Not indicated.
State of Residence at Birth of Child California	
Married to Each Other ☐ Yes ☒ No	
Other Information Both parents single. Mother's family did not know of pregnancy.	Information about the father was given by the mother.

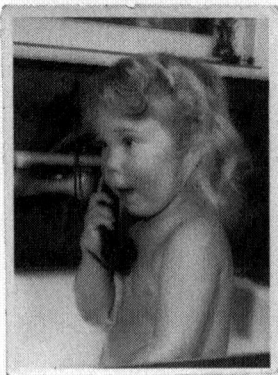

Me at 2 years

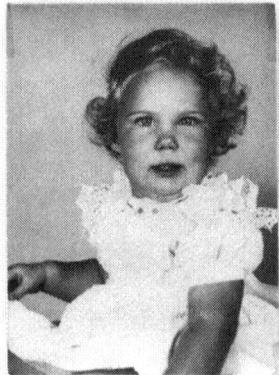

PART II:
THE QUEST

A modeling photo of my birth mother

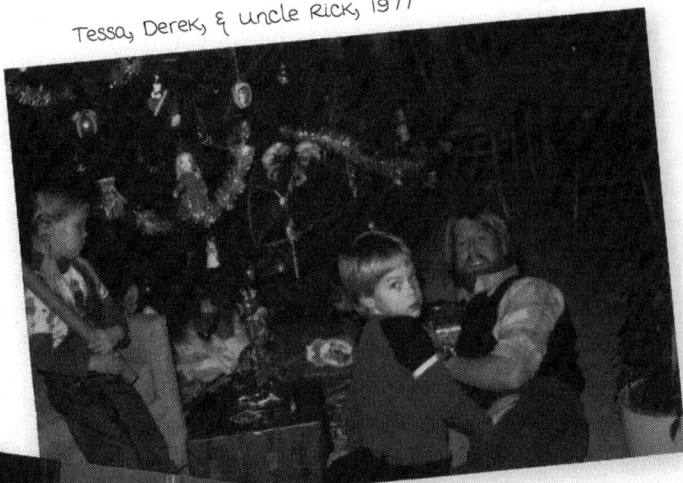
Tessa, Derek, & Uncle Rick, 1977

Me, Tessa, & Derek the
winter of the search,
1977

Derek & Tessa, winter 1977

CHAPTER 9

Deciding to search for my birth mother when we were back in Toronto was one thing, but actually starting the search once we arrived in California, moved in with my parents in Monterey for most of December, and began the preparations for a family Christmas, was another thing altogether. A torpor fell over me. The enthusiasm I'd had for my search back in Toronto began to dissipate. The momentum I'd built up through the Parent Finders meeting, the clues I'd found, and the letters I'd written, stalled. I simply had not taken into account how difficult it would be to start my search with Mom in such close proximity, peering over my shoulder.

Throughout December, each day flew by, consumed with child-related activities, Christmas preparations, and visiting old friends. There were picnics on our favorite beach near Carmel, walks to a local Monterey park with the kids to feed the ducks, and visits to the wharf, where we tossed small fish to the barking sea lions and the comical, spear-billed pelicans. I got together with friends from high school and their small children, we all went to Christmas parties and activities at Mom and Dad's church, and every trip to the grocery store or out Christmas shopping was a major expedition with the children. Mom and I spent warm, sunny mornings on the deck, enjoying the tall pines, cheeky blue jays and squirrels, watching the kids busy themselves with the toys Mom had collected over the previous months. At two-and-a-half years and at ten months, Derek and Tessa were beginning to play together, or at least play next to each other, quite happily. Mom and I nursed our second and third cups of coffee and caught up on news, anticipated our nine months together, and watched the kids. At those times, if my search happened to pass through my mind, it was immediately banished by guilt.

I gave in to the torpor. I realized that if I tried to begin my search before Christmas, and before we moved into the house we would soon be renting in Carmel Valley, I would probably spoil Christmas for the whole family. So I tried to relax, enjoy the holidays, settle back into the family activities, and wait a little longer.

When Rick arrived home for Christmas from Chico, though, driving down in his well-equipped little Volkswagen van, I did discuss searching with him in general terms. Rick was twenty-five now, newly separated and still smarting from that trauma, playing in a rock band, and preparing himself for a teaching career. I wanted to feel him out on the subject of searching, to see whether he had ever had similar thoughts about finding his birth parents. I wanted to know whether I might be able to count on him for emotional support. We went for a walk a few days before Christmas, and after talking about his situation for a while, I blurted out, "Rick, have you thought much about being adopted? Have you wondered who your original parents were and maybe thought about trying to find them?"

He mulled the question over for a few moments as we continued walking in silence and then replied, "No, I really don't think I've thought much about them at all. I think you're born as a blank sheet and your environment makes you the person you are. I know I am who I am only because of what Mom and Dad have done for me, and I don't think I've *ever* thought about finding my other parents. I know it would really hurt Mom and Dad if I did."

Of course, he asked whether something was up with me, and I told him that since Derek and Tessa had been born, I'd been considering looking for my birth parents. But I was hesitant to go into it very deeply since I now knew where he stood. I didn't feel strong enough to deal with his disapproval, because I knew that any rational arguments or emotional statements that he might have used against searching I also felt very intensely. I feared that I could be persuaded to stop my search even before it got started. So we left the subject and moved on to other things.

The day after Christmas, Harald and I and the children moved out to Carmel Valley, and still, for all of January, my search remained in a stall. There was simply too much to do in settling into and organizing our new life. We bought a used car. We joined the local babysitting co-op. I started a playgroup two mornings a week with three other mothers of two-year-olds. We enrolled Derek for two other mornings at a nursery school not far away. Harald made an initial trip to Stanford and Berkeley to stock up on research materials for his sabbatical article at the libraries there.

And I wallowed in the California lifestyle again. I loved the house Mom had found for us, perched high on the rim of Carmel Valley, surrounded by an acre of fenced-in gardens and play areas for the kids. Most afternoons I took Derek and Tessa out to the sandbox, play house, jungle gym, and swing set and either played with them or sat nearby and read or knitted. A donkey that lived next door would often put his head over the fence, watch us, and bray repeatedly until we went over to pet him, to the delight of the children. I was thrilled to have a grand piano again, and in the evenings I would limber up my fingers on it. I delved into the books I had brought along, toying with thesis topics for the master's degree in English literature that I had left half done when Tessa was born. We played on the beach, ate our fill of artichokes, and sampled the local wine.

By the end of January, two months had gone by and I still had not begun my search. An uneasiness began growing in the back of my mind. I worried that I could let the sabbatical slip by, enjoying being with my parents and Rick again, enjoying every day in the Valley, and simply let the idea of searching peter out. The intense commitment I had felt back in Toronto had become much fainter now. Yet I knew it wasn't only the pleasures of California living that were seducing me away from my search. More important were my parents. So near to them, talking with Mom almost every day on the phone and seeing them several times each week, I felt even more guilty about looking for my birth mother than I had back in Toronto. I was actually frightened when I imagined breaking the news of my search to them.

But deep down I knew that finding my birth mother was the one thing I wanted to do more than anything else in the world. I knew I would regret it all my life if I wasted this chance, these rare nine months, this opportunity to find my birth family now that we were on the spot in California, where I had been born and adopted. It was a matter of finding the right time, and the courage, to begin.

I was in this edgy state of mind when Harald and I accepted an invitation to dinner at the end of January, along with Mom and Dad, to friends of theirs in Carmel. For the first time, we left the children in the care of another parent in our babysitting co-op, and set off anticipating an interesting evening at the B---s, as he was a well-known child psychologist and she was a writer in the women's movement.

After dinner, as we all sat with our coffee around the fireplace, an elderly houseguest of the B----s, a professor emerita from Stanford, excused herself to retire into the den to watch *Roots*. There ensued a discussion of the *Roots* phenomenon. Daddy said that he thought the whole thing was fascinating: all the careful research Alex Haley had done, the meaning this endeavor must have for him personally, and for American Blacks in general. He said he could easily understand Haley's reasons for probing so deeply into his past.

Mom and I were sitting together on the couch. She then said, to everyone, but turned to me with a question as she said it, "Oh, I don't know. I'm much more of a here and now person. I don't think much about my past history and my ancestors, do you?"

I squirmed with unease as I mumbled some sort of assent. I was thinking, *You don't* need *to think about your ancestors because you have always known who they are.* But I didn't dare say anything for fear my mind would suddenly become a fish bowl to everyone in the room, or perhaps Harald would leap in at the opportunity and steer the subject around to adoption. I knew that this was absolutely the wrong place to break the news of my search to Mom and Dad, or even to throw out a suggestion, at this dinner party with people we had only just met. I couldn't help wondering, though, whether Mom's alert antennae had somehow picked up on my intention to search.

Thinking about the evening afterward, and writing about it in my journal, I guessed that Mom and Dad's very different reactions to *Roots* might indicate how each of them would react to my search. Mom would probably not want to look at it, might try to belittle it, as she downplayed the importance of her own ancestors. Mom was a person who lived very much in the present; she was a person who *acted*, who accomplished much with her time, and didn't indulge in much "navel-gazing," as she often put it. It could be very difficult for her to understand why my blank past had become so important to me, a practiced navel-gazer.

Yet I knew that my "ancestors" weren't preoccupying me much at all. It was my biological *parents* I was after, especially the woman who gave birth to me. I decided that whenever I did tell my parents about my search, I had to be careful about being drawn into a discussion of roots and ancestors and the past, because all of that was quite peripheral to my desire to search for my birth mother.

Daddy's comments about *Roots* made me feel more hopeful. He might be better able than Mom to understand why I wanted to do this. I felt that he could be more objective, for his sense of self wasn't as bound up with his children as Mom's was. Maybe he could even get excited about my search, intellectually. But if he was hurt by it too, it probably wouldn't show, for Daddy had always been much more emotionally difficult to read than Mom.

The evening at the B----s' nudged me to get moving. It pulled the search out from the shadowy back of my mind to the forefront and roused me from my torpor. The next day, I phoned the woman Jean Paton had referred me to, Mary Ramos of the adoptees' rights organization ALMA. Mary suggested that I drive up to see her in Menlo Park later in the week so we could talk in person. The powerful mixture of love, guilt, and even fear toward Mom and Dad that had immobilized me for two months at last began to break up. I felt that I at least owed it to myself to make a tentative beginning.

I looked forward to sitting down with a sympathetic person who had already searched in California. I hoped I would be able to discuss my feelings of guilt and my worries about Mom and Dad with her. I hoped she would be able to understand my feelings of being torn in two. I also hoped she could give me an idea of how long it might take me to find my birth parents and what sorts of hassles I might face, given the information I had. Did I have enough to go on in order to find my birth mother before we returned to Toronto in September? Information, sympathy, and reassurance were what I needed from Mary.

If we had rented a house nearer San Francisco, I probably would have started searching very soon after we'd arrived in California. I wouldn't have felt as constrained by the proximity to Mom and Dad. Certainly I would have been emotionally wrought in the same way, but at least I wouldn't have to explain any day-long absences. As it was, I decided to tell my parents that I was taking a "mother's day off" on Friday, packing myself and a book off to the beach. I felt very uncomfortable about lying, but I wasn't yet ready to tell them about the search, despite all my intentions about openness and honesty when we were back in Toronto. I wanted first to have a clearer idea of what lay ahead.

As if my inner struggles about hurting my parents weren't enough, now a new obstacle was arising: Harald was feeling quite strongly that I *shouldn't* search! In Toronto, and for several weeks after we arrived in California, he was all in favor of it, but now that I was moving closer to beginning, he was rapidly backing off. He argued that it was pointless to find out who my original parents were. He now felt that my problems with myself had more to do with my very "natural" (as opposed to "adoptive") relationship with Mom and that finding another mother was like going off on some wild goose chase. One of Harald's least endearing traits was habitually playing devil's advocate. When I was on one side of the fence, he'd usually be on the other, trying to be "constructively critical." I hoped that once I got started on the search, he would climb over on my side of the fence again, for I really didn't know whether I could do this thing alone.

* * *

It was strange early in the morning of February 4, 1977, driving over the Los Laureles Grade without one or both kids in the back seat, on a journey all my own. The two-hour drive gave me time to think. I reviewed what I wanted to talk about with Mary. I tried to picture what sort of person she was. I wondered whether she would be a radical adoptees' rights advocate who would come on strong, and I hoped not, for I wanted to talk openly about my worries for Mom and Dad. I itemized what I already knew and went over many different plans as to how these bits of information could be used to learn more: the name "Baby Metcalf" on the release form Mom and Dad were given at the adoption agency, the 1945 address of the agency, and the name of the attending physician on my amended birth certificate. During much of the drive, I gave in to daydreams (and daymares) about my birth parents, especially this intimate stranger, my mother.

I liked Mary the moment I saw her, a warm, intelligent woman in her late forties with no pretense in her dress, her manner, or her home. I felt comfortable as we sat down with our coffee mugs at her large oak dining room table piled high with typewriter, books, files, and papers.

Mary's case was quite different from mine. She only discovered she had been adopted after her adoptive parents died, so her difficulties were a feeling of shock and a review of her life in the light of this new information, not as in my case, trying to work a search into the existing relationship with adoptive parents. However, Mary showed a great deal of empathy as we discussed my situation. She felt, as I did, that I should tell Mom and Dad about the search soon, for it could go on for many months, and if I told them what I had done as a *fait accompli* at the end of our sabbatical, it could be a much worse shock than telling them now, because there wouldn't be enough time to integrate my search and who and what I might find into our relationship.

Mary also spoke of "widening the circle of love" as an adoptee finds herself with two families — the experience of an increase in the capacity to love for all three parties (the adoptee, the birth parents, and the adoptive parents) as they discover each other. Sitting at Mary's cluttered dining room table and thinking about my parents two hours away down Highway 101, I found this a beautiful thought, but I felt that it demanded a great unselfish love on the part of the adoptive parents. Unless they were quite unusual people, they would probably first feel threatened by the sudden widening of the family circle. But perhaps I was underestimating Mom and Dad, I mused, prejudging their reactions just because I felt so loaded down with guilt and worry.

Once we had pretty well covered that subject, and I had stopped shaking, Mary and I talked about my specific questions about searching. She told me that the quickest way of learning my birth parents' names, if I happened to be lucky, would be to write for my adoption decree from the county in which I was adopted. That was the document that transferred legal parenthood from the natural parents to the adoptive parents. California laws were in great flux in the area of adoption in the 1970s, and people were finding that some counties sent out adoption decrees upon request and others didn't. Maybe I would be lucky. Mary showed me several photocopies of adoption decrees belonging to other people she was working with. Sometimes the natural parents' names, or at least the mother's name, were written into the decree, other times they weren't, but in all cases the baby's original name formed the heading of the document. So at best, if I was sent my adoption decree, I could learn my parents' names. At the very least, I would have proof of my original name, which probably would be a confirmation of the name Metcalf. "Baby Metcalf," I imagined my decree might say, like the names on the long, legal-sized Xeroxes I was leafing through hungrily at Mary's table.

I asked Mary how I could get access to my files at the adoption agency, which I assumed no longer existed, for it wasn't in the current San Francisco phone book. Mary said that access to the files without a court order was impossible but that recently it had become possible to write to the State Department of Health/Department of Adoptions, requesting "nonidentifying background information." The department would then send a page of information about my natural parents' interests, education, family medical histories, etc., practically anything that would be in the original file except names, addresses, or other specifics that would make it easy to locate them. However, Mary said that there are usually important clues hidden within the information, and if you used some ingenuity, you could tease them out.

As for my final piece of evidence, she suggested that I drop in at the Stanford Medical School library on my way home and look up Jeanne M. Thompson, the attending physician at my birth, in the American Medical Association directories. If Dr. Thompson could tell me the hospital I was born in, that would be one step closer to finding out my mother's name, for I would then know where my hospital records were.

I left Mary with a feeling of release and a sense of purpose. This was the best I had felt about my search since we'd left Toronto! I still hadn't quite admitted to myself that I had started searching, but I figured, *Why not throw out a few feelers and see what happens?* As I drove, I mentally reviewed the first three steps of the search, which Mary had suggested, until they began to feel almost like normal, everyday things to do: Write the court for the adoption decree. Write Sacramento for the nonidentifying background information. Write to Dr. Thompson to confirm the hospital I was born in. On that last point, Mom and Dad had told me long ago I'd been born in the Shriners' Hospital on 19th Avenue, so I just needed confirmation of that from the doctor who'd delivered me, and then I could ask for my records with some confidence.

I drove straight to Stanford, walked into the medical library, pulled down a few AMA directories, and pored over the tiny print. I found my Dr. Thompson quickly. She was currently a pathologist in Modesto,

California, but in the directory she was listed as Jeanne I. rather than Jeanne M. Thompson. I thought it was extremely unlikely that there would have been two female Jeanne Thompsons practicing as residents in the San Francisco City and County Hospitals in 1945. I Xeroxed the entry on her from the directory, and I also Xeroxed a copy of my amended birth certificate for her, which was in the file of materials I had taken to show Mary Ramos. I wanted Dr. Thompson to see the date on the certificate and her own handwriting, hoping this would tweak her memory as to what hospital she had been working at in November of 1945.

It was while I was in the medical library that I suddenly realized I wasn't just toying with the idea of searching any longer, but I was actually, finally doing it. I felt like a detective working on a case with the highest personal stakes. My excitement mounted as I traced Jeanne Thompson from the 1945 directory through to the present one and then hurried over to the phone directories, pulling out the one for Modesto and copying down her present address. The name that had been going through my mind since last summer in Toronto belonged to the doctor who had actually delivered me. Hers were the first hands ever to touch me, and here she was only a couple hours' drive from where I was!

Afterward, I went out of the hospital complex and sat down under a tree on the lawn to eat my lunch. I took in the familiar surroundings with an eerie sense of distance from the student I had been in that same place ten years before. There were the red-tiled, sandstone buildings of the main campus off to my left. I remembered myself many times during those years at Stanford riding my bicycle past the very tree I was sitting under, on the way from my dorm to the shopping center, or over to the center for autistic children where I had done volunteer work, and I thought how amazed my nineteen-year-old self would have been if I had been able to peek into the future then, had seen my thirty-one-year-old self eating lunch under that tree and had known why I was visiting the hospital. I also couldn't help thinking about the last time I had been at the hospital, to have the abortion, and I reflected upon how much personal history a disinterested place contains. I studied the other people on the lawn and those passing by, wondering about their personal connections to this place.

I was bursting to share every detail of my day with Harald as I drove up the winding oak-lined road to the top of the Valley. I was hoping that my enthusiasm and the information I'd received from Mary might help him feel better about my search again. It took a great deal of self-control to talk about other things for more than an hour, for when I arrived I found Harald, the kids, and our neighbor Shirley out in the play yard. I didn't feel ready to talk about my experiences with anyone but Harald, so all my news waited until dinnertime, when I managed to blurt out disjointed accounts of my day while cutting up the children' meat, helping Tessa with her cup, asking Derek to try to his vegetables, and carrying on other conversations with the kids.

Later, after the house became quiet, with the children in bed and Harald in the back room watching television, I completed day one of my search by taking those first three steps. I typed up a letter to Dr. Thompson. I wrote to the California Department of Health asking for the nonidentifying background information from my file. And I wrote to the Clerk of the Superior Court in San Francisco requesting the adoption decree of Patricia Ann Dietterle.

That was the easy part. As I sat in the kitchen alcove that night, pulling one letter after another out of the typewriter and sealing them in their envelopes, I knew for certain that I had begun my search and was fully committed to it. What was it Mary had said with a smile as we shook hands and said goodbye that afternoon in Menlo Park? "You'll be fine, Pat. All you needed was permission to search. I'm happy I was able to give that to you."

The hard part would come the following day: breaking the news to Mom and Dad.

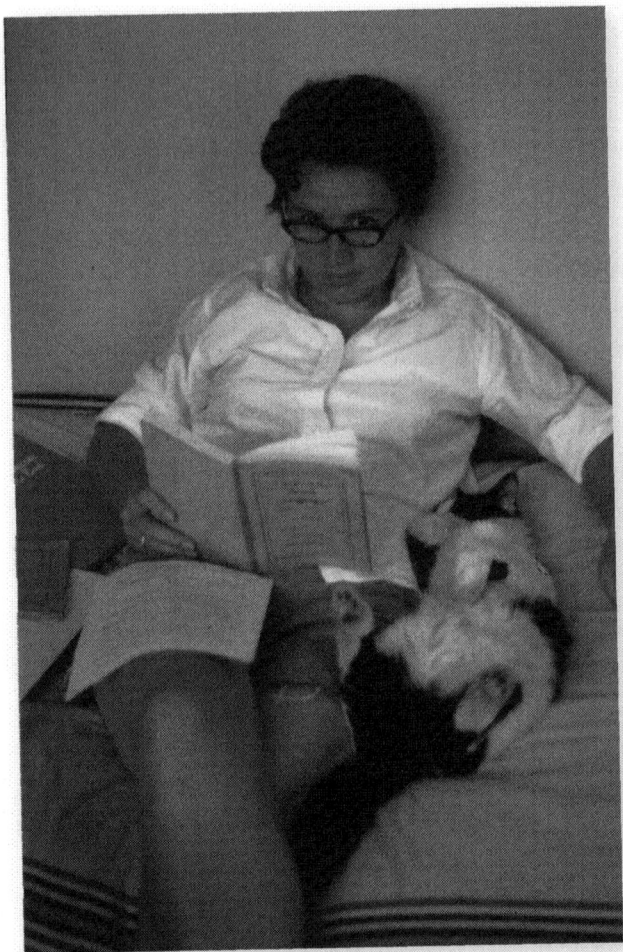

Elaine Durham, Uganda, Peace Corps, 1969

CHAPTER 10

As the four of us sat around the candlelit table in the octagonal, glass-walled dining room, the conversation did not flag. Since I'd put the children to bed, it seemed to me as if we had been talking nonstop for hours. I just couldn't find the right time to begin telling my parents about my search. At every short pause in the conversation, I considered bringing it up, but because the topic was so highly charged, and so terribly out of context each time, it seemed to me as if I would be making an announcement.

I thought an opening might come after dessert, but just as I was pouring the coffee and forming my words, Mom and Daddy suddenly began reminiscing about a neighbor of ours in Ukiah, filling Harald in on the details of his unusual life. It went on and on, with many funny anecdotes, and I felt a rush of nostalgia as memories of my childhood flooded my mind. But underneath the table my hands were shaking because THERE WAS SOMETHING ELSE I WANTED TO TALK ABOUT, and I felt helpless to change the direction of the conversation. I hoped a change of scene might help, and as if Harald were reading my mind, he suggested moving into the living room and lighting a fire.

Yet as we rose from the table, Daddy mentioned that Josephus and his sister had driven down from San Francisco that morning, and before we

97

had even settled ourselves around the fireplace, a conversation about our Ethiopian friends was fully launched: Josephus and his family, Rahel and her new husband, and Daniella and her mother still in prison back home. In the harsh light of the serious problems of survival in Ethiopia that we were discussing, my preoccupation suddenly seemed self-indulgent to me, almost petty.

In order to give Harald some background on these friends, at one point Mom explained that Josephus had been "a poor boy from the country" who had been adopted by a wealthy family in Addis Ababa. But even then I couldn't jump in. Even with that small cue of adoption, switching to the topic of my search would have seemed too stilted. Finally, I realized that in *any* context the subject I desperately needed to talk about would be out of place, so it was just a matter of screwing up my courage and *saying it*.

Mom and Dad mistook my silence for fatigue and started making noises about leaving. Thankfully, Tessa began crying then. I was glad of the break so that I could sit in the darkened bedroom, nursing her in the rocker, and clearly think out what I wanted to say.

When I returned to the living room, Harald was outside fetching more firewood. For once there was no conversation to break into, and as I closed the door into the bedroom wing behind me, I heard myself saying, "There's something I really want to talk to you both about before you leave tonight." Suddenly their relaxed faces changed, and I could sense the inventory of topics racing through their heads: "Is she pregnant again? Is there a serious problem in the marriage?"

"Don't worry." I attempted a smile. "It isn't a crisis, but it's important to me. I was wondering whether the two of you have ever talked about the possibility of Rick or me maybe wanting to find out more about our backgrounds."

They looked at each other for a searching moment, and then Daddy said, "No... No, I don't think we ever have. Why? Are you interested in finding out more about your background?"

It took an effort for me to control my whole body from trembling as I sat back down in my chair by the fireplace. "Well, I've wondered about my biological parents off and on when I was growing up," I began, "but since Derek and Tessa have been born, I've thought about them quite a lot, and I would like to know more...to know whose genes I am carrying around and passing on to the kids."

Harald entered at this point, registered the changed tone of the conversation, unloaded his armload of wood, and sat down on the hearth.

"I really want you to understand that I'm not interested in finding another mother and father," I continued, aiming at the center now. "You're the only parents I have. I'm not anticipating a relationship with whoever I might find. But I would like to know where I came from, for the sake of the children, and also just because I want to know." I told them about the experience in the labor room with Tessa, when I realized I had no information at all about my medical and genetic background, describing that interview as a sort of turning point. I felt more confident talking about a medical reason for searching because I thought they would better be able to understand that than the emotional pull I didn't fully understand myself.

But Daddy had been watching me closely and said, "Yes, I can understand why you'd want to know more about your roots." I felt my taut muscles relax a little, remembering the conversation about Alex Haley the week before and feeling grateful that a few things in life are predictable.

"You know, it feels so good to say something about this at last," I said. "I've been so nervous and worried about how to bring this up with you, and what your reaction would be."

Mom stepped in easily at this point. "Well dear, we're just sorry you've gotten yourself all steamed up about this when it really is something your Dad and I can handle. But Pat, I don't have many suggestions to make as to how you could go about finding out information. You must know that the records are sealed and that the adoption agency no longer exists."

I said that I knew where the records were; it was a question of how to get at them.

Daddy picked up on that right away. "Then you mean you've been making inquiries?"

"Well, yes, a few," I said. Then I told them the whole story that started last summer in Toronto when it became clear that we would be spending the sabbatical in California: the meeting of Parent Finders, my finding a few clues in boxes in the closet at home, my letter to Jean Paton in Colorado. And I told them, my hands shaking again, about how I had spent my "mother's day off" in Menlo Park the previous day, apologizing for having lied to Mom. I told them I had located and written to the doctor who had delivered me to Sacramento for nonidentifying background information and to the court in San Francisco asking for my adoption decree.

"You wrote to the court in San Francisco?" Mom asked, puzzled. "I don't think you'll get any information from them, because we adopted you in Ukiah, in the Mendocino County Court."

"Oh," I said, "of course.... That's right." I suddenly realized how vague my knowledge was about my adoption and how much Mom and Dad could help me by going over that information. I said, "The story I remember you telling me about my biological parents — or maybe you didn't tell me, maybe I pieced it together or imagined it — was that my...that they were married, but my mother had 'fallen out of love with my father' during the war, and that's why she gave me up for adoption...."

"Now, let me think. George, you help me here," Mom began. "All that we were told was that your mother was a music major at the University of Washington when she became pregnant. Her maiden name was... I'm pretty sure the name was Metcalf. Your father was a German-American in the Merchant Marines. But that's it. They just didn't tell us any details. You know the policies of secrecy at that time, Pat."

Shocked, I stared out the windows at the twinkling lights across the black valley. Metcalf! How fantastic to have that doctor's scrawl confirmed by Mom! But why, why then had she puzzled over that pink sheet from the adoption agency with me when I was a child, guessing that my name was "Melcoty"?

And all this time I had been assuming that I would be searching in California. I had assumed my mother's home had been in the Bay Area and that after laborious hours of research in the San Francisco Public Library, I would eventually pinpoint her as being one of, or being related to, those Metcalfs in the San Francisco phone book. Now I understood that my search must move on to Washington State.

I turned to Harald and said out loud what we both were thinking, "Elaine's in Seattle!"

"Your roommate from the Peace Corps?" Daddy asked.

"Yes. Maybe she wouldn't mind doing a little research for me."

My attention to the conversation became fuzzy at this point, for I was mentally reshuffling the few pieces of my jigsaw puzzle and wondering what things I could ask Elaine to do that would be easy for her yet could yield positive results.

The conversation with Mom and Dad was emotionally charged throughout, though emotions were never talked about. We all chose our words carefully and dealt with facts, looking at the situation as a problem to be solved, a tough nut to crack. Daddy said he would go down to the bank and look through the safety deposit box to see if there were any documents there that might help, though he doubted there was anything. And at Harald's suggestion, he said he would also write to the law office in Ukiah that had handled the adoption and request their records, though here again, both he and Mom doubted that there would be anything to help me. They didn't probe into my reasons for wanting to search, and aside from saying, "We can handle it," they didn't say how they really felt about it, and I didn't probe.

About ten thirty Daddy looked at his watch as the conversation seemed to have reached a close. I told them again how good it felt to get this out into the open and how amazed and relieved I was at their calm reaction to the whole thing.

"Well, Patty..." Mom laughed softly as we kissed goodnight, "whatever did you expect of us? We're just sorry this thing has gotten you so exercised."

"Relax, kid!" Daddy said as he hugged me. "Everything's going to turn out just fine."

The four of us walked out into the cool night air to Mom and Dad's car. Harald put his arm around my shoulder as we watched them getting settled, for my teeth were chattering, only partly from the cold. "Get inside!" they shouted cheerfully. We waved to each other, the silver Audi pulled away, and as I watched it roll down the long driveway, I felt emptier and emptier. There was no calling them back now, no turning back. And what were they really feeling?

Inside the house, I shut the heavy oak door, leaned back against it, and let out the breath it felt like I had been holding all evening. "Well, it's finally out. I can't believe how matter-of-fact they were!"

"Oh, they were upset all right, especially your Mom," Harald said. "You'll see."

* * *

The next morning, while Derek was at his play group and Tessa napped, I acted quickly on the information I'd learned from Mom and Dad. First, I wrote to the recorder at the Mendocino County court, basically the same letter as the misdirected earlier one to San Francisco ("Dear Sir: I am a thirty-one-year-old adoptee, writing to request a certified copy of my final decree of adoption....") This time, however, I was able to state confidently that my birth name had been "Metcalf."

Next, I wrote a long letter to Elaine in Seattle. Like most of my friends, Elaine knew I had been adopted, and I guessed that my search would be intriguing news to her. I told her that my birth mother had come from Washington, and as carefully as I could, I asked her whether she could find a free afternoon and go to the library for me and comb through the University of Washington yearbooks, looking for a female Metcalf music major in the early to mid-1940s. If she was successful, I continued, could she then phone the Alumni Association and ask if they had a current address for the woman she'd found or a record of a name change?

I was worried about loading Elaine down with unreasonable and time-consuming requests. She also had a little boy, just three months older than Derek, and I knew how difficult it could be to find time for library research or even phone calls with a small child around. But I also believed that Elaine's natural detective impulses would be aroused by my letter. I hoped so, because I couldn't think of anyone else I knew in or near Seattle who could do that footwork for me.

After this round of letter-writing, I stayed in the kitchen alcove awhile and allowed myself to daydream. What if Elaine turned up something very soon? What if within a week I was in possession of my mother's name and current address! What then? What would I do?

I had already thought about the first moment of contact many times back in Toronto, of course. I'd visualized how it might happen right from the beginning. But now that the detective work had begun, the possibility of actually contacting my birth mother seemed much more real. There were five things I could do, I reasoned: I could fly up to Washington, or wherever she turned out to be, and simply knock on her door. Or I could sneak a peek at her before deciding what to do. Or I could phone her first. Or I could write her a letter. Or I could ask Elaine or someone else to be the intermediary, and meet her, phone her, or write to her on my behalf and suggest a meeting.

Without the search-and-reunion manuals and websites that are available today, with their helpful recommendations for that first contact, I had only my intuition to go on and the stories I had heard in the media, at the Parent Finders meeting, and from Mary Ramos. Pondering the alternatives, I decided that just showing up at her door or even phoning could be shocking and unfair to her. I would have had time to prepare myself psychologically for that moment, but she would be caught completely by surprise. And in that vulnerable position, she might just say no and refuse to meet me at all, shutting the door in my face like that nightmarish apparition in San Francisco had done, repeatedly, after my abortion. On the other hand, asking Elaine or someone else to approach her wouldn't be fair to me! I couldn't stand the idea of leaving that dramatic first contact to someone else, even a friend who'd helped me and whom I trusted. Besides, that would put Elaine in the awkward position of persuading my birth mother to see me, a weighty responsibility.

No, I thought, it had to be a letter. In a letter, I would be able to use tact and persuasion to convince her to see me. I would make the contact, and she would have time to gather her forces mentally, emotionally, and psychologically before replying. It would be the best approach for both our sakes: direct but gentle at the same time. Forever the optimist, several drafts of that letter kept running through my mind during the next few days, like verses of a song I couldn't get out of my head.

PATRICIA MOFFAT

CREES PROBATE BOOK 30 PAGE 48

Entered March 7, 1947

FILED
MAR 7 1947
W. J. BROADOUS
COUNTY CLERK
By _____ Dep..

IN THE SUPERIOR COURT OF THE STATE OF CALIFORNIA, IN AND FOR THE

COUNTY OF MENDOCINO

In the Matter of the Adoption

of

CAROL KROLL METCALF,

a Minor.

No. 7875

ORDER FOR ADOPTION

The verified petition of GEORGE RAYMOND DIETTERLE and
KATE ELIZABETH DIETTERLE, his wife, and of the Native Sons and
Native Daughters Central Committee on Homeless Children, herein-
after called Central Committee, praying for an order for adoption
by said GEORGE RAYMOND DIETTERLE and KATE ELIZABETH DIETTERLE, his
wife, of CAROL KROLL METCALF, the above named minor, of the age
of one year and two months or thereabouts, coming on regularly
for hearing on the 7th day of March , 1947, and the said
petitioners herein and the said minor child being present in Court,
and the said petitioners being examined by the Court, each separately
and the Court having heard the petition and the evidence in support
thereof, and it appearing to the satisfaction of the Court, the
Court finds that all the allegations of said petition are true;
that petitioners are husband and wife, and are, and each of them
and it further appearing that said Central Committee has
consented to the adoption of said minor by the petitioners GEORGE
RAYMOND DIETTERLE and KATE ELIZABETH DIETTERLE, his wife, and has
authorized its Secretary, Phyllis Dunne, a resident of the City
and County of San Francisco, State of California, to execute in

tioners GEORGE RAYMOND DIETTERLE and KATE ELIZABETH DIETTERLE
and shall have the name and be known as PATRICIA ANN DIETTERLE.

Done in Open Court this 7th day of March, 1947.

_____
Judge of the Superior Court

RKE & RAWLES
TTORNEYS AT LAW
LICAN PRESS BLDG.
UKIAH, CALIF.

CHAPTER 11

Around one o'clock every weekday afternoon of February, March, and April of 1977, my ear would be cocked to the end of the driveway where the mailbox stood as I listened for the puttering of the mail carrier's little white vehicle. Day after day during that winter and spring of drought, when not a trickle of water ran in the bed of the Carmel River, the sun warmed my back as I watered the strawberries, herbs, and patio plants with soapy water saved from the lunch dishes. The light, warm air carried the scents of dust and live oaks and rosemary, and the sounds of my children playing nearby, jays scolding, the donkey braying, and the swishing of cars down on the road, while I waited, listening for the mail truck.

In the 1970s, the pace of life, and in turn the pace of searching, was slow by today's standards. Today the best place to start a search is often on the Internet or with a genetic testing kit. The steps adoptees take today in the process of finding a birth relative are just as logical and carefully planned out as they were in the 1970s, but a crucial piece of information that could have taken days, weeks, or even months to receive back then, using snail mail and the phone, might be retrieved almost instantaneously today by hitting the "enter" key or receiving your DNA results.

When I searched for my birth mother in 1977, there weren't even fax machines, let alone home computers. Thus, most of my time during the winter and spring of 1977 was spent sitting on my hands, thinking up useless things to do just to convince myself I was not giving up, and waiting for the mail to arrive every day. We didn't even have cheap long-distance phone cards then — and nothing like Skype — so rather than racking up an enormous phone bill during my search, I tried to use the mail whenever possible, or at least until my frustration shot through the roof.

I'm sure that the slower pace of life even extended to emotions during the search. It's not that the emotional impact of searching has changed. Finding birth parents today is still usually the most meaningful and emotionally charged thing that adopted people can do for themselves, just as it was in the seventies. But today searchers can get whipped rather quickly through the stages of doubt, fear, hope, guilt, terror, confusion, wonder, elation, disappointment, shame, sadness, grief, and whatever other feelings accompany a person's search. Yet in 1977, many of these same emotions in me were sustained for weeks. They were drawn out in the same way that waiting for the mail became a sustained agony.

On February 16th, twelve days after I'd sent out my first letters, the first reply arrived. I tore open the envelope with its Modesto postmark and feminine handwriting as I walked back up the driveway from the mailbox. *I have recently retired and your letter was forwarded,* Jeanne I. Thompson's graceful script declared, as my heart leapt. *I did not sign the birth certificate, but the signature is almost surely that of Jeanne Miller Thompson, who followed a class or two behind me, but on the same service at San Francisco General, as it is now known. It is the old hospital on Potrero Avenue.*

Surprised, I sank down onto the wooden swing near the patio to finish reading the letter. *There were usually relatively few deliveries on any one day,* Dr. Thompson wrote helpfully, *and if the date is correct it should not be too much of a problem to narrow it down. Hope this will be of some help.*

I lowered the letter into my lap and gazed out over the patio and yard. Derek and Tessa were playing in the sandbox, Tessa rubbing her eyes and fighting off nap time, while Harald sat on a lawn chair nearby with his newspaper and coffee. So there *had* been two Jeanne Thompsons, both young doctors in the same place at the same time! And I hadn't been born in the Shriner's Hospital on 19th Avenue after all, the hospital I used to drive by every day in 1970 with such mixed feelings. Why had I always thought I'd been born there? Probably I had misinterpreted something Mom or Dad had said one day as we drove by on a visit to "The City" in my childhood.

I wandered over to the kids, handed Harald the letter to read, and scooped Tessa up to bounce her on my hip, take her inside for a change, and put her down for her nap. It was hard to stop thinking about the letter — the first fish my net had caught — while I sat nursing Tessa in the rocking chair next to her crib. I appreciated Dr. Thompson's pleasant, helpful tone. It flooded me with optimism, in fact. I'd been a little afraid that the people I'd approach during my search would be uncooperative, would feel I shouldn't be doing what I was doing, and might preach at me or withhold information. That was the impression I'd gotten at the Parent Finders meeting in Toronto, at any rate: "Never say why you are interested in the information. Just ask." Mary Ramos, too, had stressed that you must learn to lie — or at least tell half-truths — to get the information you needed. Well, maybe it wouldn't be so hard after all, I thought. I hoped that the tone of this first letter was a good omen.

Meanwhile, what should I do with the information Dr. Thompson had given me? Drive up to the General, walk into the records department and ask for my file? What name would it be under? I felt it was very unlikely they would just hand it over to me, whether I appeared in person or sent a letter. No, I needed to be patient until I knew more. I decided to wait until I received the nonidentifying background information from Sacramento, which might have some important clues about my birth parents, and wait till I'd heard from Elaine. Then I'd have more to go on in approaching the hospital — hopefully my mother's full name.

* * *

Two days later, I could hardly believe what I pulled out of the mailbox. I knew I'd hit the jackpot as soon as I saw "Mendocino County Clerk" stamped in the upper left-hand corner of the fat envelope. Surely they wouldn't have sent such a heavy letter if they were turning down my request for my adoption decree! Surely a thin envelope or a terse postcard would have sufficed.

I wanted to have time to read the document through without interruptions, so I controlled my impatience and didn't even open the envelope until I'd cleared the patio table of the lunch dishes and Harald had agreed to sandbox duty again. Then I sat down at the picnic table, opened the envelope carefully, and unfolded the three long Xeroxed pages of the document. There on the first page, framed by legal jargon and typed in full caps, was my full birth name:

CAROL KROLL METCALF

I stared at the name until it danced on the page. With a fluttering heart and an unnerving sense of dislocation (*I am myself and yet I am not; I am myself but I was once someone else*), I read slowly through the document. I learned that I had been legally adopted by Mom and Dad on March 7, 1947, when I was sixteen months old, though I had been with them for over a year by that time. I read that my natural mother, whose name was not mentioned, had signed a statement of relinquishment on December 4, 1945, when I was sixteen days old. I also learned that the name of my adoption agency had not been "The Babies' Aid," but incredible as it sounds, "The Native Sons and Native Daughters Central Committee on Homeless Children." Perhaps The Babies' Aid had been a sort of clearing house for babies that were finally judged "okay for adopting."

When I reached the final paragraph of the document, thundering with capital letters, I had to wipe the tears from my eyes several times in order to finish reading it.

NOW, THEREFORE, IT IS ORDERED, ADJUDGED AND DECREED
that said minor CAROL KROLL METCALF, be adopted by the petitioners GEORGE RAYMOND DIETTERLE AND KATE ELIZABETH DIETTERLE, husband and wife...and that said minor shall hereafter bear the family name of said petitioners... and be known as PATRICIA ANN DIETTERLE.

Reading and rereading the document, I was flooded with emotions. I was amazed that my birth mother had given me a name! In those empty weeks before I had been passed on to Mom and Dad, my name had not been "Female Baby Metcalf," as was the case on most of the adoption decrees Mary Ramos had shown me. My mother had given me a name, though she knew she would never see me again.

But I had always been Patricia Ann Dietterle: Pat, Patty, Patricia. That had been my name and my identity all my life. I'd never thought of it as a second name overlain upon a first. One of my earliest and proudest achievements in school was laboriously printing my name in large letters with a fat red pencil: "Patty" — that magical symbol of myself, printed on blue-lined newsprint.

But when I saw my original name for the first time, and when I read the last paragraph of the adoption decree, I saw a transformation of one person into another, an obliteration of one identity in the taking on of another. In effect, Carol Metcalf died at sixteen months of age. I wondered what she would have been like if she had grown up, what her family would have been like, where she would have lived, whether she would have had sisters and brothers, what her interests and talents would have been, where her life would have led her if she had grown to be thirty-one years old. How would Carol be like Patty, and how would she be different?

I felt dizzy, I felt split, as if I'd disintegrated into twin parts. Rather than feeling energized because the document held valuable new information for my search, as I continued to sit at the picnic table a few minutes longer with the strange thing in my hands, I could only weep.

* * *

Three days later, I was back playing detective at the Monterey Public Library. I was relieved that the adoption decree had verified the name Metcalf, now almost certainly my mother's maiden name. But an unexpected new clue was the name "Kroll." Even before my tears had subsided as I finished reading the document, I had concluded that Kroll was my father's name. After all, Kroll was a German name — Harald confirmed that — and Mom had said they'd been told that my father was a German-American.

Why else would my birth mother have stuck the name Kroll in the middle of my name, if he weren't my father? It looked so out of place between the very English "Carol" and "Metcalf." More tentatively, I also thought there was a good chance that my father's name was Carl Kroll. If I'd been born a boy, I reasoned, my birth name might have been Carl. But since I was a girl, they might have just stuck an "o" in the name. So when I went to the library a few days later to pick up a new stack of picture books for the kids, I headed first over to the shelves of telephone books and pulled out the current Seattle phone book. Several Krolls were listed, and two of them were Carl Krolls.

That evening, still in detective mode, I took another step. I dashed off a letter to the California State Registrar of Vital Statistics in Sacramento in an attempt to spring my original birth certificate. I knew from Mary Ramos that it was extremely unlikely they'd send it to me, for the original certificates for adoptees are sealed by the courts, and only the "amended" versions are given out. But I figured I'd take a chance. What harm could it do? The document would be very helpful, if I could get my hands on it. It would tell my mother's full name, her address, and occupation at my birth, and might confirm my hunch about Carl Kroll too. Perhaps in that long shot of writing for my birth certificate, I was just practicing how to lie; lying seemed such an important skill in searching, and my lying capabilities needed developing.

Dear Sir, I wrote boldly, *For purposes of applying for Canadian citizenship, I am required to present a copy of my birth certificate....* I gave my name as "Carol Kroll Metcalf," included my birth date and place of birth, and sent along $2.00 to cover photocopying and mailing. I was hoping the clerk would be confused by my letter. "If she's adopted," he might have reasoned, "then she'll want her original certificate to find out what her name is. But she already knows what her name is! She signed the letter Carol Metcalf. Maybe there was some mistake and this certificate shouldn't have been sealed. Oh well, if she needs this for Canadian citizenship, I guess I may as well Xerox it."

Five more days crawled by. By February 23rd, only one more piece of information had come in. Not surprisingly, a clerk at the Superior Court in San Francisco wrote to say there was no adoption decree on file for me there. I was still waiting for the nonidentifying background information from Sacramento. And after two weeks of waiting, I still hadn't heard anything from Elaine.

So I phoned her. I was glad I did, because somehow Elaine hadn't picked up on the sense of urgency I'd thought was screaming out from every sentence in my letter. She hadn't realized how eager I was to find my birth mother within the few months we were spending in California.

But she had done something already. She'd phoned the Alumni Office at the University of Washington and asked whether they gave out current addresses of graduates. The answer: not unless there's a compelling reason such as a medical emergency. They said that I could write a letter to my mother, which they would then *read* (!) and perhaps send off to her, but they couldn't give me her address.

My blood began to boil at the idea that a stranger would consider it her right, even part of her job, to read a personal letter to a birth mother, and then act as gatekeeper and censor! It hit me with full force then that in the eyes of the bureaucracies in our society adopted people are never grown up. We're always treated as "adopted children."

Elaine and I talked about the disturbing business of lying. She said that when she called the Alumni Office, she'd told them the truth: that a friend of hers was trying to get information on her birth mother. Perhaps if Elaine had cooked up a story, like she was trying to locate old friends for a reunion, the person she talked with might have been more cooperative. This was my fault, I realized. I should have warned Elaine in my letter about the need to be cautious — to "just ask" and not reveal the reason for her questions.

Elaine said she'd be able to check out the yearbooks in a couple of days and would let me know right away if she found anything. When I mentioned that my father's name was probably Kroll, and that Mom and Dad had said he'd been a Merchant Marine, Elaine said she'd talk to her brother-in-law, who had been in the Merchant Marines, to find out where old ships' records might be. Elaine had also heard of a new organization in Seattle that helped adoptees who were searching and promised to send me the address.

By the end of our conversation, Elaine was fired up and ready to get going. She said if she got on to something "really hot," she'd phone on the weekend.

* * *

The next day, February 24th, when the little mail truck puttered up the road, it brought the long-awaited sheet of nonidentifying background information from Sacramento. Excitedly, I quickly scanned the single page — a standard form with the left side containing information about my mother, the right side for my father — and then returned to the top, devouring every crumb of information, seeking in every phrase clues that I could put together to form even a hazy first picture of my birth parents. It was a picture handed down from outside observers and at least twice removed from the original, my mother. Some clerk in the Department of Health must have recently gone through my adoption file and summarized in his or her own brief phrases the descriptions of my mother that were jotted down probably by more than one social worker more than thirty years before: *5'5" tall, blue eyes, medium brown golden hair, very pretty, poised, charming,* began the typewritten description of my mother. *Above-average intelligence according to psychological report of*

Wechsler-Bellevue IQ Test. What a couple they must have made, I mused, skin tingling, as I read the description of my father: *6 foot tall, reddish blond wavy hair, blue eyes, fair, well built.*

Unfortunately, the information didn't verify what Mom had said about my mother being a music major at the University of Washington when she became pregnant. It merely gave her place of birth as Washington, and my father's too, stated that she had had two years of university by the time I was born, and that her interests were singing, dancing, and dramatics.

It was possible that she didn't finish university, I thought, for her age at my birth was given as twenty-four, several years older than I'd expected. A twenty-four-year old pregnant sophomore? Well, in wartime perhaps her education had been broken up; perhaps she'd worked in between her university years, because her occupation was given as waitress. Or maybe she'd just been working as a waitress to support herself while she was pregnant in California. It was also quite possible that her two years of university had been in California, not in Washington at all. Maybe she moved to the Bay Area to go to college and then got pregnant by a friend back home. There were so many possibilities. It bothered me that my mother was twenty-four when I was born, though. I felt that could complicate things a little in trying to trace her. Yet it also resonated. I, too, had become illegitimately pregnant at an age when I should have known better: twenty-four.

The information on my mother's family could turn out to be helpful in going through old city directories, I realized. I would need to hunt for a Metcalf family with both parents alive in 1945 and five children: two boys and three girls. Also sad but potentially helpful was the fact that an uncle had died of TB. The death certificate might turn up something useful, if the man was her father's brother and had the name Metcalf. The list of survivors could include my grandfather, with his address at that time.

The information on my father was much sketchier and less helpful. At least it confirmed the only information I already had on him: his German background and service in the Merchant Marines. His age was given as twenty-three, a year younger than my mother. It did list his interests as singing and radio work and said he had a "very good singing voice" and was studying singing. I pondered that information for a while, letting a tall, well-built, blond, and blue eyed young man (named "Carl Kroll"?) materialize in my imagination on a dark stage in the spotlight, holding a microphone. Would his voice have been tenor or baritone? Would he have preferred opera or jazz?

It was a surprise to me that both of my parents had been singers. I certainly didn't have a great singing voice. It was good enough for a choir but too thin for a solo voice. In fact, both my parents were talented and interested in areas of the arts that were more outgoing and social than solitary. They weren't painters, sculptors, pianists, writers, but were involved in theater, singing, dance, radio. That contrasted with my interests. I'd never had the slightest inclination to be in a play and could work up stage fright just thinking about it. Although I'd played the piano for audiences dozens of times, I'd always been nervous about it. Maybe I'd inherited my parents' musical talent but not their fearlessness.

Because of the little note at the end of my father's half of the page ("Information on the father provided by the mother"), I reread the information on him carefully, looking for clues into my parents' relationship. Everything she said about him was complimentary, so I hoped she had been in love with him. *They'd given me away, let me go, shut the door, gone on with their lives, but surely they had loved each other....*

I was surprised that the background sheet contained a few details about my birth. Somehow I'd thought that the information in my file would only be based on interviews with my mother when she was pregnant. Yet the information sheet stated that my mother's health was good when I was born, that she was Rh negative, just as I am, that there had been no complications in the pregnancy, but that I had been a breech birth. I found that last fact arresting. The breech birth could be marginally helpful in getting my hospital records, I thought, but mostly it just interested me personally. I realized that my birth must have been much harder on my mother than Derek's and Tessa's births had been on me. It was possible she was under general anesthesia and never saw me at all.

Another detail from the report consumed my imagination for much of the rest of the day: "Mother's family did not know of pregnancy." How could that be? That must have taken a lot of lonely courage on her part, unless her relationship with her family had been poor. But even then, surely she'd have needed to confide in someone — a sister maybe. Perhaps her keeping her pregnancy to herself indicated that she was feeling terribly disgraced, and she chose to go through it alone rather than bringing any shame on her family. Maybe having my father with her was enough in the way of emotional support. (But was he with her? There was nothing about that at all on the sheet.) Thinking about my abortion as the only experience I could compare to hers, I simply had to tell Mom! I needed her support, even though it was a very painful thing for her to have to share.

So this charming, poised young woman, my mother, had been a strong and self-reliant person: pretty, blue-eyed, golden haired, smart, healthy, and strong. On the other hand, I wondered, had she been in a state of numbness, flying on automatic pilot? Was she just aiming to get through her ordeal as quickly as possible, without upsetting anyone in her family, so that she could forget about it (me) and get on with her life?

* * *

I now had three large pieces of my puzzle in hand: the name of the hospital where I'd been born, my own birth name, which confirmed "Metcalf" as my mother's name and suggested "Kroll" as my father's name, and the nonidentifying background information, which was filled with tantalizing hints about my birth parents and also contained many little clues that I could use in finding them, especially my mother. What I needed next in order to move forward very far was my mother's first name.

I phoned Mary Ramos for advice. She agreed with me that the hospital records should be the quickest source, but the problem was how to get them. She suggested that I first try going to the hospital in person, preferably between twelve and one o'clock, when the main staff should be at lunch! Request the records for medical reasons, she advised, and don't mention adoption at all. If that didn't work, she suggested I enlist the help of Dr. John Davidson, a Palo Alto doctor who had occasionally helped adoptees obtain hospital records. She gave me his address.

In mulling this over after we'd hung up, I worried that if I tried to get the records in person and failed, it could jeopardize my chances of getting them through Dr. Davidson, for the medical records staff would have been alerted. I decided to contact the doctor first, and soon. I would explain my situation and see how receptive he would be to helping me.

That evening Elaine phoned. She'd talked to her brother-in-law, the ex-Merchant Marine, who said that there was no general roster of men, but if I knew the name of my father's ship, I should be able to get a 1945 address. Scratch that idea, I thought; I couldn't imagine how I could learn the name of the ship before being certain of my father's name. Elaine said she planned to nose around the university the next day and would contact the registrar's office and the Alumni Association again ("I'm really afraid I blew it the first time!").

Elaine had also contacted Jean Jones, the head of Birth Right in Seattle, an organization of adoptees who were searching, like Parent Finders in Toronto. She gave Jean all the information we had so far, and Jean actually went to the library that afternoon and thumbed through yearbooks, locating a Mary Jean Metcalfe at the University of Washington in the mid-forties. I doubted this person was my mother, although it was slightly possible her name could have been misspelled in the yearbook. However, everything needed to be followed up, and I didn't totally rule out Mary Jean Metcalfe. But more important, what amazed me was that Jean Jones, contacted by a perfect stranger about another stranger's search, would take her own time to go off and do library research!

Elaine gave me Jean's address and phone number, so I phoned her right away and thanked her. Jean said she'd been glad to do a little research for me. As it turned out, she was being filmed by a local TV station in the morning, and they'd wanted some footage of her "at work," so she had thumbed through the yearbooks for me with the TV camera beamed on her. How bizarre, I immediately thought, if my birth mother might watch the program, completely ignorant of the fact that she was watching herself being searched for!

* * *

On Tessa's first birthday, February 26th, we had a post-nap afternoon party out on the patio with just the four of us and Mom and Dad. While I baked and frosted the cake, Derek was busy in the kitchen alcove, coloring blue and pink designs on the white paper napkins with marking pens. Then he helped me hang balloons from the plum tree on the patio, which was just breaking out in pink blossoms.

Sitting in the high chair in her new pink-and-blue-checked party dress, the birthday cake with its one big candle blazing in front of her, Tessa looked up in amazement as we all sang "Happy Birthday." Then she shrieked and dug her fingers into the cake. After the cake and ice cream, we all moved over to the lawn for presents. Tessa was more interested in the shiny, crinkly wrappings than in the presents until she got to the xylophone "Nana and Apa" had given her, and she banged it with great smiles. She liked the ball from Derek, too, and said "ball" over and over as she rolled it across the grass, crawling after it at top speed.

It was an idyllic afternoon in Carmel Valley. This was what we'd come to California for, I mused with pleasure — the chance to spend time with Mom and Dad like this, the chance to miss a long, freezing Canadian winter, the chance for the children to be this happy and healthy. On the spur of the moment, Mom and Dad agreed to stay on for dinner to continue the birthday celebrations, and we moved inside.

In the middle of dinner, the phone rang. "Elaine," Harald mouthed silently from the kitchen doorway. I felt a little sheepish as I excused myself from the dining room table and hurried off into the bedroom to talk on the extension out of earshot.

"Patty, this could be it! I think we've got a name!" Elaine announced. She'd gone to the library that afternoon and had found a "Kay Metcalf" in the 1942–43 Seattle city directory. "And guess what her occupation was?" Elaine drew out every moment of the suspense. "Waitress!" The same job given for my mother in the nonidentifying background information.

Quickly, because I felt pressed to return to dinner, Elaine and I discussed what we should each do next. She had talked to a parish priest who worked at a Seamen's Club on the Seattle waterfront. He said he would scout around and see where the records of Kroll might be! As well as checking in with the priest again, Elaine had a few ideas on following up blood types for my mother based on my blood type and the fact that my mother was also Rh negative. She would also find out where census and birth and death records from various years were kept in Washington. I felt that the most important thing at my end would be to check the San Francisco city directories, hunting for a female Metcalf who popped up after 1943. With luck, she would be "Kay"! There were other avenues I could pursue, such as searching for a birth announcement in the newspapers and checking out homes for unwed mothers in San Francisco, but the city directories would be first.

Kay, Kay. Could this really be her? We would have to get confirmation from at least one other source, and I tried to talk myself into remaining cautious, but still, this was encouraging news! If Kay was indeed her name, the task of tracing her to the present day had just become a whole lot easier. Compressing my lips to remove the grin from my face, I almost floated back into the dining room to rejoin the family.

PATRICIA MOFFAT

Mom & me at
her and dad's
50th Wedding
Anniversary
Party

Mom, Monterey, 1986

Mom with helper Derek

CHAPTER 12

M om and Dad had not mentioned my search since I'd broken the news to them. In the three weeks since then, although we saw each other a couple of times each week and spoke on the phone almost every day, the subject was not discussed. I had been letting them know the important bits of information that were trickling in, but they showed no interest in talking about that information or in helping me think things through.

Nor had Daddy checked the safety deposit box or written to the lawyers in Ukiah, the two things he'd promised to do. Harald or I reminded him of these things a couple of times during February, and each time he said he just hadn't had the time to get around to it. I'd never known Dad not to follow through on a promise, and I began worrying about whether his "forgetting" signaled an unease about my search under the surface.

More likely, though, his inaction was in deference to Mom's feelings. I had the definite sense that more was boiling under the surface in her than in him. The morning after Tessa's birthday party, I dropped in to see Mom, taking Derek with me. As Mom walked up the hill to the car with us when we were leaving, she announced, "Pat, I have a few things to say sometime about this adoption business." *This adoption business.* To my ears, her tone and choice of words had a forceful ring, as if she were about to issue some sort of ultimatum.

"Good," I said evenly. "I'm sorry we haven't had a chance yet for you and me to sit down and talk about it." But inside I was actually frightened. That old fear of being the naughty child arose within me, anticipating punishment for having done something wrong.

The child in me had been afraid of telling Mom and Dad about the search in the first place. But my adult self said it had to be done, that this search had to be open and honest. I was afraid that Mom, especially, would be very hurt, and that she might express her hurt by lashing out at me and being punishing and rejecting. But when I finally worked up the nerve to tell them about my search, they didn't react with the emotions I'd braced myself to deal with. They were surprised but offered to help. They acted as if this was not as big a deal as I'd been making it out to be, after all.

But by the end of February, and especially with Mom's comment about the "adoption business," I knew that the hurt or anger I'd expected from her was now surfacing. The negative feelings she'd tried to suppress when I broke the news must have been intensifying over the ensuing weeks as she saw that I really was going ahead with the search and was beginning to get information.

I wondered what exactly Mom intended to say to me and hoped I could deal with it sensitively. The most important thing would be to let her know that I loved her and that only she was my "real" mother. I knew this would be difficult for me, for my relationship with my parents had never been demonstrative. We had never been spontaneous huggers and had rarely even said "I love you." Yet while I needed to reassure Mom, I also had to make sure she knew that my search was very important to me and that I wouldn't turn back. Could I explain this convincingly, with love and regard for her feelings, when I didn't fully understand this intense commitment myself?

As if the subject was too loaded for one sitting, during the next couple of weeks Mom and I talked about my search in two separate phone calls.

On February 28th, the day after Derek and I had dropped in for a visit, Mom phoned. After the usual chit-chat about the kids and daily activities, she told me that she didn't want to try to convince me to stop searching, but she asked that I take it easier, not go at it so intensely. I had to smile, listening to this familiar message. How many times had my parents said this to me in my life? But if I did "take it easier," it would be less likely that I would find my birth mother before our sabbatical was over at the end of the summer. I wondered whether Mom would actually have preferred that. But I kept quiet and heard her out.

"When you reach the point where you know who your birth parents are, Pat, and you know where to contact them," Mom continued, "please just stop and consider all the possible consequences before you do anything." I assured her that I would be very careful, that I didn't take that first contact lightly at all, that I had already been giving serious thought to it, since I didn't want to rush in and disrupt someone's life.

It was only after we had hung up and I sat in the kitchen alcove for a few minutes staring out the window at the live oak trees that I understood what Mom was really trying to tell me. It wasn't concern for my birth mother, caught unawares and possibly shocked, that was uppermost in Mom's mind. Surely it was concern for herself as my mother, concern for our relationship, and for our family. I realized that what she was really asking me was something like: "Won't it be enough for you to know who they are, to know what sort of people they are, what their backgrounds are like, and what they do? Will it really be necessary for you to talk to them and see them? Think of what this could do to our family."

If that was what Mom really meant, I just didn't see how meeting my biological parents could hurt our family. I felt so certain that I would be strengthened psychologically by knowing who and where I had come from, and that could only be a good thing for all my relationships, including with my parents. Even if what I discovered might be disappointing or upsetting, at least it would be real, and that void at the beginning of my life would be filled. Yet I could see that Mom might feel threatened by the thought of my natural mother and me sitting and chatting over coffee, something I really hadn't thought much about because I was very caught up in the momentum of the search. I'd decided to make the first contact in a letter, but beyond that, I just hadn't spent much time envisioning how we would meet and whether a relationship between us would develop.

* * *

Almost two weeks later, Mom and I finished that phone conversation and finally got deep enough to touch the emotions driving each of us. After the kids were in bed, on the night of March 7th, Harald and I watched a TV program on adoption. Somehow, listening to other people's stories gave me the courage to phone Mom. I thought she might have seen the program too and that we could start off by discussing it. But she hadn't. She asked me whether I'd learned anything.

I told her what the three people interviewed had said about adoption searches from their own viewpoints. The adopted woman had put it very simply: "The adoptee lives her whole life with the knowledge that somebody gave her away. The search is to answer the question of *why*. A person can't help feeling rejected, no matter how happy he or she is in the adoptive home. There is a real need to know the reasons for the giving up of the child." I told Mom that it made me feel relieved to hear my own thoughts expressed by someone else, to know that other people were feeling the way I was, having grown up in loving homes too. There was also, continued the interview, a great need to find "someone who looks like me." Mom and I chuckled over that, because the adoption agency's aim of "matching" had been so successful in our case.

Then I recounted that the birth mother spoke of remembering the child's birthday every year. She said she would give anything to know whether the child was all right, happy, and in good health, but given the present laws, there was no way for her to find out.

Next, the adoptive mother spoke. She admitted to feeling a little threatened by the search, worried that she might become supplanted if her daughter was successful in finding her birth mother.

That encouraged Mom to talk to me for the first time about her own fears. "I guess the thing I'm most afraid of, Pat, is that if you find your biological roots, your biological mother, I will become simply a friend — a good, close friend maybe, but no longer your mother. 'Blood is thicker than water.'" She said that she did not want to share me with someone else, and she couldn't stand the thought that our family could be destroyed. "Ever since the adoption went through, your dad and I have managed to block out that other mother's existence; we just obliterated her from our minds and from our life," Mom continued. "You were our little girl, not someone else's originally, but *our* little girl. Now I have to adjust to the fact that that other mother may enter our lives."

Mom didn't think it was likely my birth mother wouldn't want to see me at all. She thought that curiosity would overcome her, even though meeting me might be disruptive to her life. In fact, Mom said she was worried that my natural mother might want to play "quite an active mothering role" in my life once she met me. "Really for the first time in my life, I'm feeling very negative feelings," Mom said. "I'm feeling threatened, I'm feeling jealous, I'm feeling resentful and helpless that this situation could have come about. I just don't know how to handle these feelings; they're so strong. I'm trying hard to get them under control, Pat, but it's damned difficult."

She also said that my search had taken her back to her hysterectomy, and that she'd been struggling through it all again in her mind, confronting the fact, "unimportant until now," that she was "a woman unable to bear children."

As Mom's words tumbled out, a wave of respect and love swept through me. For the first time that I could remember, Mom was revealing her own vulnerability. I was very moved, because her role was always to be the strong one, the one whom others depended upon, not only within our family but in the larger community too. Yet that night on the phone, she was telling me that inside she was floundering. She was admitting what she had been unable to do the evening I'd broken the news about my search: that my finding my birth mother was not such an easy thing for her to "handle" after all; it was not something she could easily "deal" with. It was a relief to be facing real emotions at last.

On my side, I tried to make sure Mom understood that my search was in no way a rejection of her as my mother, but that it was a positive step in my own growth. I told her how all my life I had never been able to forget that I had been "given away" by my "real mother," how my dogged achieving all through school was an attempt to earn her and Daddy's love and to make me feel worth something. For the first time, I told her about my fantasies about my birth mother as I played the piano: how as a child and teen I'd hoped that something I did might somehow make that other mother proud of me too, even though she'd given me away. I managed to tell Mom that I loved her, and that she and Daddy were, and always would be, my only "real" parents, but that at the same time I just had to find the mother who had given me up, to find out what she was like, and why she hadn't kept me. If I didn't, I told Mom, those questions would persist for the rest of my life, continuing to work against my living fully in the present.

By the end of the call, I felt that Mom and I were closer than we had been in years. Finally we said we loved each other and said goodnight. I went off to bed feeling emotionally drained but more at peace than I'd been since beginning my search.

PATRICIA MOFFAT

Elaine Durham
and her
son Charlie,
around 1974

Elaine Durham, Uganda, Peace Corps, 1969

CHAPTER 13

During March my search progressed haltingly, with one baby step forward and two steps back. A few threads that had seemed promising in February suddenly unraveled, yet new bits of information just as suddenly materialized. My emotions were like a yo-yo as I felt alternately hopeful and discouraged. As the weeks wore on, I also felt increasingly squeezed by the time pressure. I still wanted to find my birth mother before we left California at the end of the summer.

I tried to understand and put aside the unraveled threads and the dead ends as best as I could. In a phone conversation with Jean Jones of Birth Right in Seattle, I learned that the city directories did not, after all, list dependents, just individuals, addresses, and occupations. They would not be helpful in finding that Metcalf family in the 1940s with three daughters and two sons. I also received a form letter back from Sacramento stating that they could not release birth certificates without the full names of both parents. I thought that replying with "Kay Metcalf" and "Carl Kroll" was too much of a long shot to bother with.

The most discouraging news concerned the hospital records, one of the three big puzzle pieces that I'd thought were securely in hand. On February 28th, I'd phoned Dr. Davidson in San Francisco. He had been kind and supportive and offered to try to get my hospital records for me at the General if I would write him a letter describing all my pertinent information. He suggested that in the letter I should concentrate on my lack of medical information as the reason for requesting my file, stressing the difficult pregnancy with Derek.

The reply that came from the hospital on March 16 was even harder to take because Dr. Davidson had been so helpful and encouraging. *Your attached request is being returned to you because*, began the short, impersonal form letter — and the following item was then checked off: *Patient not registered here; no record found in files.* Patient not registered there! So I had *not* been born at the San Francisco General after all, as Dr. Thompson had believed. I felt depressed about this all that afternoon and annoyed Harald by following him around and thinking out loud about what to do next.

Meanwhile, in Seattle, Elaine was turning up similar goose eggs: census records after 1900 were sealed, and while death records were kept in Olympia, birth records were filed by county, not in one place in the state, as they were in California. Red Cross blood donation records only went back ten years and were confidential except in paternity suits. Nevertheless, Elaine seemed undaunted by this run of failures and was enjoying her detective role. I felt incredibly lucky to have such an enthusiastic partner in my search. In early March, I received a letter from Elaine describing how much she had learned since her first phone call to the University of Washington Alumni Association:

> *...people I approach either in person or by phone may or may not get my name and phone number. No one, not even the parish priest, has gotten your present name or address. I have always identified you as a friend from Eastern Canada who is down in the Bay Area now, looking for information on relatives.*
>
> *The general story I give out on Miss Metcalf is that she was a young woman who got mixed up with a merchant seaman*

during the war, who hasn't been heard of since her baby was put up for adoption, and the family decided to pretend she never existed. (One lady of the appropriate age looked me in the eye today and said, 'A lot of us got to know merchant seamen during those years,' smiled sympathetically and led me to the appropriate city directory.)

I try to imply that this gal is one of those cousins — every large family has one or two — who disappeared into the throng during the war and you want to know about her to tidy up a messy corner of your genealogical charts. A casual comment on how every chair in the genealogy section of the library is occupied and a mention that I just finished reading Roots *usually clinches the request. I always considered myself a successful salesperson (my other career while in school) and I guess I haven't lost my touch. What does surprise me is how much of a con artist I have become!*

* * *

But like the yo-yo, what goes down does come up. For every few pieces of discouraging news that Elaine and I received, the search seemed to take a positive step forward. On March 1st, when Harald was up at Stanford stocking up on more books and I was alone with the kids for a few days, I found some free time in the morning while Derek was at his play group and Tessa was napping, sat down at the kitchen phone, and dialed the San Francisco Public Library. Within a minute I was connected with the City Directories desk. Taking a deep breath and acting as if it was the most normal request in the world, I asked the clerk at the other end of the line if he had time to check the books for 1942 through 1945. I asked him to look for a new entry for a female Metcalf, that is, a woman of that name who pops up and moves into town sometime during those years. "No problem, if you don't mind hanging on for a few minutes," he replied.

Oh dear, I should have said I'd phone back, I worried as I sat waiting, drumming my fingers on the table. But then it might have been hard connecting with the same clerk again. I might have lost him, along with whatever information he might have for me. I thought I might not have been sitting waiting on the line like this if Harald had been home, and I hoped I'd be able to get to the next phone bill before he did. The time crawled by horrifyingly slowly. Finally, after a full ten minutes by the kitchen clock, the clerk came back on the line.

"Well, I only found one new entry by that name," he reported. "In the 1943–44 book there's a new entry for a Kay W. Metcalf."

My heart almost stopped. "What's it say for her occupation?" I almost whispered.

"Occupation, let's see — it says 'beauty salon operator,'" he replied, obviously reading from the book. "Funny thing, though, is she disappears in the next directory, the '44 to '45. She comes up just that one time."

Thanking the clerk profusely, I hung up and found I was longing for a cup of coffee. As I stood at the stove waiting for the kettle to boil, I tried to make sense of what I'd just learned. Was this the right person or not? Was this Kay Metcalf my mother? It made sense that she would pop up in San Francisco the very same year she disappeared from the Seattle directory. But why then would she disappear again in 1944–45? I knew absolutely for certain, with no detective work needed, that I had been born on November 19th, 1945 in San Francisco. So how was it possible that my mother wasn't listed in the directory for that year? Also, how could a waitress in Seattle suddenly move to San Francisco and open a beauty parlor? Maybe it was her aunt or some other relative who owned the beauty salon, and she just worked there while she was pregnant, and they got the information slightly wrong in the book. *Well, I decided, it's probably not the same person after all.* It probably was just a coincidence of names. Before I'd believe this was her, I'd have to search harder and find another instance of "Kay."

But I was fired up with adrenaline after the call and ready for more action. Taking my mug of black coffee back to the phone, I threw caution and the dreaded phone bill to the wind and dialed the number of the San Francisco Public Library again. This time I asked for the newspaper room. I told a pleasant but obviously harassed male librarian my true story and asked if he could check for a birth announcement for "Carol Kroll Metcalf" in the major papers from November 19, 1945 to about twenty days afterward. He told me that he'd recently worked on another case like mine and had found the birth announcement two whole months after the birth. He said he'd check as far forward as he had time for and would send me a Xerox if he found anything. But he warned me that he was so far behind in his work that it could take him two to three weeks to even start looking for my birth announcement, and then he might only be able to spend an hour on it. I said I'd be grateful for any help at all.

A Xeroxed birth announcement from the newspaper room never came. I wasn't surprised. Why would my mother have publicly advertised her shame? Phoning the newspaper room was just one of those wild-card things to do, those desperate ideas Elaine and I took a chance on, as unproductive as the search for my mother's blood type or my father's ship.

Rethinking the hospital mistake was different, though. I had to pursue that trail further. Obviously I had been born in *some* hospital in San Francisco, and my records, and my mother's full name, would be on file there. But which one?

As soon as the kids were bedded down on the evening of March 16th, the day I had received the discouraging letter from S.F. General, I phoned Elaine. I asked her to go ahead and search the birth certificates in Seattle-King County for any female Metcalfs born in 1920, '21, or '22 and to send me photocopies if possible. She also promised to phone the music department at the University of Washington, asking for female Metcalf music majors in the early forties, and said she'd phone the registrars at several other colleges asking for female Metcalfs registered between 1938 and 1945. Now I was hopeful that we'd get a pool of names to work on. Then we could go back to the city directories, follow up marriage certificates on several of the names, and just keep tracking them down until one fit. I was worried that all of this could take months.

All the next day, St. Patrick's Day, the hospital mix-up continued to bug me. I retraced my steps, trying to figure out at what point I'd stumbled onto the wrong path. Maybe the hospital had made a mistake was my first thought. Maybe they didn't have files on babies, just on mothers, and maybe she used a false name. But no, I reasoned, how could she have done that if she'd already arranged the adoption through a reputable agency?

My second thought was that perhaps Jeanne I. Thompson was wrong and that Jeanne M. had been at a different hospital, even for a short time. I chewed on that most of the afternoon, and finally, at night when the house was quiet, I began hunting for a needle in a haystack. I said to myself with flagrant optimism, "Any doctor who started working in the Bay Area would not want to leave it." So I called information in San Francisco and several suburbs asking for the number of a Dr. Jeanne M. Thompson until I actually found her! A husky voice answered the phone.

"Hello," I began. "Is this Dr. Thompson?"

"Yes, speaking."

"Dr. Thompson, you will probably think this a strange request, but I think that you were the doctor who delivered me in November of 1945. I wonder whether you could tell me what hospital you were working in when I was born."

"Well, let's see. In '45 I was out of residency. I wasn't working in obstetrics at all then. Are you certain that your information is correct?"

My heart sank and continued to sink lower as we talked, trying to piece the past together. *What in the world has gone wrong this time?* I wondered.

Finally the voice said, "I wonder if it's my wife you wish to speak to."

I stammered, hunting for words, blushing into the telephone. No wonder that woman's voice sounded so deep!

Humbly, I waited for Jeanne M. to come to the phone. When she did, I repeated my story briefly.

She said, "No, in 1945 I wasn't at the General. I was at the University of California Hospital in San Francisco — U.C. Hospital. I'm sure that's where your records would be."

136

Thanking her excitedly, I hung up and immediately phoned Dr. Davidson at his home and relayed this new information. He gave me the name and phone number of a friend of his who worked at U.C. Hospital and would be able to get the records there more easily. Dr. Davidson said he'd send my letter on to Dr. Preston and suggested that I write him a brief note too. Which I did as soon as I hung up.

Now I holed up for another wait to hear from Dr. Preston, to hear from Elaine. It took a week.

"Patty, are you ready for this? Hold on to your seat!" Elaine said as soon as I picked up the phone on the afternoon of March 24th. "A *Kay Metcalf* was registered at the Cornish School for the Allied Arts sometime between 1938 and 1945. That's all they could tell me over the phone, but here's their address, and you can write for more information."

Elaine had phoned several colleges and universities in and around Seattle and found no female Metcalfs registered during those years at all. And then finally, a *Kay*! Kay, Kay, Kay: the waitress in the Seattle city directory who disappears in 1943; the beauty salon operator who turns up in San Francisco the same year. And just a few days before, I had been telling Mom and Dad how discouraged I was about not being able to uncover my birth mother's first name. Since our phone conversation in early March, when Mom and I had laid our emotions out in the open, we had been talking a little more easily about the search. Now, in response to my discouragement, Mom said, "Wait a minute. When you mentioned the 'Kay' in the directory the other day, it seemed to ring a bell. Now that I think of it, I'm pretty sure they told us her name was Kay, or Katherine, or Kathy Metcalf. Something like that, anyway."

I was both excited and perplexed by this news. Mom's name was Kate. If the adoption agency had told her my biological mother's name was "something like Kay or Katherine or Kathy," surely she would have remembered it, even after all those years. I wondered whether she had blocked the name out on that first night we had talked (as she said she'd blocked out my birth mother's existence through the years), or whether, terrible thought, she'd remembered it but chose not to be too helpful. I'd probably never discover the truth, but the important thing was that the puzzle pieces were beginning to fit together again!

On the phone that late March afternoon, Elaine and I analyzed all the occurrences of the name Kay. It certainly was tempting to just zero in on Kay or Katherine Metcalf. Yet I still worried about heading off on a tangent and felt it would be wiser to wait for the U.C. Hospital records. That seemed the only documented verification of her name that would be available to us, at least the only connection between her name and mine.

* * *

But this time the wait was very long. The yo-yo spun down and stayed there, swinging uselessly, agonizingly, for more than a month. What little information came through was negative. Elaine discovered no records of any female Metcalf births in Seattle-King County for the years 1920–22. No records at all. That meant that my mother had been born somewhere else in Washington than the state's most populous county. But where? I, meanwhile, had written to the Cornish School of the Applied Arts, asking for a current address for the Kay Metcalf who had been registered there in the late thirties or early forties ("Kay Metcalf is a relative of mine who vanished during the war..."). A stiff reply came back, referring to the "federal law respecting the privacy of students," which prevented the release of any further information. By April 8th, Dr. Preston at U.C. Hospital had still not responded to my St. Patrick's Day letter, so I phoned him at the hospital. He apologized, saying that he just hadn't had time to get around to my request. I thought I detected a note of apprehension in his voice too, though, about getting involved, and I was worried that he might keep putting it off. I felt helpless and discouraged during our conversation. Afterward, I mentally reviewed what I'd said. I was sure that my request must be far down on his priority list because there were serious, life-threatening situations in patients' lives that he had to deal with every day. Yet I hoped I'd managed to get across to him how important that hospital file was to me, and how he was the only person I knew of who could get hold of it.

Our personal lives began mirroring the discouragements in the search. As the weeks wore on, both Elaine and I began — or continued — having marital problems. One problem was that Elaine's husband, Joe, was worrying about possible legal or ethical repercussions because Elaine was so involved in my search, and he was counseling her strongly to back off. Harald, meanwhile, had become increasingly irritated with me because of my "Metcalf obsession," as he now termed my search. He would often pick fights to stir things up, calling the whole enterprise into question, especially at times when he knew I was trying hard to think about my puzzle pieces logically rather than emotionally. To try to regain some peace in the household, I did slow down the searching in late March and April. I tried to sit back and simply hope that Dr. Preston would come through with the hospital records soon.

When I phoned Elaine on April 11th, she sounded as down and tired as I was, and not so eager any more to go combing through dusty old files and directories. Aware of Joe's opposition, I feared that I had been burdening her with too much, or that she had taken on too much, in helping me. She suggested that I contact the Salvation Army in San Francisco, which for a token fee of $1.00 would hunt down missing persons. She also suggested I contact the Children's Home Society in Oakland (where Rick was adopted) and see whether they could help. I wasn't eager to do either of these things. I knew I'd much rather conduct the search myself than turn it over to the Salvation Army. Maybe I was just being stubborn, but I felt very strongly that this was *my* search for *my* own past. Having a friend help was one thing, but having an agency do it or hiring a private detective — that I couldn't do. I thought it might be worth a try to see whether the Children's Home Society would have some advice, since it was the biggest adoption agency in the state. But I hadn't been adopted through the Children's Home, and besides, I had the strong feeling (perhaps an unwarranted prejudice) that an adoption agency was the last place one should expect to get help in locating birth parents.

When Elaine and I hung up that night, it felt to me like we were quitting. I could feel the search quietly slipping away through my fingers. I'd lost my on-the-spot detective. And giving in to pressure from Harald, I'd come to a standstill myself. It would be many years, if ever, before we had the chance to be out on the west coast again for such a long time. In those long-ago days before Google, it would have been much harder to conduct the search all the way from Toronto. After the phone call, I stood up from the kitchen alcove with a sigh, went into the back porch, and groped for the pack of cigarettes hidden in a cupboard, and stepped outside into the cool, windy night. As I huddled under the eaves by the back door and lit up, smoke and tears stung my eyes.

PATRICIA MOFFAT

CHAPTER 14

In late April I decided to plow ahead on the assumption that Kay Metcalf was my mother. At that point, so late in the spring, who cared if it all turned out to be a waste of time? I figured I just might luck out and waste less time in the long run than continuing to wait passively for the elusive hospital records.

At that turning point, I phoned Mary Ramos for advice. I wanted to know her opinion on how best to approach Sacramento Vital Statistics for marriage licenses. If Kay Metcalf had married in California, the license would provide me with her married name and perhaps all sorts of other useful information: home address at the time, birth date, parents' names and occupations. But her married name was what I was primarily after, and I didn't want to make a mistake and blow this chance. As usual, Mary cautioned me not to mention adoption but rather to cook up another story when requesting the license.

She also suggested I try concentrating on Kroll for a while, because often it's much easier to trace the father than the mother simply because his name wouldn't have changed. Mary suggested putting an ad in the personals column of the Seattle papers and also sending postcards to all the male Krolls in the phone book, asking for information on Kay Metcalf.

To me, those measures sounded a little drastic, because they would allow me to surface. They might warn a relative that I was searching, and depending upon who the relative was, that could have a negative effect. The background information from the Department of Health had stated "Mother's family did not know of pregnancy." It was possible they still didn't know or that if one member suspected, he or she might want to make sure it was kept quiet. In writing to the Krolls, I just might contact my father without knowing it, and he might not want to be found. He could back off before I had time to be sure who he was. The more I thought about Mary's suggestions for pursuing the Krolls, the more nervous I became. I decided to put Kroll on the back burner a while longer and concentrate on getting Kay Metcalf's marriage license.

After the phone call with Mary, I called Sacramento Vital Statistics. I was surprised at how easy it was to get a photocopy of a marriage license. The marriage records were public information, so you didn't even need to state why you wanted the license. All I needed to do was send a letter telling the person's maiden name and the years I wanted to have checked. The clerk I talked to suggested asking for a search from 1945 to the present in case she had married more than once or married late. That night I wrote the letter to Sacramento requesting the marriage license of *Kay Metcalf.* I hoped all this wouldn't be a waste of time, since there was still no conclusive proof that "Kay" was actually her first name.

I then phoned Olympia to ask how one goes about requesting marriage licenses in Washington, since there was no guarantee that Kay Metcalf, if indeed she did turn out to be my birth mother, had married in California. I learned the discouraging news that in Washington, marriage licenses were filed not in the state capital but instead in each county. "Oh no!" I wailed. "How many counties are there in Washington?"

"Well," replied the clerk, "I think about forty." He suggested trying Seattle-King County first, as Elaine had done in checking for my mother's birth certificate.

But Mary's suggestion to focus on Kroll for a while, simmering away on my mental back burner, must have penetrated my subconscious. On

April 28th I awoke with a dream still vivid in my mind. It stayed with me all day, as if refusing to disappear until its message was acknowledged.

I dreamed that my birth mother was in a mental institution and I was sitting in a little cubicle inside the hospital, waiting to see her for the first time. When she was brought to me, she was enormous, so tall that she had to bend way down at the waist to squeeze through the door. She was an ugly, lumpy person, pasty-faced with stringy hair. But it was her size that impressed me most: she was gargantuan.

After gazing at her wordlessly, the scene changed and now I was outside of the institution. There I saw my birth father from a distance. He was about twenty years old in the dream and was hanging around outside the hospital with several other youths. Even in my dream, I was reminded of groups of young men I had seen in Germany in the sixties. He was dark blond and rather nondescript, with greasy hair, a poor complexion, a leather jacket, and he was smoking.

Of course, the dream revealed my old fears of what I might find at the end of my search. What worse nightmare could there be than meeting your mother for the first time in a mental institution or in prison? But what struck me most about the dream, as I allowed the images simply to rest in my mind during the day, was the relative sizes of my parents. When my mother squeezed herself into my cubicle, it was as if I was a very small child, only knee-height in comparison to her, and she, the giantess, was visiting my playhouse. On the other hand, my father, because I observed him from such a distance, was tiny. In comparison to my mother, he was insignificant; he was a Tom Thumb figure.

The dream truthfully represented the relative importance of those two unknown people in my life, both in my child's unconscious and in the way I had been conducting my search. When I was growing up it was my birth mother who preoccupied my imagination, not my father. With her I felt a sort of mystical inner communication, but I rarely even thought about my father. As an adult, the abortion and the births of my children turned my thoughts toward my mother, not so much toward my father. And when I made the decision to search, I said I was hoping to locate my birth parents, plural, but deep down I knew it was my mother I was really looking for. I wanted to find her first. Since February 4th, the day I started my search in the Stanford medical library, I hadn't followed up a single lead that might have taken me to my father, while I had made a flurry of phone calls concerning my mother, had stayed up late at night writing letters requesting information about her, or had sat for days and weeks in frustration waiting for news of her to arrive.

Mary Ramos knew this already, of course. That was why she suggested concentrating on the Krolls for a while. But until my dream, I wasn't ready to hear her. Before I went to bed that night, I drafted a short note to send to the male Krolls in Seattle, trying to put myself in the position of that unsuspecting man (my father) and thinking up phrases that were nonthreatening. All I wanted from him at that point was to know whether he knew the present whereabouts of an "old friend of mine" named Kay Metcalf.

* * *

Having made the decision to concentrate on my father, a few days later, on May 2nd, I hit paydirt on my mother. That afternoon as I walked into the kitchen with Tessa on my hip to warm up her naptime bottle, the phone rang. Dr. Murphy, a pleasant young intern at U.C. Hospital in San Francisco to whom Dr. Preston had apparently pawned off my request, said he had my hospital birth records right in front of him and could read the information aloud to me if I wished. Shaking with excitement, I gently deposited Tessa on the kitchen floor with some newsprint and crayons, and sat down in the kitchen alcove to listen.

My mother's name was "Catherine Metcalf" — Catherine with a "C" — related Dr. Murphy. She was Rh-negative, and her San Francisco address at the time was 621 Taylor Street. Dr. Murphy volunteered the information that Taylor Street was now a run-down part of town consisting mainly of old apartment buildings and boarding houses. He read on, almost as if to himself, the delectable information that as well as being a breech birth, I had been born with an infection in my fingernails.

146

I was elated finally to have proof of my mother's name. I told him how frustrating it had been, not knowing her name for sure, and how grateful I was for what he'd done. Now I could move forward in my search with so much more confidence. "But isn't there anything else about her in the file?" I asked. "Her parents' names or anything?"

"No," he replied, "that's it. I could try to get *her* hospital records, I suppose. You'd probably get a lot more information there."

Funny, I had assumed that if I requested my file, it would contain all the information about her too. I hadn't even realized, and no one had told me, that babies and mothers have separate hospital files. So I asked Dr. Murphy to please, yes, if it wasn't too much trouble, go ahead and try to get her file. He estimated it would take at least a week, because the old files were in "the morgue" across town, and the medical records office would have to send over a special messenger. Well, I'd waited this long, I thought as I thanked him and we hung up, so I could wait another week or so. But the main thing was that Catherine/Kay (now I felt certain they were the same person) was The One!

* * *

My plan now became double-pronged. I would wait to hear from Sacramento Vital Statistics, hoping that Kay Metcalf had indeed married in California. If so, I would soon have her married name, which would put me very far ahead, and I could then begin tracing her changes of address to the present. If no document turned up in Sacramento, I would begin the more difficult task of writing to request her marriage license from all the counties in Washington, starting with Seattle-King County. I respected Elaine's need to back off from the search and felt that I could handle those letters easily myself from California. Secondly, I would move ahead on the Kroll front right away. Perhaps I truly could short-circuit the laborious process of tracing my mother by finding my father first.

* * *

On the morning of May 4th, while Harald was up in Berkeley again for a few days, Mom drove out to Seaside with Derek and me for his weekly swimming lesson. We left Tessa with Daddy and Konjo, my parents' friendly Keeshond dog, who was at that time Tessa's favorite creature.

Mom and I were still keeping in close touch, checking in with each other often on the phone whenever we didn't actually manage to see each other. Mom and Dad frequently drove out to Carmel Valley for dinner, and the four of us also went into Monterey to see them. My search still wasn't Mom's favorite topic of conversation, but she and I had become more at ease discussing it as the weeks went by.

"Watch, Nana!" Derek shouted happily from the pool as Mom and I sat in deck chairs on the sidelines. Six two- and three-year-olds, all wearing orange water wings, suddenly began paddling and kicking their way to the far end of the indoor pool. A simple abacus, with large, brightly colored beads on a wire in a wooden frame, was set up at each child's starting position. When they swam back to home base after two laps, they moved one bead on the abacus over to the right side of the frame. Whoever moved three beads first was the winner. I had mixed feelings about instilling competitiveness at such an early age; on the other hand, the teacher was very encouraging and patient with the kids. They all were obviously having a wonderful time and were learning to swim quickly and with confidence.

As Mom and I waved encouragement to Derek and oversaw the moving of abacus beads, we managed to have a stop-and-go conversation. I told her the latest news: that I had heard from the hospital and that my birth mother's name was "Catherine." She thought, as I did, that Kay and Catherine had to be the same person. Then, later, Mom surprised me by saying, "You know, Pat, sometimes I have a warm feeling that what you are doing will be good for all of us." It was hard for her to elaborate, but as I toweled Derek down after the lesson and helped him into his dry clothes, I was glad and relieved that Mom was having some positive feelings about my search at last. I often thought about Mary's happy-ending idea about enlarging the circle of love, and I still hoped that that could happen. *If* I ever did manage to find my birth mother.

After the swimming lesson and lunch with Mom and Dad, I left the kids with them for half an hour while I dropped into the library to exchange books. As soon as I got there, I made a beeline to the phone books, opened the current Seattle directory to "Kroll," and lugged it over to the Xerox machine. *Sorry, out of order*, read the sign taped to the machine. So I took the phone book to an empty spot at a reading table and began copying down the names, addresses, and phone numbers of the male Krolls in the margins of the morning newspaper, the only thing I found to write on in my bag. I skipped over "Elizabeth Kroll" and "Kay Kroll," finished the list, and headed over to the children's section to pick out a dozen new books.

Driving home to the valley that afternoon through the blond hills, with Derek and Tessa enjoying the ride in their car seats in the back, the name kept pounding in my head. Just an odd coincidence of names, I tried to tell myself. Kay wasn't an unusual name. Kay *Kroll* though... Who could she be?

That night as soon as the kids were asleep, I settled into my usual place at the kitchen alcove under the phone and attempted to read *The Mill on the Floss*. I was still thinking about thesis topics and almost every evening would immerse myself in George Eliot. That night, with Harald away, the house was unusually quiet. I couldn't seem to finish reading a paragraph without my own thoughts intruding noisily. After several attempts, I put the book aside and surrendered to the argument raging inside my head.

How could she be my mother? If she married Kroll, then why did she give me up for adoption? Maybe that old story about her falling out of love with him is true? Or maybe she married him sometime later? No, no, it's so unlikely. The best I could hope for is that she's a relative of my father who might be able to give me some information on my mother. But realistically, that's also unlikely. She's probably someone completely unconnected either to my father or my mother. Just an odd coincidence of names. Look at my two Dr. Jeanne Thompsons.

Finally, I had to satisfy myself that she wasn't the person I was looking for. I reached for the receiver on the wall above my head, called Seattle information, and asked for her number. I dialed the number several times until after nine, but there was no answer. However, by now I was charged up and in the mood for a treasure hunt. I dug out my list of male Krolls and dialed Carl H.'s number. "If Kay Kroll won't answer," I said to myself, "I'm determined to get *some* results!"

Feeling rather foolish and foolhardy, I told Carl H. that I was trying to locate a man named Carl Kroll who must be about fifty-five years old and had been in the Merchant Marines during the war. He was very nice, said the age was almost right on, but he hadn't been in the Merchant Marines. He wished me luck and we hung up.

By ten thirty, and after several more tries, Kay Kroll still hadn't answered her phone. I had a tremendous, virtually uncontrollable urge to talk to her, for no other reason than to stop her name from buzzing in my head, just to satisfy myself that she was *not* Kay Metcalf. I doubted very much that I would have given into that powerful urge and kept on dialing if Harald had been home that night. I knew he would warn me against using the phone in that way. But it was already May, and I still felt very far from the end of my search. I was impatient with the seemingly endless waiting for bits of paper to come in through the mail, for phone calls eventually to be returned. Yet I knew that dialing that number was risky. If Kay Kroll did happen to know my mother, she might steer me away, she might warn my mother, she might place obstacles in my path.

I tried one last time and still got no answer. Reluctantly, I gave up, turned out the kitchen and living room lights, slipped quietly in to check on the kids, and climbed into bed with *The Mill on the Floss*.

PATRICIA MOFFAT

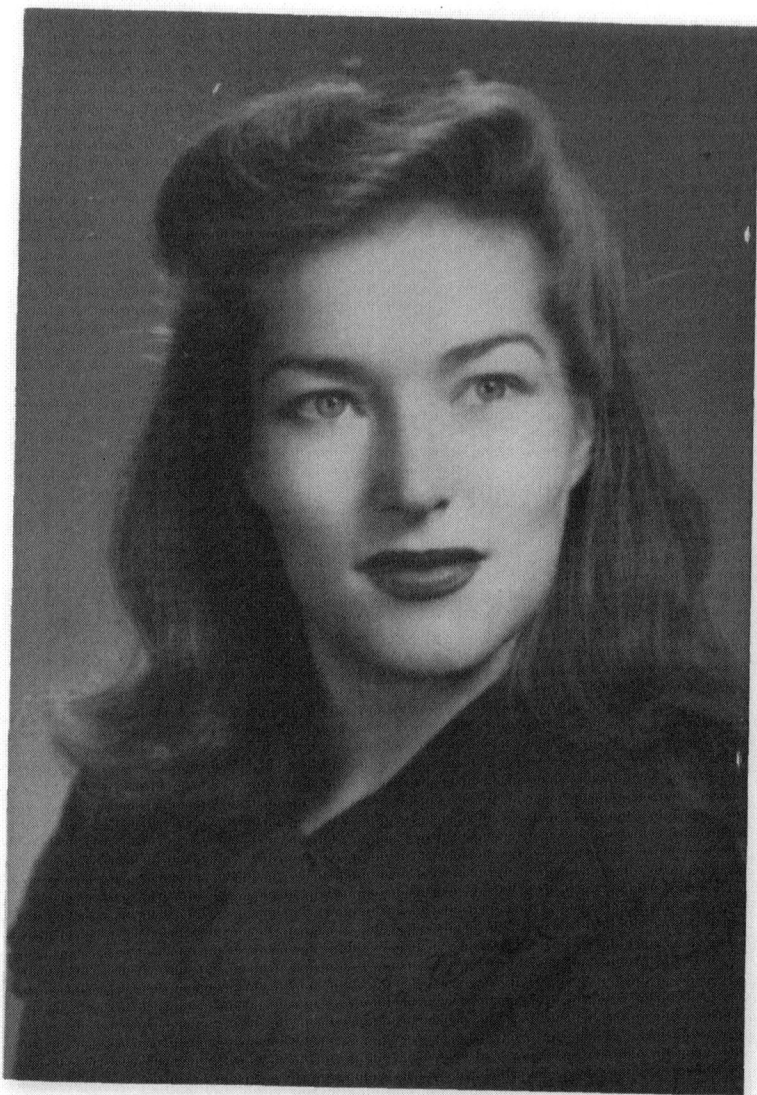

Kay Helen Metcalf, San Francisco, July 1945.
She was 5 months pregnant with me at the time.

CHAPTER 15

All through the next day, May 5th, I tried to banish the phone number I had unwittingly memorized from my thoughts. I was glad it was my morning to host Derek's play group, for organizing finger-painting and snacks for five three-year-olds and watching Tessa at the same time certainly helped to focus my attention on the here and now. Harald was still in Berkeley, so after the play group and lunch and Tessa's nap, the kids and I spent a leisurely afternoon outside and then had an early dinner. By eight o'clock I was back at my post by the phone. As had happened the night before, I dialed and dialed and got no answer.

At 9:15 I dialed the number for the umpteenth time, and this time a soft, pleasant woman's voice answered, "Hello?"

"Hello," I began. "Is this Kay Kroll?"

"Yes," she said with no trace of apprehension.

"I'm phoning you from California on a wild hunch," I heard myself saying calmly and confidently. "I've been trying to find a woman named Kay Metcalf, and I wonder if by any chance you might be Kay Metcalf Kroll?" Amazing. I hadn't meant to be so direct.

"Yes, I'm Kay Metcalf," she responded after barely a pause.

"You *are*?" I almost dropped the phone. Though I should have known better, I had not prepared myself for this response. I had no mental script ready for whatever came next. My mouth went dry.

"What is the...? Is anything the matter?" she asked. I could hear the sudden concern in her voice, and I tried not to panic. I began staring at the white globe of the kitchen ceiling lamp, concentrating on the most ordinary object in sight, trying hard not to break down. Now I knew who she was, but she didn't know a thing! My God, why had I been so reckless? What about my plan to write a letter first? Oh, but I couldn't scare her. I had to hold on to her somehow!

"Well...I... It's hard to know what to say next..." I managed to say. "When I was a baby, my name was Carol Kroll Metcalf." I heard a quick intake of breath, and I rattled on hurriedly, almost apologetically. "Now, I don't know whether we are related or not, I really don't, but there's a chance."

"When is your birthday?" she responded calmly and distinctly.

Now my heart was pounding, and I was trying harder than ever not to cry. Who but my mother would ask such a question? "November 19, 1945."

There was a pause, and then she said in almost a whisper, "Yes, I think we are related."

"Oh, I can't believe it!" I burbled ecstatically into the phone. "Look, am I calling at a bad time? Would it be better if I called you back later?"

"Why don't you write me a letter?" the gentle voice replied. "I hate to have you phoning long distance."

Oh no! I couldn't go back to the letter now. It was way too late for that. I just had to hold on to that voice.

"Oh, that's all right, really," I said, desperately trying to sound casual. "I have a friend in Seattle, and we've been phoning long distance very often in the past few months. I'd really like to phone you again, if that's okay." I didn't care if we couldn't afford another phone call. This one I'd have spent the grocery money for!

"All right, then," the soft, slightly husky voice of my birth mother replied. "This is sort of a difficult time to talk. Can you phone me tomorrow night about the same time?"

"Yes, I'll call you as soon after eight as I can, okay?"

"That's fine."

"Are you feeling all right?" I asked just before hanging up. Along with my euphoria, I was also worried that she might be shocked, that her world had just been turned upside-down, that this phone call might create severe difficulties in her life.

"Yes, I'm fine," she replied.

"Good, I'm glad. I'll talk to you tomorrow then. Goodbye."

"Goodnight."

As soon as we hung up, I gave in to my tears, sobbing for many minutes in the silence of the house. Then I poured myself a glass of Chardonnay and paced with it barefoot across the polished hardwood floor of the dining room and living room, gazing out over the black valley alive with twinkling lights like stars, feeling as if I were striding across the roof of the world. Then I returned to the kitchen and phoned Harald at his friends' house in Berkeley.

Despite Harald's negative attitude toward my search during the previous months, now that it was over, he seemed almost as jubilant as I was and yelled out to Gerd and Kirsten (and into my ear), "Hey! Pat found her mother just now! In Seattle!" He offered to come home to be with me when I phoned the next night. I assured him I would be fine on my own. In fact, I wanted very badly to finish this quest alone, to savor the prize on my own. Just the thought of having someone else, anyone else, sitting and listening in on a very private conversation with my birth mother felt like an intrusion. Harald told me to pour myself a glass of wine (I said another glass of wine was just what I didn't need!), take a warm bath, go to bed, and not make any more phone calls. "Okay," I said, and as soon as we had hung up I dialed Elaine's familiar number in Seattle even though it was after ten thirty.

"Elaine, I found her! I found her! Just now, an hour ago — Kay Kroll, right in the phone book!"

"Whaaaaat! Patty, that's fantastic! Just a minute, I don't believe this," and Elaine reached for her telephone book. "There can't be a Kay Kroll in the phone book! I'm sure the name would have leapt off the page at us weeks ago. Think of how many times we've looked through that list of Krolls. Must be a new phone book." But she found the page, and there was the name.

"Just shows you," I said, "if you have a fixed idea in your head, you can stare right through an elephant."

"We never even noticed the female Krolls, we were so busy focusing on the men. Amazing! Well! What did you two say?"

At the end of our conversation, Elaine said, "Patty, I've been backing off for the past month, you know that. I've just had this feeling that you were getting awfully close. I guess maybe without even realizing it, I wanted you to do the last part all on your own."

Elaine said she'd scout around the next day, and if she found out anything interesting about Kay, she'd call me before I made my evening phone call.

After Elaine and I hung up, bed was still far from my mind. My muscles were aching from fatigue, but my mind was hyped up and exhilarated. I pulled out my spiral notebook journal and wrote down the conversation with my birth mother word for word. At that moment it felt as if every phrase was burned into my memory, but I knew that if I didn't write it down that night, within a few days our words could become hazy.

After half an hour of writing, I was still at loose ends. There were lots of people I could call, I thought, but all were far away, in different time zones, and I'd sort of promised Harald that I'd control myself. One call I knew I couldn't make was to Mom and Dad. I was glad it was after their bedtime, because I wasn't ready to tell them. What a reckless thing to do, I told myself again, phoning out of the blue like that! It would have been so much saner to have waited until I was sure of who she was and then written that letter. Still, I didn't feel the slightest bit sorry that I'd done it this way, so against my better judgment. I knew that for the rest of my life I would never forget that moment of recognition, that sudden connection with her soft voice at the other end of the phone.

And yet a small feeling of uneasiness wormed its way to the surface of my consciousness, and I tried unsuccessfully to squelch it down. Her voice: so gentle, so pleasant, so unruffled, so controlled...so cool? She sounded so calm and in command of herself. There was no obvious surprise, no expression of excitement, hardly even any upset. I felt like my emotions and my words were careening all over the place, and it was only by concentrating very hard, homing in on the reality of her voice, that I managed to form sentences. Could it really be that she was unruffled by my finding her? Was it possible that she might after all be the "cold fish" I'd suspected as a child, when Mom told me she'd put me up for adoption because she'd fallen out of love with my father?

But no, surely not! Maybe in moments of strain or excitement she reacted by being super-cool. After all, people had said that of me often enough. My students — "Miss Pat, whatever we do, you always stay so calm and patient." Maybe she was shaking under that surface calm. I wondered whether someone might have been sitting there with her, making it difficult for her to talk to me. Or maybe she just went numb and needed a day to collect herself.

I was so shocked to discover that the name in the phone book really was my mother that in a way I felt relieved to have some time to think about it all too and prepare myself for the next conversation. I knew the waiting would be agonizing, though, especially since I'd planned to take the kids into Monterey the next morning. I didn't think I'd be able to tell Mom about the phone call then. I knew so little about Kay Metcalf Kroll, and maybe if I told Mom what had happened, she would spend the whole day in worse anticipation and suspense than I would. Better to wait, I decided, until Kay and I had a chance to talk longer.

But Kay Kroll, Kay Metcalf Kroll.... The name played through my head as I paced the living room floor till long after midnight, willing myself to get tired. Why was her name Kay Kroll? Did that mean that she did marry my father? Or his brother? Or did she name me after the man she was intending to marry and not after my father at all? And why was she listed on her own in the phone book? Did that mean they were divorced? Separated? Or that he was dead? So many questions!

Knowing how early Derek and Tessa woke up in the mornings, I finally forced myself to take my exhilaration and my slight uneasiness off to bed.

Waiting and patience. Waiting and patience. I'd waited my whole life to talk with my mother. Now I would have to wait one more day.

* * *

At Dennis-the-Menace Park in Monterey the next morning, I watched Derek and Tessa scramble around in the warm sand. I pushed them in the swings and hauled small pails of water from the drinking fountain while they played with spoons, cartons, and wet sand. Then we went to Mom and Dad's for lunch. Daddy wasn't there, and the kids and I didn't stay long. I found myself watching Mom carefully, and whenever I thought of telling her about the previous night's phone call, my mind went into a sort of paralysis. Mercifully, Mom didn't inquire about the search. I gave her a big hug as we left and drove back to the valley to spend another long, warm afternoon of waiting.

At five thirty, as I was frying chicken and the kids were playing on the window seat in the living room, Elaine phoned. "Hold on a minute," I said, putting the receiver down on the alcove table, for in 1977 we didn't have cordless phones, let alone cell phones. I dashed over to the stove to turn the chicken down and into the living room to take a quick peek at the kids, and then returned to the phone. "Hi, Elaine! Did you have a busy day?"

"Listen, Patty, you are really gonna like her," Elaine began.

"What? You mean you've seen her? You've talked to her?"

Obviously enjoying every moment of the suspense, Elaine narrated her day to me. First, she had staked out Kay's apartment. Elaine, with her three-year-old, Charlie, and her sister-in-law, Corinne, in tow, drove over to Kay's apartment and inspected the outside of the building and the neighborhood.

"She lives in the university district, a fairly high-rent area. I couldn't see much because she lives on the second floor, but I jumped up and down to try to see in the windows, and Patty, she's a Plant Person!" We both burst out laughing at the ridiculousness of the scene and the fact that we took it as a good omen that she was a Plant Person — "Hanging baskets with big healthy plants all over the place," Elaine continued.

Ironically, wonderfully, Elaine could almost see Kay's apartment by looking out her living room window. They lived almost directly across the canal from each other. So during all those phone calls when we were wondering where in the world that Metcalf woman was, and how to go about finding her, there she was, practically right under Elaine's nose.

The first mission accomplished, the trio returned home and Elaine phoned the city directories desk at the library and asked for the current entry on Kay Kroll. She learned that Kay owned and operated an imported fabric boutique. Next, Elaine phoned the Better Business Bureau and found that Kay had started the business in 1973 and had changed location twice since then.

Clutching the current address of the shop, Elaine, Charlie, and Corinne *went there*. Feigning interest in the batik fabrics, Elaine studied my mother. "I asked her a few dumb questions about the material — why some pieces were priced so much higher than others — things like that, just to get her talking."

"Just a sec," I said, hearing shrieks from the living room. I quickly appraised the situation, decided Derek and Tessa weren't doing much damage to each other or to the window seat cushions, and hurried back to the phone.

"You're really gonna like her," Elaine repeated. "She comes across as very professional, competent, and pleasant. She's shorter than you, about my height, and has dark hair with a bit of gray at the temples."

"Really?" I said. "I'd always imagined her as a tall blond." I was breaking out in gooseflesh, imagining Elaine actually talking to her, looking at her. I felt grateful to Elaine, but mostly envious!

"Yeah, I was surprised too," Elaine continued, "but aside from that, there are obvious resemblances. Her eyes and cheekbones are very similar to yours, though her face is different around the mouth and chin. Her nose has a bump in it too, not as much as yours, but it's there. You can see it. She's a very attractive, stylish, natural-looking lady, good figure. But the thing that really freaked me out was that as we were talking, I swear she reminded me so much of you that it could have been you and me talking. There's something about her voice, something about her whole manner that is so much *you*!"

* * *

At eight o'clock I was still trying to get Derek to bed (Tessa having folded earlier), reading him a couple of extra stories in the hope that he would stick his thumb in his mouth and get droopy around the eyes. When he was finally asleep, I sat in my usual place in the kitchen, watching the clock, picking up the receiver and putting it down again, gathering my thoughts, trying to decide what to say first. Strange how easy it was to dial her number the night before, when I was calling in almost total ignorance. Now, I was so nervous that I finally phoned almost a full hour after I said I would.

She picked up the phone after the first ring.

"Hello! Is this Carol?"

"Well...it's Pat. I'm sorry, I forgot to tell you my name last night."

I told her my married and maiden names, both of them polysyllabic German-sounding ones, and she repeated them thoughtfully.

"Well, how does Metcalf sound to you?" she asked.

"It sounds really...regular!" I answered, and we both laughed.

"How did you ever find me?" was her next question.

I gave her a brief run-down of the search, including the accident of just finding her name in the phone book the other day.

"I'm sure you must want to know about your birth and why I had to give you up for adoption." Without my even asking, she plunged back into 1945. She was twenty-three and working as a waitress at the Olympic Hotel in Seattle, and also singing at a Merchant Marine Club frequented by men about to ship out. She had never felt herself to be in love and had had practically no sexual experience, she said. "I was beginning to wonder whether there was something wrong with me." Then one night my father, who had heard her singing at the club the evening before, walked into the hotel where she was working as if he was looking for her. "He was the handsomest man I'd ever seen — tall, with blond, curly hair, a great build, and these beautiful blue eyes with long, black eyelashes. I said to myself, 'If you can't fall in love with this man, there is definitely something wrong with you!'"

They went out several times, and finally the inevitable happened. "But I didn't see any stars after all. No fireworks exploded inside me, and I knew I wasn't in love with him."

Soon after that, my father shipped out, and Kay went ahead with her plans to see if she could get into the movies, and she moved to Los Angeles. (That detail surprised me, since Elaine and I had been assuming she would have lived only in San Francisco.) A month after her arrival in L.A., she discovered she was pregnant. During the early part of the pregnancy, she worked as a photographer's model, and then when she began to show, she moved to San Francisco. She told her employer that her husband was away in the war, which was so common in those days that no one questioned it.

I was very surprised when she told me that my father's name was Bobby Z-----. I had gotten used to the idea of Carl Kroll as my father, and this new name sounded strange and foreign. She actually knew very little about Bobby Z-----. He was in the Merchant Marines, he seemed "very intelligent"; he sang well and had told her he'd done radio work; he had lived in Yakima, Washington for a while, she thought, but she wasn't even sure of the spelling of his last name. She didn't try to contact him when she discovered she was pregnant because she thought he might offer to marry her out of a sense of obligation. She knew she didn't love him and didn't want to begin a marriage with "two strikes against it." When she had been in San Francisco for some time, and was obviously pregnant, Bobby tried to contact her at her hotel, having gotten her address from someone in Seattle, but she asked her friend Carl Kroll (!) to tell him that she wouldn't be able to see him. Hence, my father did not even know of my existence.

"I've been thinking and thinking about the name you gave me on the phone last night — Carol Kroll Metcalf. I have no idea how 'Kroll' got into it. I named you 'Carol Metcalf.'"

We pondered together how this could have come about. Carl had registered her at the hospital, and maybe in the confusion a clerk just transferred his name onto my birth certificate. "Anyway, it's not important how it got there," Kay said, "but it's just lucky it was there because it made it easier for you to find me!" Any remaining fears I might have had about her possibly being "cool" toward me evaporated at that.

"I guess you'll want to find your father too, won't you?"

"Probably sometime," I said. "How would you feel about that?"

She thought for a moment and then said, "I can handle it." (Funny, I thought, Mom's exact words when I first told her I wanted to find my birth parents.)

"I must tell you," she said, changing the subject, "that your two half-sisters were sitting here with me waiting for your phone call tonight because they just wanted to say 'Hi' too, but finally they had to leave to go over to the Island and tell your grandfather that he has another granddaughter."

"What?" I gasped. "Two half-sisters and a grandfather? Tell me about them!"

She told me that she and Carl Kroll married a couple of months after I was born. They were together for nineteen years and had three children: Keith, now twenty-eight, Kandy, twenty-seven, and Keeva, twenty-five. Ten years ago, they divorced. Carl was now remarried and Kay had a "steady boyfriend." (The boyfriend, Henry, was with her the night before when I'd phoned, and that was why she asked me to phone back.)

The children learned about me at the time of the divorce. Their reaction was sadness that they had a sister "out there" whom they wouldn't be able to know. I asked whether Kandy and Keeva had any mixed feelings about me now that I'd turned up. (Keith didn't come into this part of the discussion because he was living and doing research in the Netherlands. He was married, with a six-year-old son.) "Oh, no!" Kay said emphatically. "They've been terribly excited all day. I phoned them right after you called last night. They really read me the riot act — 'Mom, how could you have been so dumb? You didn't even get her name or her phone number! What if she doesn't call back?'"

She told me a lot about Keith, Kandy, Keeva, Gramp, and her mother Eunice, who died sixteen years after a stroke left her partially paralyzed. She told me about the most difficult period in her family's life, when Keith developed testicular cancer at seventeen, just around the time of the divorce. The cancer had metastasized, and his survival was touch-and-go for many months. He still suffered aftereffects from the surgeries, she said, with scar tissue in his stomach sometimes causing him a great deal of pain. She also talked about my two aunts, two uncles, and numerous cousins. Names, occupations, characteristics, lifestyles of all these people began swimming confusedly around in my head. But two half-sisters, a half-brother, and a grandfather!

"You know," she said, "I'm so happy you've found me, but I'm not really surprised. I kind of expected it, kind of thought I'd hear from you one of these days. That's what I told my sisters just this past February. We have never talked about it in all these years, I never even told them about you back when it happened, but then suddenly in early February — I can't even remember how it came up — we talked about it, and I told them that I just had this feeling that I'd get a phone call sometime."

"In February?" I asked, startled. "I started looking for you on February 4th!" I broke out in goose bumps, and we talked about thought waves and ESP.

"Tell me about your parents," she said, and I gave her a glowing description of Mom, Dad, and Rick, adding that Mom was having a hard time coming to grips with my search.

"Oh, I'm sorry," she said, genuinely surprised and disappointed. Then, "Do you believe in reincarnation and karma?"

"Um...what are you getting at?" I asked cautiously.

"Well, I believe in reincarnation. It's part of what we were raised on as kids. I've had the very strong feeling ever since I gave you up that I knew your mother and father in a past life...that I was very close to them, and that I had done something that had hurt them, and because of that I owed them a debt. The payment of that karmic debt was you...because...." The easy tone of our conversation changed. My throat tightened painfully, and I heard her voice breaking as she continued slowly and carefully. "Because you don't give a baby away.... You just don't give your own little baby away to strangers. You give her to friends."

We both cried, not even searching for words to cover up.

Finally she said, "I want to meet you very much. But I know it will be a very painful experience for me too, coming to know you, and to know what I have missed all these years." Again she began crying before she reached the end of her sentence.

With tears streaming down my cheeks, I said, "I want to meet you too, very much. But I'm probably quite different from the way you imagine me because of Mom and Dad and the environment I grew up in."

"Oh, I think environment is much stronger than heredity in shaping a person," she said. "I haven't earned the right to be called your mother. Your mother is the person who raised you and loved you every day of your life. All I contributed was the biological accident of your birth, and half of your genes. I just want to see you...but your adoptive mother is your real mother. When you talk to her, please try to tell her that from me."

We talked for over an hour, filling each other in on the important events of our lives in the most incredible phone conversation I'd ever had in my life. I told her about Derek and Tessa, and she was amazed and delighted to have "two more little grandchildren," a phrase that triggered momentary ripples of worry in me.

"I've been terrible, talking on and on like this. This phone call is costing you money!"

"Yes, it is," I admitted. "It's a good thing Harald is in Berkeley tonight."

It was much harder to end the conversation than it had been to begin it. We exchanged addresses and both said we would look into cheap ways for me to get to Seattle. Finally we managed to say goodnight and hung up.

Afterward, I didn't feel the same wild exhilaration mixed with worry I'd experienced the night before. I was astonished at how lucky I was to find her so open, so glad to be found, but the wild euphoria I'd felt after the first phone call was replaced by a feeling of serenity. I'd found her, and already I loved her. No pacing the floor and staring pensively out over the dark valley was necessary now. No drinking white wine, either, or any more phone calls. There was only one thing I felt like doing. I hoisted up the lid of the baby grand and played Debussy and Chopin until I finally felt I would drop.

* * *

Before seven thirty the next morning, I dialed Mom and Dad's number.

"Well, Patty!" Mom answered the phone, obviously surprised. "What's on your mind so bright and early?"

"Mom, I'm sorry to call at this hour, but..."

"We've been up since the crack of dawn as usual. You know you don't have to apologize for that. What's up?"

"Well, I wanted to talk to you before the kids wake up and before Harald gets back from Berkeley...just to tell you...that I phoned Kay Metcalf last night, and she *is* my birth mother."

"You did? She is? Hold on just a minute! Your dad's halfway out the door. George! Pat phoned Kay Metcalf, and she *is* her birth mother!"

"She did? How about that! That's great!" I heard him say. The front door slammed shut, and Mom came back on the line.

"So it's happened," she said. "You really did it." And she began to cry, apologizing for her tears. "I knew this moment would come. I've been trying to prepare myself for it, Pat, but it's hard."

"I know, Mom," I said gently, but no tears came. "Mom," I continued, "it's okay, it's really okay. You're the only Mom I have. You know that, don't you?"

"Sure, I know that, honey. It's just the shock, I guess."

"Would you rather I didn't say anything more?"

"No, no. I'll be all right. Of course I want to know about her! What's she like? How did she react?"

"Well, she wasn't shocked. She wasn't even very surprised. She said she'd kind of been expecting a phone call."

"Was she happy?" Mom asked. She was beginning to sound genuinely curious now, and I loosened up a little.

"Yes, she was glad I'd found her," I told Mom. "She said she felt relieved. She also said something that will probably sound strange to you, at least it did to me. But it shows that she feels a connection with you and Daddy." I told her about the reincarnation idea, of Kay thinking she had hurt Mom and Dad, her close friends, in a previous life, and me being the "payment of debt."

"Well," Mom laughed gently, "it's understandable, though. I guess it's made it a little easier for her to live with it all these years. How about other family?"

"She's divorced and has three children, a boy who's three years younger than me and two girls in their mid-twenties."

"Oh no, poor Rick," she cried, and fresh tears started.

"What do you mean, 'poor Rick'?" I asked.

"Please don't tell him about this yet, Pat. I'm just afraid he'll think, 'First my wife leaves, and now my *sister* too.'"

"Oh, Mom! That just couldn't happen!" Keeping my promise to Mom not to tell Rick about my search had been hard during the past several months. I could hardly believe that she still wanted me to keep the deception up, especially now that the search was over.

"Pat, the fact is you have two families now," Mom continued. "Don't you see that? That family in Seattle, they'll greet you with open arms. What are you going to do then?"

"Mom, I don't know for sure how they'll react. I've thought so little about finding other 'relatives.' Anyway, they all know I'm not Carol any more...that I already have a family."

"Well, I don't know how important we will be to them, really. I think they'll want to welcome you back into the fold."

"All I know is how Kay feels about it," I replied. "She said that all she gave me was the accident of my birth. She said she doesn't deserve to be called my mother, and that only you are, because you've loved me and raised me. She asked me to tell you that."

"Well, I appreciate her saying that...but saying is one thing," Mom concluded. "If she sees you, she may feel something else, and who could blame her for that?"

CHAPTER 16

The rest of May was a time of waiting, for I had decided to fly up to Seattle the first weekend in June. In conversations and visits with Mom and Dad, there was very little mention of my upcoming trip. Yet whenever Mom did say something about Seattle, I felt that her words were the tip of an iceberg, and I sensed worries and maybe anger underneath. My relationship with Rick felt like it was on hold, for Mom was still firm in not wanting him to know yet about my search. I felt that Rick was being left out of something important, which could affect his life too, but since he was living five hours away in Chico, it wasn't hard to go along with Mom's wishes.

At home, Harald and I increasingly snapped at each other as the month wore on. He was feeling pressured by time, because the writing block he'd experienced with his doctoral thesis had resurfaced in his work on his sabbatical article. As I became increasingly preoccupied with who and what I would find in Seattle, Harald complained that I was "less than half there" with him and at home.

To cool my frustration with our arguments and my tension and worries about Mom and the upcoming trip to Seattle, I would escape out to the backyard most evenings after the kids were asleep, sit on the woodpile, breathe in the dry, herbal scents of the valley, stare up at the starlit sky, and smoke a cigarette. This infuriated Harald even more, since he had decided that now was the time for both of us to quit smoking.

Two important items from my search arrived in May, anticlimactic now that I had found Kay. Sacramento sent the marriage license of Kay Metcalf and Carl Kroll, which arrived the day after my second phone call to Kay. So if I had curbed my impulses and waited until Harald had returned from Berkeley before dialing that Seattle number, I would have found her not by fluke but rather by logical detective work only a couple of days later. I would have known for certain beforehand who the "Kay Kroll" in the current Seattle phone book really was.

I was a little startled by the date on the Xeroxed marriage license. January 9, 1946 sounded familiar to me. Flipping through my still-expanding "search" file, I found what had twigged my memory: the date on the pink medical discharge sheet for "Baby Metcalf" was also January 9, 1946. So on the very same day that Mom and Dad were picking me up at the adoption agency in San Francisco, when I was six weeks old, Kay and Carl were getting married in Inglewood, a suburb of Los Angeles.

The other thing I received in the mail was Kay's complete hospital file, which Dr. Murphy had kindly Xeroxed for me: eleven pages of medical forms, psychological assessments, and a detailed report on my delivery. I was very interested in the hospital social worker's report:

> *Mrs. Metcalf was referred to Social Service routinely by Mrs. Erwin of Women's Clinic, as she is illegitimately pregnant. She is in her seventh month and expects her baby in December, 1945.* [So I was somewhat premature, like Derek.] *Mrs. Metcalf is a very attractive young woman of 23 who seemed self-assured and quite definite about plans for herself and the baby. Her husband is aware of her condition and married her secretly to give the baby a name. Neither her family nor his know anything about the marriage. She states that her husband has been wonderful to her. He has told her that the decision about keeping or releasing the*

baby for adoption is up to her and that he is quite willing to have her keep the baby if she wishes. They plan to live in Los Angeles after her delivery and start a new life together. At present, she is living alone and working at the soda fountain of a drug store. She is certain that she will be able to manage financially on this and her savings. At this time she feels quite certain that she wishes to release the baby for adoption and would like assistance with this. She was given interpretation about resources in the community where she could obtain assistance.

I found much food for thought in this report. From Kay's own information on the phone and from the filing date on the marriage license, I knew that she had lied to the social worker. But why hadn't the social worker seen through her? There are so many holes in my twenty-three-year-old mother's story: How could she have been "illegitimately pregnant" if she were married? Why would Carl Kroll have married her "to give the baby a name" if she had already decided to put me up for adoption? If they were married, then why was she living alone and supporting herself on her job and savings? The cooked-up marriage seemed a transparent, face-saving device. Underneath Kay's poise and self-assurance must have been shame at being pregnant and the need to pretend she was married even to strangers, in order to try to preserve her self-respect. She had also changed her name from Kay to Catherine in all her dealings with the hospital and the adoption agency. I felt this was a touching little lie. I sympathized with her need to cover up her identity but also with her basic honesty in not changing her name too much.

This ambivalence was also evident in her medical history sheet, where in the blank after "religion" she boldly wrote "Atheist." Then she seemed to reconsider and wrote "Prot." in parentheses afterward.

When I got to the last report, the detailed medical account of my birth, I saw her self-assurance breaking down. I imagined my own distress at the time of my abortion magnified many times in her. A young Dr. Jeanne Thompson wrote of Kay's labor:

Patient's membranes ruptured spontaneously one hour ago and since then she has had mild pains about 10 minutes apart. She enters in an extremely nervous state.

Impression: Rh-negative primipara with ruptured membranes in premature labor with breech presentation.

As I read through the hospital records, a clear picture of my young mother materialized before me, like a photo from an old Polaroid camera gradually developing in my hand. Here was an attractive, confident, self-respecting young woman caught in a situation that was foreign to her upbringing and her image of herself. She lied in order to maintain her self-respect throughout the interviews with social workers and the physical examinations, and then when the final moment arrived, her poise abandoned her and she became frightened. In her loneliness and fear, she leaned on her friend Carl, and six weeks after my birth she did what she told the interviewer she had already done: she married him, despite the odds against the marriage working out. Not for the first time, I considered how profoundly Kay and I had affected the course of each other's lives. Would she have married Carl Kroll, had three children by him, and divorced him nineteen years later, if she had not given birth to me and relinquished me for adoption?

Kay and I exchanged several letters and talked on the phone once more during May. Our first letters, both written the day after the second phone call, crossed in the mail. In my letter, Kay discovered that I had graduated from Stanford, while in her letter I discovered that my half-brother Keith had also graduated from Stanford. I had gone to the overseas campus in Germany while he had gone to the campus in Austria. We had just missed each other: I graduated just as Keith entered as a freshman.

In my first letter, Kay discovered that I had spent two years teaching in Uganda; in her letter I learned that a Ugandan student had lived with the Krolls in the early sixties. Both of us had had experiences living abroad, Kay with her growing family in Australia and Holland, where Carl had exchange teaching positions, and I in Germany and East Africa. We also

172

shared a love of music. Although Kay did not finish her music degree at Cornish, she had a deep appreciation of music and fostered the musical talents of her children. While I was practicing my Czerny exercises and giving piano lessons to several small children, Keith was playing the bass with the Seattle Youth Orchestra and a jazz trio, while Kandy and Keeva studied and taught ballet.

More important, our letters explored and revealed our feelings as we attempted to explain who we were and to discover each other through writing. *I honestly feel that you did the most motherly thing you could have at that time,* I wrote to Kay on Mother's Day. *I remember so clearly my powerful emotions at the births of my children, and to have given them up in order to provide a better life for them would have been a devastating thing for me. I really hope that...my finding you won't open an old scar.*

In her letter that crossed mine in the mail, I found that she, too, was revisiting the time of my birth: *When I was talking to Gramp he said, 'Well, little sister,' (that's his pet phrase for all his daughters and granddaughters too) 'I wish you had brought that baby home for us to raise. We would have loved to have one more around here.' I know that's true, and I knew that would have been true then, but that's where you'll have to decide whether you would have liked that life better than the one you've had. The family ties and the love would have been there, but in a small community there would have been the stigma of the unwed mother background and then — well, when you see the house and place that would have been your home, you may not think it was such a bad decision. He's a real character and you'll love him, but he is a character. I guess we all are.*

Pursuing it further, she continued: *I think that most people go through the same thing — searching for their identity. But when you don't know your natural parents, you think that finding them will tell you who you are. I think for you with all you've done and experienced, you really know pretty much who you are by now, and meeting some of your blood relatives may satisfy your search for your roots and probably reinforce some of your feelings about yourself without actually telling you too much that you don't already know. However, it will be very interesting to hear your comments*

*after you've been here a few days and even to hear years later how much —
or if — it has affected you. I hope you will always be completely candid and
honest about it to me. I promise I won't be overcome with remorse or guilt if
I decide I did the wrong thing because for that time and at that time it was
the only decision I could have made. I just think it would be very interesting
from a psychological point of view. You should keep notes and write a book!
I'm sure there are many people...who would be very interested in how this
experience has affected both of us.*

In another letter I wrote to her, *I want to reassure you that my need to
find you does not mean that I had an unhappy childhood or that my parents
haven't loved me as they would have loved their own biological child, or that
I have psychological problems as a result of having been adopted...*

And in the letter I received from her the next day was what seemed
like an indirect reply: *Does your mother still feel uneasy about this? I'm
very concerned about her feelings. I don't want her to feel that our getting
together will take anything away from her. I really feel that raising a child
is being a mother.... She has made you what you are much more than I
did by bringing you into the world. Also I believe that you don't just love
someone because they are your biological mother or your father. There are
bonds between people that can't be explained, and blood has nothing to do
with it.... I don't know how science or psychology explains these bonds that
seem to exist between people when they first meet, but to me reincarnation
offers a very logical explanation. I wish I could meet your parents. They must
be very wonderful people. Please try to convey some of this to them.*

It was such a change during May to be listening for the mail man's
puttering motor because I was hoping for a letter from Kay, rather than
waiting for more puzzle pieces in my search to come in. I found her
letters fascinating and reread them frequently. I loved the fact that she
wrote so easily, clearly, and naturally. Reading the letters over again even
years later, our words still seem to me to be singing back and forth and
together, as if in a duet.

Yet despite my delight in discovering her through her letters, I often
felt during that month of waiting I was walking an emotional tightrope

in relation to Kay. Sometimes I would feel a rush of powerful feeling toward her, knowing that I would love her unconditionally. Other times I maintained a more cautious stance. It's only human nature to put one's best foot forward in letters and phone calls. Maybe once we were together in person, I would discover things in her that I wouldn't like, and she might feel the same about me. Then, later, it would be difficult to backtrack from our initial enthusiasm.

That was only half of it, of course. A large part of my caution toward Kay stemmed from my heavy burden of guilt toward Mom. While I was searching, Mom had been able to cloak her own anxieties under her motherly worries for me: I might be rejected again by my first mother, she feared, or I might be upset by whatever and whomever I might find. Now, though, since it was clear I was being welcomed in Seattle, Mom's fear of losing me became stark. She was much more preoccupied with the "tie of blood" than I was. In talking with her, I often got the impression that she felt a psychological battleground was being prepared, with Kay and herself as antagonists. She said she was afraid that, despite Kay's protestations to the contrary, Kay would want to "mother" me and that I might "submit" to it under the emotion of the moment, and then what would happen to our family? Mom spoke of the danger of my being "overwhelmed" by the family in Seattle, of being "swept off my feet."

So when I talked to Mom, I tried to reassure her, downplaying my strong emotional pull toward Kay and my intense curiosity about the rest of the family. Instead, I focused on my doubts when I talked with Mom and on my desire to go to Seattle as an independent adult, a mature person. I spoke to her not of my joy or of my relief at having found Kay and being accepted so warmly by her; I mainly spoke of complicated questions of identity and independence. Not surprisingly, because of this stance with Mom, as the month wore on, in some ways I, too, began thinking of Kay and Mom, even Kay and me, as antagonists — as if she were rushing to engulf me, and I was struggling to maintain my identity as Pat, not Carol, and above all, not as her daughter, but as Mom's daughter. Sometimes I felt as tense as a rope in a game of tug of war, with Mom pulling on one end and Kay — or my concept of Kay — on the other.

At home, Harald reinforced Mom's point of view forcefully, for his own reasons. He felt that I had already become distanced from him during my search, and like Mom, he was afraid I would be overwhelmed by Kay and the family in Seattle, that I would lose my head and become confused about who I was. As long as I had known him, Harald had been distrustful of powerful feelings, and in our long, draining conversations throughout May, he relentlessly tried to bolster up my analytical side and chip away at my emotional side. He must have realized that my search and my contact with Kay were changing me in some profound but as yet undefined way, and he worried about the change, perhaps fearing it could have repercussions on our marriage. What a long way Harald and I had come from that evening in Toronto almost a year before, when it was he who had suggested this quest in the first place!

Harald picked through Kay's letters with a fine-toothed comb, bringing to my attention her occasional inconsistencies, her moments of superficiality, and her "take-charge" attitudes toward me. He was annoyed that she had not offered to meet me halfway in my trip to Seattle. He felt it would be a better beginning to the relationship if we would meet not in Seattle, which was "her turf," but somewhere in between, say Portland, Oregon. Like Mom, Harald read a battlefield into the situation and saw it as a "surrender" that I would be meeting Kay for the first time on "her territory." Failing a halfway meeting place, he felt she should have offered to split the cost of my airline ticket. We had long and heated arguments over Harald's analyses of the situation.

Aside from the pressures from Mom and Harald, I was also struggling internally with questions about how I could go to Seattle very clearly as Pat, not Carol. For my own sake, I did want to meet my birth mother as an adult, as an independent person, not as the baby she had given birth to and given away thirty-one years before. Why was this important to me? I believed that if Kay had a false idea of who I was, if she saw me as Carol, not as Pat, I would feel very uncomfortable and would probably let the relationship lapse after we returned to Toronto. I wanted an honest and open relationship. I wanted to know her as the person she had become, and for her to know me as the person I had become. I expected we would share family memories — that I would learn about Keith, Kandy, and Keeva's childhoods, and that I would tell them about my growing up — but I knew that those events were wholly in the past and that there was no way that thirty years of memories could be lived over together in words. I could never be her daughter in the way that Kandy and Keeva were her daughters. When Kay looked at me, she would see not the continuum of years, not the shared memories and the gradual development from baby to adult. She would see me as a familiar-looking stranger with a painful memory as the main backdrop to the present. We simply had to start in the present — as Pat, not Carol — if the relationship were to grow into something valuable for both of us.

In the light of my identity struggles and resolutions, I detected occasional signs in Kay's letters and our phone conversations that disturbed me. In her eagerness for me to come to Seattle, I felt that she didn't fully grasp that I was a wife and mother with responsibilities at home and that it would be difficult for me to just take off alone immediately for a rather lengthy visit. Keeva was planning to drive down to Santa Rosa, not too far north of Monterey, for a job interview in June. Kay suggested that I take the bus up to Santa Rosa and drive back to Seattle with Keeva, without realizing that this would take up too much time for me. Harald still needed time to work on his research, and it would have been difficult for him to do that while looking after the children for ten days or so. Another thing was that I had never been away from the children, even overnight, and I wondered about their (and my!) ability to cope with the separation. Kay suggested that I leave the kids with Mom and Dad if this would be too long a period for Harald, without understanding what mixed feelings Mom would most likely have about that arrangement. She was upset enough about my trip to Seattle, and to ask her to take care of the children while I was there would have been rubbing salt into the wound, I thought.

I did see what Harald meant about Kay's "take-charge" attitude toward me, but I attributed it more to genuine eagerness for us to meet than to an attempt to "control" me. However, her ideas about my trip did come across forcefully in her letters. I knew it would be easy for me to relax and just go along with her suggestions, but I felt I had to help her see exactly what my situation was with Harald, Derek and Tessa, and Mom and Dad, and why my plans had to take all of them into consideration.

I relate well to older women — older, sensitive, intelligent, interesting women — and have had at least one older woman among my close friends ever since high school. I have wondered whether this is because I was adopted and have been subconsciously searching all my life. I knew that Kay was sensitive, intelligent, and interesting, but also very forceful. And since she was my real, biological mother, not just an older woman friend, I did agree with Mom and Harald at some level that I could become "overwhelmed," and I did not want that to happen.

I already had a mother. I was not looking for another mother in the sense that Mom was my mother. For the previous ten years, at least, I had been trying to become independent from Mom yet remain close, a tricky balance. What I did not want was to leap into another mother-daughter relationship with similar tensions. But what I did want is harder to define, because there were no models for this relationship in our society, at least in 1977. One could have two sisters, two daughters, two grandmothers, two close women friends, but what about two mothers? Not a mother and a stepmother, not a mother and a mother-in-law, but two real live mothers, one who gave birth to me and from whom I have inherited many characteristics and with whom a relationship has begun, the other who raised me, disciplined me, put band-aids on my scrapes, stayed up worrying when I came late at night, helped me work out countless major and minor problems in my growing up, and whom I call "Mom."

The difficulty in defining this new relationship first became clear to me when I started writing to Kay. On the phone, I didn't remember calling her anything. We never found ourselves in a twist of the conversation where we needed to address each other. But as I sat down to write to her the next day, I toyed with the pen and stared out the window for several minutes before beginning: *Dear Kay, It's difficult to know what to call you, but I hope 'Kay' is all right with you.* I felt that it was important to have this established in the beginning, without making a big deal about it. And yet when I received her letter that had crossed mine in the mail, she signed it quite naturally and affectionately, *Lots of love, Kay-Mom.* I recognized this as a lighthearted compromise, and without thinking much more about it, I began my second letter to her: *Dear Kay-Mom.*

As I was finishing the first page of the letter, Harald, walking by with a fresh mug of tea, peered over my shoulder, did a double-take and exploded. "What in the hell do you think you're doing, Pat? How can you possibly think of writing such a thing?"

"Why? She signed her letter 'Kay-Mom,' and I don't see any reason why I shouldn't—"

"You don't? Don't you see how cruel that is to your Mom? How would she feel if she read that letter?"

Silent remorse from me. That guilty child again.

"What's going on inside of you anyway, Pat?" he continued. "You're getting completely sucked in, aren't you?"

Seething with anger at his tone, I put the letter aside. When I returned to it many hours later, I took out a fresh sheet and began, *Dear Kay, I doubt that this letter will be as coherent as the last. We've just had a little birthday celebration here for my dad and it's quite late...*

* * *

I planned my trip to Seattle under the increasing tension of trying to steer the course of the relationship that was unfolding and trying to maintain my identity as Pat. At first I thought I would take Derek with me. Having him along would establish me in the role of mother as well as daughter. It would signify my adulthood without anything having to be said about it. He would also remind me, in case I did begin to be "swept away," of who I was. There was a very empathetic connection between Derek and me, and I knew that in his sensitive and forthright three-year-old way, I could count on him for comfort if I needed it. Also, I thought he would love the trip — the plane ride, playing with Elaine's three-year-old, Charlie, visiting Gramp's farm, and I thought Kay would love to meet him too. However, our bank account wasn't able to manage his two-thirds priced ticket.

Mom suggested I take Tessa along, for her presence would serve the same function as Derek's in relating to the Seattle family, and since she was under two, her plane ticket would be free. But I felt that taking Tessa along would inevitably mean that my three and a half days there would revolve around naps, bottles, and diapers, and that I wouldn't be able to give in as much to the experiences of getting to know Kay and the family, which was the purpose of the trip. I didn't want to ask Elaine to help look after Tessa because her fifteen-month-old's needs would take up too much of Elaine's time. More importantly (and it was Harald who pointed this out to me), taking Tessa could have been too heavy a trip for Kay, because Tessa (chubby, blond, blue-eyed, still a little unsteady on her feet) might have been too strong a reminder of the girl child she had given up.

So I decided to go alone and to take pictures along of Mom, Dad, Rick, Harald, Derek, and Tessa. I also asked Elaine to meet my plane and to let me sleep at her apartment each night. I wanted to use Elaine's home as a base I could return to each night and think things out, hash things out with her if I needed to, and where I could relax completely. I wanted to spend each day, all day, with Kay and other members of the family and then be able to collapse quietly at Elaine's. Projecting my balancing act onto Kay, I thought she would appreciate this set-up too and would like to have some breathing space and time to reflect quietly on what was happening between us.

Wrong! Soon after I wrote to Kay about my ideas for the trip, I received this reply: *Please reconsider your plans to stay with Elaine, though I know how you might feel about it being a rather heavy trip, but since I have to be at the shop part of the time, it isn't as though we'd just be sitting in my little apartment all the time.... If you arrive Saturday sometime during the day, we couldn't all meet you because someone would have to be in the shop — and we do all want to meet the plane. By all, I mean Kandy, Keeva, and I. I asked Elaine about having you stay with me, and I guess it's just thinking it might be too emotional that would be the main thing against it, but I think that's crazy. Emotional experiences are the pinnacles of our lives. It's boredom and safe, sane security which are to be avoided. It's like taking tranquillizers for the exciting happy events of life — how terrible to dull those feelings. Life itself gets dull enough at times — that can't be helped sometimes. Four days is a very brief time. I'm sure even if we find this whole experience not at all what we imagined that it's better to find out the worst rather than going on with some fantasy.*

Kay's direct, gutsy statement produced a whirlpool of confused feelings in me. I responded immediately to the verve and emotion in it, and then I reflected upon how I had changed in the past several years. Ten years ago, at the height of my relationship with Paul, I never would have sought to cushion the emotional impact of the trip. I would have leapt right in, making no provisions for catching my breath. But I knew that I had changed since then and had become more cautious. I did want to give in to the experience, but I also needed to step back and consider the meaning of it all.

I reacted strongly to some of Kay's statements. I didn't feel life was dull; at least, my own life had rarely been dull, yet it sounded as if she thought I was inclined to be "safe, sane, and security-minded." Maybe she really didn't know, I hadn't let her know, how deeply moved I was by finding her. Maybe I had been too concerned with controlling my feelings in writing to her for fear of overwhelming *her*. The faintly derogatory use of the word "fantasy" bothered me too. She had said previously in a letter that she worried about living up to what my childish fantasies of her must have been (*I've been a dream who never got angry or cross with you and who always would have loved and understood you and been proud of everything you did*), and my reply hadn't seemed to dislodge that concept from her mind. I hated to see Mom and Harald's battleground developing, but I saw that both Kay and I were two strong-minded Scorpios. (Her birthday is exactly a week before mine.)

I hadn't formed an answer to Kay's letter, when the next evening as I was preparing dinner, the phone rang.

"Pat? Hi! This is Kay."

"Kay! How are you?" My heart surprised me by fluttering like an adolescent in love.

"Fine. Well, actually, I'm kind of upset. At first I thought I shouldn't call, I should just let things go on, but I finally decided I'm a person too! And I just had to say something."

"What is it? What's the matter?"

"Well, I've been talking to Elaine again this afternoon about your visit, and I just have to find out how much is you and how much is Elaine in these plans. Do you really want Elaine to meet your plane, and do you really want to stay at her place?"

"Yes...I thought it would be good for both of us to have a chance to kind of sit back and take a deep breath, that's why I want to stay with Elaine. And I thought she should pick me up at the airport and drive me to your apartment, and then you and I could meet each other quietly, and have all afternoon to talk, without having to meet in those crowds and not being able to really say much to each other."

It never occurred to me that there was anything odd about standing in the kitchen in a soiled apron at six o'clock in the evening, with one hand holding the phone to my ear and the other waving a dripping spatula to emphasize my points, as my long-sought birth mother and I launched into our first argument.

"Well, I don't think I'll be able to stand that!" Kay's voice, usually so soft and husky, came through almost stridently now over the phone lines. "I'll be pacing the floor, waiting, wondering whether you've arrived or not. It was always like that when Keith used to come home from Stanford. Carl would go out and pick him up, and I'd be left alone pacing the floor. I just can't stand the idea of going through that again. Anyway, I love airports! The excitement of the whole scene. I can't miss it! Especially with you coming now for the first time!"

"Well, I don't know, Kay, — I have a funny feeling about airports," I replied, backing off a little while still pursuing my line of argument. "It seems like whenever I've traveled alone and been in and out of airports, it's always been a powerful thing for me. I've always been saying goodbye to people I love, or saying hello after a long time, and I thought this time it would be good to avoid it and just meet at your place."

"So what if it's emotional?" she retorted immediately. "So what if we shed a few tears? What do we care about those other people watching?"

Joy welled up in my chest as I listened to her. For a few moments I forgot all about Mom and Harald and my own internal identity struggles. I loved her for saying what she felt! I loved her for caring so much about meeting my plane! I felt that I had been too cautious in making my plans and that I should relax.

But then she said, "Listen, I have always made my children's decisions for them. I just feel that you've done enough work. You've made enough decisions in all it took you to find me. Now you just leave this part of it up to me."

Any lightness in her words eluded me. "Wait a minute!" I said, like a porcupine suddenly cornered, and the spatula in my right hand sprang into life again. "I'm not sure I like that. I'm a pretty independent cuss, you know!" My words startled me. They were Mom's words in moments of stress, repeated from her crusty father, Grandpa Boyd.

Kay paused and then laughed gently. "Yes, I guess you are. I didn't mean that quite the way it sounded."

"Well, you know," I said, matching her appeasing tone, "I guess I've been mostly considering myself in all this. You're sure right — you are a person too! Look, why don't you meet me at the airport, but I'll stay at Elaine's apartment at night?"

"Okay. How about if you stay with Elaine the first two nights, and let's just leave the third night open. If it feels right to stay at my place, then do. How's that?" We were bargaining, both of us determined Scorpios, grown-up women, mother and daughter.

"That sounds fine! Let's just see how it goes for the third night." I began laughing with relief and at the ludicrousness of the situation. If only I could have tuned in on this conversation three months before, when I was starting my search! "Kay, I'm so glad you called. I can't wait to see you!"

"I can't either! I'm sure we won't have any problem recognizing each other, but just in case I'll wear a bright orange coat. You can't possibly miss it."

We ended the conversation by going over the details of the flight arrival, and all I was thinking about was that incredible moment of seeing her for the first time. Yes! That was how I wanted it to be too — at the airport, with all the crowds and chrome and garbled messages over the loudspeakers! The heck with what Harald thought, and sparing Mom's feelings! This was *my* life, and I wasn't going to spoil one of its most dramatic moments! This was *my* quest, and I wasn't going to deny myself the prize!

Harald had walked into the kitchen partway through our conversation. As I hung up, he looked at me, shaking his head and smiling ironically. "So you backed down, huh?"

"We compromised," I corrected him, bristling.

PATRICIA MOFFAT

One of Kay's modeling
photos from 1945-46

John Metcalf (Gramps), born March 31, 1897
Eunice Grannis (grandmother), born Oct 30, 1898

Eunice Grannis, age 16

Frank Metcalf
(great-grandfather)
with one of the
violins he made,
Pasadena 1937

PART III:
BLOOD TIES

On the beach on Whidbey Island:
Keeva, Kandy, Gramps (John Metcalf), me, Kay

Kandy, Keeva, Kay, & Keith

Kay when I first met her, June 1977.
She was 56 years old

Me at age 14,
the same age as
my siblings

CHAPTER 17

Somnolent, caressing, the deep voice of the hypnotherapist guides me through my trance. *"You are sitting in a train compartment which is yourself. We will be traveling backward in time. Through the windows, you will look out onto scenes from your life. The train will slowly gather speed, rushing back through your life like a film running in reverse. It will begin slowing down as you get smaller and smaller, younger and younger, until it comes to a complete stop at the moment of your birth. When that happens, when the train brings you to the moment of your birth, you will tell me.*

"Ready now.... All the muscles in your body relaxed, all your muscles very heavy and relaxed, the train slowly begins to move. 1977, 1976, 1975, 1970 ... back, back, back in time, watching the scenes of your life through the window of the train as we move backward in time."

Spring in Carmel Valley. Harald and I talking under the pink flowering plum tree in the patio while the children play in the long grass, the breeze soft, the morning full of promise.

Back. A delivery room, white walls, shiny steel instruments, masked figures in green cotton smocks and surgical gloves gathered around my raised knees. Pressure prying my body open till I howl that it will crack in two. Someone cries with life, someone cries with joy.

Back. Harald and I at the indigo water's edge, reciting vows of idealistic promise. Daddy against the rough gray oaks, reading of love from the Bible.

Faster back. Laying my head on Paul's shoulder, the smell and caress of soft suede. Watching the foaming breakers at Carmel Beach, feeling the baby inside.

Back, back. Lithe black girls in blue-and-white school uniforms. Brilliant red flame tree arching over a dusty road. Thin old men pedaling bicycles barefoot.

Back. Flipping through new fiction in the Stanford bookstore one gray, dreary Thursday morning when the world stops. Dallas, November 22, 1963.

Back. Ginger and I aimlessly wandering the green, pine-scented streets behind Monterey High, cutting English, our favorite class, just to see how it feels.

Back. Moving day, August 5, 1959, the four of us and Grandpa Boyd cramped in the pink station wagon, so hot that the kittens are panting like dogs.

Back. Picking raspberries in the early morning, red ones like jeweled beehives, little black ones like beaded caps. Eating my way down the sun-flecked, thorny arbor.

Back. Scared, carefully leading Ricky up the hill to the house. Stepped on sharp glass, he's sobbing as we watch his white sock and sandal turn wet crimson.

Back. Sunday dinner at Grandma and Grandpa Dietterle's. Black pitted olives that fit satisfyingly onto my ten fingertips, to be sucked off in turn. When Grandpa plays ragtime, the canary sings.

Back, slowly back. Mama in the living room, talking on the black daffodil telephone while I'm in the bedroom painting each toe and fingernail red, orange, pink.

Back, very slowly back. Reaching through the crib slats to Daddy's brown dresser, pulling one, two, three drawers a little bit out. Straddling the crib in cold wet diapers, grasping the dresser and backing down, feeling the way with my toes.

Now the images stop coming. The windows of the train are black. Black and silent in my head. "Stopped," I say from deep inside my train tunnel.

"Now the train has stopped," the comforting voice says. "The train has stopped, and Baby Pat is about to be born. Baby Pat feels nice and warm and dark, doesn't she? Now Baby Pat wants to be born. What do you feel, Baby Pat?"

No answer. Serene nothing, silence.

"Do you feel a pressure on your head, a squeezing?"

Mutely, my head shakes no. Head fine, am comfortable, lying down. But now I feel a pulling on my feet and legs. My legs begin to twitch, muscles quivering uncontrollably in the therapist's recliner. Large hands pull gently at my ankles, and I'm moving now, squeezing, slipping, sliding from warm tight dark to cold rushing light, supported, suspended, pulled from the warmth, hanging in space.

"Baby Pat is born!" the voice announces. "What is it like to come into the world, Baby Pat? What is it like to be born?"

"Terrible!" the word shouts from my mouth. "It's terrible!"

Jolted, my eyes pop open. For a moment I am back in the hypnotherapist's office, shocked, staring at the pastel prairie watercolor on the wall. I wail, I cry with all my body as if for the first time in my life. "Terrible," repeats the therapist softly. "Why is it a terrible thing to be born, Baby Pat? Tell me."

I close my eyes, still crying, and am sucked right back into deep trance. "Terrible because I have to leave my mother. I have to go away now, all by myself."

My baby self is being pulled away from her. Buoyed by the large warm hands, I float from the green room where I have just been born into a gray corridor, a long tunnel, outstretched born-first feet leading the way, being steadily sucked away from her, alone and lost. I see her behind me, receding, her body on the table, knees up, bleeding, her beautiful face turned away, her long amber hair spilling over the table.

"But your mother loves you, doesn't she, Baby Pat? You know she loves you and you love her, and she is giving you up so that you will have a better life."

"Maybe she loves me. But she's worried about herself. I'm part of her, but I have to leave her...going away all alone."

"But you will have a good life, won't you, Baby Pat? You will miss your mother, but you will learn to be strong and independent, and soon you will have other parents who will love you."

Yes, all of this is true. As I float farther into the new tunnel, the tunnel leading to my life, my baby self pushes down the aching and the tears. She watches her mother, my mother, until she is doll-like in the distance, and the green room disappears. Then she takes a deep breath and looks forward, all alone now, and peers with anticipation toward her new life.

* * *

"On behalf of your captain and crew, I wish you a pleasant stay in Seattle. Please remain seated with your seatbelts securely fastened until the aircraft has come to a complete stop."

I am not brave enough to be the first passenger off the plane, so I busy myself with my travel gear for a few minutes. Then, so as not to be the last person off, draped with shoulder bag, camera, and Mom's raincoat, smiling and apologizing, I elbow my way into the stream of similarly laden people moving down the aisle. God, how I wish I could command my legs to stop shaking!

Exuding a surface calm but feeling that my heart may burst at any moment, I walk through the dog-legging covered ramp from the airplane toward the arrivals area. Not receding this time, but ever moving toward her, I walk through the gray tunnel toward the light. Peering around the bobbing forms in front of me carrying packages, briefcases, and children, I scan the faces of those waiting up ahead, searching for her excitedly, half-fearfully. The man in front of me veers slightly, and suddenly there she is! She's standing like a beacon at the end of the tunnel in the bright orange coat she promised to wear, alone, waiting, eagerly watching the stream of emerging passengers.

Something surges inside me, threatening tears. But I must not see her for the first time through a blur of tears! I want to see every detail of her face clearly. I swallow, smile, and wave hugely. Her face lights up, she smiles, and waves back. Thirty years have brought me back to this familiar stranger. Pulled away helpless at my birth, I now walk back to her of my own accord. Finally, I emerge from the tunnel and stand before my mother for the first time.

There is a moment's pause, a moment of drinking in the features of the other person before she says "Hello" and I say "Hi" at the same time.

Laughter wells up in both of us, and we reach out and hug each other a little gingerly, as if the other might break. Then I hold her by her shoulders, almost at arm's length, unabashedly staring. I am astonished, totally unprepared for her youthful physical beauty. I know she's fifty-five years old, yet she appears to be in her early forties. Somehow, the few pictures she sent didn't capture her essence at all. Everything about her is glowing, translucent, luminous — her smooth skin, her clear blue eyes, her soft brown hair silvering at the temples. Her cheekbones are high, her features beautifully proportioned. She radiates health, energy, serenity. How can this lovely person possibly be my mother?

"Am I...do I look anything like what you'd expected?" I ask, trying to turn my perspective around, wondering what her first impression is of me. It really doesn't matter what I say.

"Well, I did have a mental picture from the photographs," she says, her eyes making me feel giddy again, "but I'm positive I would have known you right away, even if there was nothing to go on."

No tears. We can't seem to take our eyes off each other, but there are no tears. Only this enormous wonder, this tingling exhilaration.

As she leads me through the maze of the terminal to the baggage claim, she looks closely at me again. "Your eyes are so like your father's," she says. "Funny, I haven't thought of those eyes in thirty years."

"Do they bother you?"

"Oh no, not at all! Your father was a very handsome man."

I'm a little disturbed by this sudden turn in the conversation, a little protective of my father, whoever he is, that handsome man with the odd name whom she spent a few days in 1945 not loving. He's as much a part of me as she is, though he's ignorant of my existence.

Pleasant small talk, verbal stroking as we walk through the terminal. I am captivated by her; never in my life have I been so instantly drawn to anyone. I steal looks at her, studying her features over and over again. I notice her graceful hands, her long, thin fingers. I take in her slender figure, wrapped in a simple but exotic cotton batik dress under her open, hand-knitted coat. I try to put together the gentle, slightly husky voice I already know from the phone with this astonishingly attractive woman. I am surprised by her spontaneous, almost girlish laughter.

* * *

"When I was born, did you see me? Did you touch me?" We are heading into Seattle on the freeway in Kay's dark red Plymouth. I know this is probably the wrong time to leap into the heart of the matter, but the small talk has been getting to me.

"I didn't hold you, but I did see you," Kay replies evenly, without surprise, keeping her eyes on the road. "In the excitement of the birth, one of the nurses just forgot the circumstances, and as soon as you were born, she held you up to me and said, 'Look! Here's your beautiful baby girl!'" Suddenly she struggles to control her voice, and I am sorry that I've asked, here in the car, but I'm dying to know. I am so attentive to her every word and nuance that my whole body feels electric. "I just took one quick look," she continues, "and then I turned my head away. I couldn't bear to look at you or to hold you, knowing that I couldn't keep you."

Her voice catches, and for a moment her self-control gives way to tears. My heart is pounding now, my throat aching. I switch direction slightly.

"Did the adoption agency tell you anything about Mom and Dad?"

"Oh, yes. I think it was when I was about seven or eight months pregnant, they told me they had picked out possible parents for you. They said they both had college degrees, that your father had been in the navy and was a teacher, and that your mother was a social worker."

"Sure sounds like Mom and Dad," I say. "Isn't that odd, though? They didn't know anything about me or anything about you until the day before they picked me up, when I was six weeks old."

"Six weeks old?" She turns to look at me, surprised and worried. "All that time the agency knew who your parents were going to be, and they didn't give you to them until you were six weeks old?"

I flash on Derek and Tessa at six weeks of life, both of them distinct personalities by that time, Derek insistent and physically active, Tessa quieter, observant. Both of them were smiling widely, toothlessly at six weeks, responding with their whole little bodies to the voices, faces, and smells of familiar people. Where was I for those first six weeks? Was I given enough attention so that I learned to smile?

"Maybe they wanted to make sure I was healthy and normal before they gave me to Mom and Dad. Observation period or something."

"Yes, I know that's true," Kay says, "or at least it was true when I was working for the Children's Home Society later on. But back then, somehow, I assumed your parents would come to the hospital to pick you up right away."

"Well, it should be that way! Natural parents have to take what they get, so why shouldn't adoptive parents too?" I am beginning to feel a little angry, similar to the anger I felt at "the system" when the nurses kept Derek away from me in the hospital for his first few days of life.

"It's so much better for the baby, that's the main thing," Kay continues, warming to the theme now. "You know, back in those days I was so ignorant. I thought that a baby was just a little organism that needed to be fed and have its diapers changed. I thought it didn't really matter to the baby who took care of it, when it was that small, as long as it was handled gently, given enough milk, kept dry. But today the views on infants are so different — so much more is known — and that first period in a baby's life is so important! The baby's identification with the mother begins right away."

There's that feeling of hollowness and dislocation again, that sense of being lost, like when she talked about my father's eyes. All I can think about is the bald fact that I wasn't able to bond with *my* mother, neither Mom nor this lovely woman sitting beside me, when I was that small. "Well," Kay says, taking her eyes off the road for a moment to smile at me, "thank goodness you don't seem to have suffered from early deprivation."

"No, I don't think so," I agree. Yet I can't help slipping this in, for maybe she doesn't realize the impact of what she's just said. I smile, "Of course, I smoke. I guess that oral thing could be due to not being breastfed."

She doesn't smile back. She looks worried again. And she doesn't succumb to a possible segue into breast vs. bottle, bad habits, smoking, drugs.

"When I worked for the Children's Home Society, part of my job was transporting babies from the hospital to foster homes, and from the foster homes to the agency where their new parents would pick them up," Kay continues. "I always felt so much for those little babies, those helpless little beings totally alone in the world, being taken care of by paid foster mothers who must have been kind but also couldn't allow themselves to get attached — being driven around by a stranger from one place to another, not understanding any of it. They'd just lie there in their little baskets—" she indicates the passenger seat I'm occupying, "completely alone."

I'm speechless, trying to process this information. How could she have done that? Forced herself to confront her own past and her guilt every time she transported a homeless baby?

I ask the obvious. "Did you work for the Children's Home as a way of working out your feelings about having given me up for adoption?"

She turns to me, surprised, and looks at me blankly, shaking her head. "No, no, I don't think I ever once thought about it that way."

* * *

Preparing the coffee in her sunny kitchen, Kay is a little bustling, a little too quick in her movements, apologizing for the instant coffee and trying to explain away the smallness of the apartment. We'd become quite comfortable with each other in the car, even though the topics we talked about were highly charged. But now there is a slight reticence and nervousness again. We chat about her jewelry projects, spread out on the kitchen table, about her collection of miniature vases, about Keeva's cat, which has appeared in the kitchen, meowing and rubbing against Kay's leg at the sound of the fridge door opening and shutting.

Moving into the living room and settling into opposite sides of the couch with our coffee mugs, I notice the baskets of large, healthy plants hanging in the window, just as Elaine had described. There's a dark, pleasant, relaxing feeling in the living room. An exquisitely detailed batik in navy blue, cream, and brown hangs on the wall above the couch, Indonesian shadow puppets decorate the walls, and teak sculptures sit in recesses in the bookshelves, all evidence of Kay's interest in the crafts of Indonesia, her several trips there, and her business.

Now there's a sense of expectancy in the air again, as if the small talk is over. I feel momentarily awkward, at a loss as to how to begin. Visual aids. "I brought some pictures along," I say.

We go through the glossy prints one by one as I share my present life with her: Derek, Tessa, Harald, Mom, Dad, and Rick. Kay is especially interested in the kids and Rick. "Gee, wouldn't it be neat if Rick could drive up here in his camper and visit this summer?" she says. "The girls would absolutely love him!" We laugh, caught up in the improbable notion of Rick falling for one of his sister's half-sisters.

Now it's her turn, and out come the albums. It's eerie for me, turning the thick pages, guided by Kay, studying the photos of ordinary family scenes, of my half-sisters and brother growing up. If she'd made a different decision, I would be in these photos too. Carol would be here, opening Christmas packages, playing in the backyard after an uncommon snowfall, waving from the boat bound for Australia. She'd be three years older than Keith, with blond pigtails just like her little sisters Kandy and Keeva.

Who am I? Who would I have become if I had grown up in my biological family? Two waves of sadness wash through me simultaneously: sadness that I missed growing up with my "real" family by blood, and sadness that I could have missed having Mom, Dad, and Rick as my family. I don't want to even try to express these conflicting feelings to Kay.

Along with the family pictures is a breathtaking portfolio of Kay as a photographer's model in Los Angeles not long after my birth. Here is a glamorous, classically beautiful vision of a mother far surpassing any of my childhood fantasies.

"Wow! No wonder you tried to make it in Hollywood," I say, remembering details from our second phone conversation, which at the time I'd brushed aside as a young woman's daydreaming.

"Here," she says, thumbing quickly, almost in businesslike fashion, through the portfolio. "Keep that one if you like. I was four months pregnant with you."

The face in the black and white photograph is fresh and young, the dark blond wavy hair brushed lightly back and tied with a ribbon. The full breasts of early pregnancy are evident in the bathing suit, in contrast to the later modeling pictures. Here she is, twenty-three years old, blooming, and I'm a small curled thing inside her. They say it's loud in there, that the fetus can hear the pulsings and gurglings of the mother's body, as well as muted voices, noises, and music on the outside. They say that fetuses pick up the emotional states of the mother.

"Did you feel any resentment toward me — I mean, toward that baby you were carrying — because your movie career was blocked?"

"Toward you? A little baby? Oh, of course not. It was all such a glamorous dream then, but if it had worked out it may not have been a good life at all." I am transfixed by her beautiful profile as she pauses to sip her coffee, and at her slim, girlish figure in the batik dress. "I feel that most of the time the things that happen to us in our lives have some purpose," Kay continues, turning to look at me warmly. "There are experiences we have to go through which may seem like the end of the world at the time, but which help us grow. Maybe we can't see the purpose or the growing until years afterwards." Her sentence trails off, and her eyes suddenly fill with tears.

"My worst fear when I was growing up," she continues, "was that I might get pregnant and have a baby before I was married. I don't know why I was so afraid of that particular thing. It seemed to be the one thing I could imagine that would mean I had ruined my life. I've thought about whether that fear was some kind of signal that that experience was what I really had sort of subconsciously planned for myself in this life. Of course, when it actually happened, I never thought about that, I just worried and suffered and tried to think about how to get my life back in shape and make the best decision for you."

How long do we sit talking on the couch? One hour? Two or more? I am completely unaware of the time as we move through topic after topic, filling in the years. I fight the feeling of dizziness, of sensory and informational overload that is similar to what I experienced the first time I went to Germany, when I was concentrating so hard on understanding the language.

Kay tells me in greater detail the story of my birth: how her water broke when she was at her hotel, how she took a taxi to the hospital and Carl met her there, how very painful the contractions were, and she begged the nurses for more painkillers. When I remind her that I was a breech birth, and that probably explains the extra-strong pain, she is astonished. "Do you know, I never knew that? I guess I really must have been out of it!" She tells me about her difficult marriage with Carl. We talk about abortion: yes, she would have had one at the time if she could have. Do I think badly of her? And when I tell her about my abortion, she sympathizes, saying it must have been harder for me to do that than most girls, knowing my own mother could have done the same.

"I thought a lot about you around the time of my abortion," I tell her. "I don't understand how you could have pushed your experience away, carried it around with you for so many years, and not talked about it. Didn't you ever have to cry, just to let the pain out?"

She folds her slender hands in her lap, massaging her left hand with her right, and is silent for a long moment. "Mainly I was feeling numb, I was trying to block it all out, to push it all to the back of my mind and just go on somehow," she replies. Her phrases are sounding so familiar to me. Mom. When something unpleasant happens, it does no good to "stew" about it. Just carry on, keep moving forward, chin up.

"Yes, I used to be very good at bottling things up. You know, I didn't cry during that entire time. Just the stoic, going on. Wait a minute — there was just one time, I remember it now. Carl and I went to a movie in Los Angeles not long after you were born. It was called *Sentimental Journey* or something like that. In the movie there was a young couple who couldn't have children, and they'd just learned there was a baby ready for them to adopt. I remember this scene so clearly now. They were fixing up the nursery for the baby. They were both so happy, so eager to get the child.

I started crying there in the theater. I told Carl I couldn't stand to watch it, so we got up and left. I was still crying as we walked out of the theater. But even then I don't think I got it all out. It had taken me by surprise, and the tears just started coming. But still I pushed it down, didn't let myself give in completely."

She pauses again, sits very still, and stares out the window. "You've read *Gone With the Wind*, haven't you?" she asks finally, and I nod. "You remember at the very end of the book, Scarlett says something like, 'I'll think about it tomorrow'? When I read that, I had to read it over and over; it struck me as being so true for me. Sometimes I think that's the story of my life. I pushed it away, thought I might think about it some other time.

"I think that's why I felt such a tremendous sense of relief when you phoned. Suddenly I knew you were alive! You were all right, you'd been placed in a good family, and you'd grown up to be well adjusted and secure. I just felt that in your voice during that very first phone call. And I felt light, really physically light, like a burden I had been carrying around all those years was removed, and I hadn't even realized how heavy it had been!"

Yes, she always remembered my birthday, she says — it's exactly a week after her own — and she always imagined a blond, curly-haired little girl growing up somewhere in California. Later, when she worked for the Children's Home Society, she came to know many "difficult-to-place" teenagers who had been shuttled from foster home to foster home, sometimes due only to some small physical defect or because they'd developed serious behavioral problems. Then she began worrying about whether I had met a similar fate. But no, she didn't do anything about it, she didn't try to find anything out about me. It was practically impossible, she says, even though she was working in the area of adoption.

Now I feel like burying the past for a while too. I feel that we've dealt with as much of it as we can. My head feels cleared. I'm ready to talk about things that are not so deep and painful. All the time we've been sitting on the couch, my eyes have been returning to two oil paintings on the wall: a serene blue bay surrounded by tall trees and a large abstract that suggests a high, impenetrable stone wall with colonies of ochre spheres exuding from it like bright fungi. The suggestions this painting brings to mind are somber, but the colors are pleasing. I ask Kay about the paintings and am surprised when she tells me that Keith painted the abstract when he was seventeen, soon after he learned he had cancer. The seascape is her own. I feel a rush of connection to the paintings and to the creative energies of this new mother and brother. I tell Kay that I draw and paint too, but I like watercolors more than oils.

Still in pursuit of less painfully charged topics, I ask Kay to tell me more about her ideas on reincarnation.

"Well," she begins with that lilting girlish laughter, "if you aren't into it, it will all sound pretty weird..."

"That's okay! Let's go!" I feel like Alice falling down the rabbit hole as Kay guides me through the wonderland of her New Age beliefs. Each soul lives many different lives as it grows. Each lifetime is like a new classroom, with new tests, experiences, challenges. How we meet these tests helps determine the conditions for our next life, our next incarnation. Karma is the balancing out of the successes and failures of all our incarnations. If we overcome a certain obstacle in one life, we won't have to meet that same problem in another life. But if we bungle it, we'll have to make it up sooner or later. "That's what I meant about owing your parents a 'karmic debt,'" she explains.

Kay believes that some souls tend to stay together throughout many lifetimes, choosing to reincarnate together. "I think families often stay together," she says, "like in a past life you and I may have been sisters, or maybe I was your daughter, or maybe we were close friends. The roles change as the souls work things out together."

It's very rare, she continues, but some people can remember bits of past lives. Sometimes people find those memories through years of meditation, or even drug experiences. But for most of us, knowing about our past lives is like peeking in the back of the textbook to find the answers. That would be like cheating, rather than honestly trying to meet the challenges of our present life. "But I believe we do receive direction from our higher selves, from a higher level of reality, which reminds us of our purposes in this life, but we receive the help unconsciously, through dreams and intuition." Part of skillful living, Kay adds, is learning how to tune in to one's higher self and receive guidance.

She tells me about the "really far-out book" she's reading now, titled *Seth Speaks*. Seth, who is "an entity no longer focused in physical form," speaks through a woman named Jane Roberts. According to the material channeled from Seth, this life, or what we call reality, is actually a dream, while our real life, our true reality, takes place in dreams and in the spirit state between incarnations. In those states, our souls set up the situations we will meet in a particular life and monitor how our present personalities deal with those situations. "It's repeated over and over in this book," she says, "that 'you create your own reality.'"

My once-Presbyterian mind is struggling. "Who or what is the soul, then?" I ask. "In different lives, are you the same person, the same personality just in a different body, or what?"

All the incarnations are part of the soul or the higher self, she answers. Seth suggests there's an "oversoul" that directs all our incarnations, and it's as if all our lifetimes are taking place not in earthbound linear time, but all are happening simultaneously. This means that if my twentieth century personality is having difficulty with a certain problem, it may be able to get some direction from my fourteenth century self or my twenty-fourth century self, if I can just tune in well enough to my intuition and connect with my higher self.

"Well, who knows?" Kay concludes. "It may be true, or it may all be just a fantasy. But it makes sense to me. It makes life have more meaning, and besides, it's fun to believe it!"

Washing up in the bathroom and changing into my jeans, I feel as if I'm reentering my body after a trip to another planet. First there was the long talk about my birth and all Kay went through then — a journey into the past that was highly charged with controlled emotions — and now this plunge into spiritual theories light years away from my much more earthbound frame of reference.

Is there a connection? It feels like we switched gears late in the afternoon, moving from the achingly personal to the omnisciently impersonal, and yet.... Quickly, she turned her head away, it was over for her, she had signed the relinquishment papers, she didn't dwell on it, and like Scarlett O'Hara, she thought she might think about it tomorrow. But perhaps she was actually calm then, more calm than numb, because she believed that my soul had chosen to incarnate into this particular baby, knowing ahead of time it would be separated from her, pulled, taken away at birth. Perhaps she believed that my soul had planned this life in advance, with this trauma at its beginning, this particular challenge, and this quest to complete. The responsibility for the relinquishment, then, would be mine. "I guess it's made it easier for her to live with all these years," prescient, sensible Mom had said. Splashing my face with water and looking up into the mirror, I notice that my eyes have dilated. The pupils are huge and black, ringed by thin halos of blue.

The three sisters on the ferry for my
first visit to Whidbey Island:
Keeva, Kandy, and me

CHAPTER 18

As Kay and I walk into her shop, Batiks Indonesia in Pioneer Square, I'm aware of the smell of burning incense, and my peripheral vision registers racks of colorful, intricately patterned batik clothes, panels of similar material on the walls, and jewelry and art objects crammed into a small space. But my attention is riveted to the two attractive young women sitting together at the back of the shop by the cash register. They stand up, smile, and wave excitedly when they see us. They look so familiar!

The counter is in the way, so we don't hug. We grasp each other's hands over it and begin talking all at once. "Keeva! Kandy!" "Pat! Hello! Welcome!" Both of them exude almost palpable, loving vibrations toward me.

We're relishing the physical resemblances. Keeva and I are about the same height, 5'8", while Kandy is a few inches shorter like Kay. Kandy's eyes are brown rather than blue. But otherwise, the similarities are striking: general body frames, dark blond hair, clear, tanned skin. And there's something else that's familiar about my two sisters, something more intangible that I sense immediately. In manner they both have a surface calm covering an inner intensity that is also me. Is this is what is meant by a blood tie, this instant recognition?

Soon we're all talking rapidly. It's funny that Kay thought my eyes were like my father's, because Keeva and I are looking into each other's eyes again, enjoying the spooky feeling of looking into a mirror. They're both saying what a difficult thing it must have been to find "Mom" and how happy they are that I did. And I'm saying how lucky I feel to have found two sisters. I've always wondered what it would be like to have a sister, and now I have two!

Back at Kay's apartment, while Kay and Keeva prepare dinner in the kitchen, Kandy and I talk in the living room, sitting together on the couch where I spent most of the afternoon. I feel close to Kandy and comfortable in her presence. Her manner is warm and open. As the fragrance of sautéing onions and mushrooms begins filling the apartment, Kandy tells me that the three of them had quite a discussion about tonight's menu, since she is on another of her diets. She's "always fighting this darned weight problem," she explains with an apologetic smile.

I ask her how she felt that night Kay told her she'd had a phone call from me. I am alert to the slightest signs of resentment in my two new sisters, a little worried that they might feel I'm horning in on their mother.

"Oh, I felt so excited!" Kandy replies. She beams her warm, open smile on me. "We all did! You see, it really affected me when I first heard about you when I was about fourteen. I just could hardly believe that my *sister* had been given away! I wondered about you, where you were, and what you looked like, but at that time I never dreamed I'd meet you someday."

She recounts the scene she's never forgotten. Kay was busy in the kitchen while Carl and the three teenagers were in the living room. It was during the time Kay and Carl were deciding to separate, and there was "a lot of tension and pretty vicious arguing" going on. Kandy thinks her dad was trying to hurt her mom and that he didn't stop to consider the effect his words would have on his children when he told them their mother had had a baby before they were born and put it up for adoption — and what did they think of their "fine, pure mother" now?

"Of course, instead of blaming Mom," Kandy tells me, "we said, 'Really? Why did she give the baby away? Was it a boy or a girl?' Mom came in then and said, 'Carl, what in the world are you saying to the kids?' Then we heard the whole story, and all we could think of was, 'You mean we have another sister out there somewhere and we'll never get to know her?' We just felt sympathetic to Mom and really, really sad."

Kay and Keeva walk in with the dinner plates and join the conversation. Over a soufflé and salad, and for three hours afterward, the four of us hardly pause. How do you squeeze whole lifetimes, even just the highlights, into one evening? As we sit talking, I am aware of two levels of communication: the conversation itself, as we exchange summaries of the important events in our lives and our feelings around them, and a more unconscious level of communication consisting of body language, nuances, and emotions. I feel very much at home in this second, deeper level of communication, so much so that at times it strikes me as bizarre that we know so little about the details of each other's lives and experiences and that we must spend these hours attempting to catch up.

They tell me more about the divorce. They tell me about Keith's cancer, which was discovered around the same time, and how close to death he was. I am very curious about this brother and wish he weren't so far away in Europe now. They fill me in on each person who will be at the family gathering tomorrow on Whidbey Island, all the relatives I will be meeting for the first time. How wonderful that they've organized this for me! I feel nervous and excited in anticipation. It's Gramp I'm most interested in.

"He's wonderful in so many ways," Kay begins. Sitting in the rocking chair in her batik dress, with the glossy hanging plants behind her, she reminds me of a graceful tropical flower. "He's so young for his years, the way he lives out there in that old place, always with a couple of students sharing the meals and the work. He's never been concerned about money. In fact, he really believes that money is the great root of all evil. He lives mostly for enjoyment now. He'll spend all day driving his truck over to eastern Washington in the summer, picking fruit and talking to people. He'll bring back a whole truckload of fruit and sell it, but never for profit — just enough to pay for his gas."

Gramp is a "very ethical, very spiritual person," I learn. He's always been concerned about the progress of his soul. Along with being Christian, quite fundamentalist in some of his beliefs, they admit, he also believes in reincarnation. He was an early follower of the psychic healer Edgar Cayce.

As they've been talking, I've been remembering the black-and-white picture Kay sent me of a strong, handsome old man with twinkly eyes, full head of white hair, long, gnarled fingers. He was wearing a plaid lumberjack jacket in the photo, a striking individual against the dark feathery background of evergreens. Anyone's vision of Grandfather.

They explain that Gramp took part in the first therapeutic experiments with LSD in the U.S. in the 1950s, and since then he's tried most of the mind-expanders as they've come along. His current "thing" is carbon dioxide. "He has this huge cannister of pure CO_2 in his living room," Kay explains. "You'll see it tomorrow, unless someone has managed to hide it. He inhales it until he almost blacks out. He says that at the point just before you black out, you get this rush, this hallucination of truth. I haven't tried it myself. I don't like the idea of passing out."

"Have you...ever tried anything yourself?" I venture, looking over at my beautiful, batik-clad birth mother, sitting demurely in her rocking chair.

"Oh yes, I guess I've tried most of the stuff being passed around — not a whole lot of anything, but just enough to get the feel of each trip." She itemizes her experiments with marijuana, mescaline, and LSD, lingering a while on a lovely LSD trip in which she lost herself in the veins and patterns in the leaves of her plants and began feeling that she *was* a plant. "I've never looked at a plant since then without reliving some of that sensation of being the plant and really feeling its beauty. I don't know... we don't know...how you feel about this, what your experiences have been with drugs."

The ball has just been passed to me. But I'm so caught up in a disorienting sense of role reversal that for a moment I don't know what to say at all. I mean, where I come from, your *mother* isn't out there experimenting with drugs and giving testimonials about the mind-expanding qualities of certain chemicals. She's warning you, with great seriousness and concern for your welfare, about the addictive qualities of marijuana after she's just found out you've had your first joint. I learned from Daddy long after the fact that Mom had actually become physically ill after reading a letter from me from Stanford in which I described my initiation to hashish (which involved several hours of communing with a tank of tropical fish). And now here I am, across the small room from this disarmingly innocent-looking person, also my mother, and feeling out of my depth, as if — poof! — suddenly I'm dressed in a matronly tweed suit with sensible shoes while everyone else in the room is barefoot and in kaftans.

I tell them that my experiments have been few, just marijuana and hash. I pull out my repertoire of horror stories of a few friends and acquaintances who either lost their grip on reality permanently or who never woke up.

"Wow, that's really heavy." Kandy nods sympathetically. "With those sorts of bad trips happening around you, I can see why you'd steer away."

That's only part of it, I'm thinking. Always having to maintain control over my body and my experiences. The same thing, really, as trying to control this trip in such detail ahead of time, making certain I would be staying with Elaine, not allowing myself to walk off a cliff into the unknown. I feel it's all connected to that old fear of falling, floating, in that silent dark void that has always yawned underneath my life. But I did search, didn't I? Doesn't that argue against the over-cautiousness I'm blaming myself for now? And that's what this trip is all about, isn't it? More mind-blowing than any drug trip, surely! Experimenting with being "out of myself" — out of this body entirely — not as a plant, not as a fish, but as another person I might have become.

As this topic exhausts itself, Kay says she really wants to hear more about my childhood and my parents and the kind of life I've had. I'm surprised to find myself suddenly feeling entirely comfortable again. Thinking about Mom and Dad and Rick, Ukiah and Monterey, makes me feel centered and normal. I take a deep breath and sink back into my "real" life, trying to convey to my new family who I am and where I've come from.

At the end of my probably too-rosy monologue, Kay wants to probe Mom's negative reactions to my search. She doesn't understand Mom's attitude. "I feel so strongly that when your children leave home, they are completely independent and on their own," she says. "The love and the ties will always be there, but they have to go their own way. You don't own them! And you, Pat, have left home for some time now. I think your journey to find me, to find us, is part of your independence and your growth. How can your mother not feel happy about that? When I first talked with you on the phone, I just assumed that our meeting would be a happy experience for everyone, that your parents would be excited about it too."

I feel compelled to defend Mom, to explain her jealousy. "Maybe it's harder for a mother who hasn't borne her own children," I say. "I mean, you know that your children come from you, and there's no one else who could ever take your place. So maybe you can feel confident when they leave home, and you can let go fairly easily. But when she adopted me, Mom knew that there was another mother out there somewhere, and maybe she had to block out that thought — 'obliterate it,' is what she's said — all those years because it was so hard to face her own inability to have children. She says that fact wasn't important after Rick and I came, but it sure seems to be important to her right now. Maybe the apron strings are tighter with adopted children."

"You know, I think I *can* relate somehow to what she must be feeling," Kay says. "When Keeva was married to Dan, she began spending a lot of time with her mother-in-law. They seemed to be getting very chummy. And I must admit, I did feel little twinges of jealousy. I told myself it was stupid and that nothing had changed between us, but there was someone else in a sort of motherly role. Yes, I guess I did feel it then!

"Well, I hope we can all work this out. I hate to feel that she thinks our getting together is taking something away from her. Because she is really your mother. I think you and I may become good, close friends, but I'm certainly not your mother in the way she is."

The irony of it, I'm thinking, as I bask in this interest, acceptance, even (already, yes) love emanating from Kay, Kandy, and Keeva. What was it Mom said a month or so ago? "I guess I'm afraid that I won't be your mother any longer. I think we'll always be good, close friends, but that other woman will become your mother."

But Kay wants to pursue this further. It's as if she's playing with the idea of having kept me after all, trying out that alternative decision so long after the fact, and finally justifying again, for her own peace of mind, her act of relinquishment. She says she considered several alternatives to putting me up for adoption. "I thought about keeping you and raising you alone," she explains. "But that was such a horrifying thought in those days. We both would have been branded as outcasts by society. And then there were so many problems in starting the marriage with Carl, just back from the war, having lost an arm and all. I just thought that being a father to someone else's baby would have been very difficult for him."

"Mom, I'm sure you were right in that," Kandy offers. "Dad always felt a stronger connection with Keith because he was a boy. It would have been awfully hard for Pat, being a girl and not even his own child." Her words are like a heavy curtain drawing aside, allowing me to see wounds in Kandy that have not healed.

"And then the idea of leaving you on the Island with Mama and Daddy," Kay continues her train of thought after looking at Kandy for a long moment, "that was the only real alternative, and that's a very hard thing for a child, too, being raised by relatives and calling their mothers 'Auntie'...."

The air in the room is becoming thick with our emotions. I sense shared regret and wondering and melancholy. "I think you did the very best thing you could have, Kay, for everyone," I tell her, always the diplomat and peacemaker. Yet there's a sharp lump in my throat as I say the words.

* * *

Elaine bounces down the steps of her apartment building to greet the four of us. It's after 11:00 p.m. and I'm still keyed up. Plump, freckled, and chatty, Elaine cuts through the intensity of our evening with her jolly banter and puts everyone at ease. As she hugs me, I find myself crying for the first time all day. Tears of relief and wonder meant for my mother and sisters spill onto my old friend's shoulder.

"You okay, Patty?" Elaine laughs and pats me on the back. "Hi, Kay! Good to see you again! And now, which is which?" After names and faces are sorted out, Elaine steps back a few paces and declares, "Amazing! There really is something to heredity, isn't there?"

After small talk about the weather and a discussion of tomorrow's plans, I hug Kay, Kandy and Keeva goodnight, haul my suitcase up the stairs behind Elaine, and wave as Kay's red Plymouth pulls away.

Charlie and Joe are long since in bed. Elaine has been working on lesson plans for her knitting class and waiting up for me. I tug off my sandals, sink into the couch, and move the magazines and children's books aside to put my feet up on the wooden coffee table. "Thanks, I really need that, I'm so hyper," I say as Elaine walks in from the kitchen carrying two tinkling glasses of Scotch. After two sips, I can feel the muscles in my body begin to relax.

"Well, how's it going?" Elaine asks, and I launch into a description of my day.

When my head finally hits the pillow, I'm so tired, I'm dizzy. Visions of Kay dance in my head: her fine features, her gracefulness and youth, her fascinating manner and way of speaking. Is she really my mother?

PATRICIA MOFFAT

Gramp's house on Whidbey Island

Coffee gathering at Jack & Norma's
Back Row: Keeva, Norma, Jack, Gramp, Kandy
Front Row: Me and Kay

Gramp & me

CHAPTER 19

It's warm already as Kay, Kandy, Keeva, and I drive through Seattle to the ferry landing. On the ferry, we leave the car and stand at the upstairs railing to enjoy the sunshine and the dark, glittering water of Puget Sound. I back up and take portraits of each of them with my telephoto lens, imprinting their voices and their laughter on my mind as I imprint their faces on the film.

The ferry docks, and we drive several miles through Whidbey Island, through stands of forest, meadows, along the shore, and through a couple of small, lazy towns. The land is lush and spring-green, a new color to me after the golden-brown hills of California's drought. First stop is Lou and Earl's, Kay's older sister, my aunt.

Lou and Earl come out of the house to greet us, looking like they walked right off the set of *The Waltons*. Lou is plump, with graying hair, healthy-looking, and cheery. She and Kay seem ten years apart rather than two. Earl is tall, bony, and ruddy-cheeked, with a bobbing Adam's apple, and shy, although he pumps my hand enthusiastically. Earl is from Alberta and has family in Ontario, so we chat about Canada at first.

Lou serves coffee, and we all settle into the simple living room. Noticing an amber glass ashtray on an end table, I ask if it's all right to smoke. "Oh, sure," Lou says. "Better have one here before you go over to Gramp's."

"Yes, we've already warned her he doesn't allow cigarettes at his place," Kay says.

"That's okay with me." I smile. "I'm not sure I'd allow him to drop acid at my place." We all laugh.

"Is Emmeline coming today?" asks Kandy.

"Oh, she wouldn't miss it for anything," Lou says. "I'm sure she's consulted with her doctors and they've said she's up to it."

"Who's Emmeline?" I ask.

Emmeline, it turns out, is Gramp's seventy-year-old Soul Mate, with whom he's been having a spiritual and perhaps sexual affair for the past twenty years. Grandma Eunice finally died with this going on, but Emmeline's husband is still alive, and she divides her time between him and Gramp. Her doctors, treating her for cancer, are departed ones she consults through séances. They're all shaking their heads in amusement, while I'm unable to hold back my incredulous laughter any longer.

It is only a couple of miles from Lou and Earl's to Gramp's house, a roomy, weathered, two-story cabin sitting a hundred yards or so off the road toward the sound. Tall grass and buttercups line the gravel road sloping down to the house. There's a barn, fruit trees blooming pink and white, and a horse grazing in the field. The Metcalf family property contains the three types of land on Whidbey Island: a long stretch of beach, pleasant farmland, and tall fir forest. As we step out of the car, I breathe in the beauty of the place on this sunny, warm morning. Across the dark water is the forested mainland, with the white cone of Mt. Baker levitating above it on a carpet of low-lying clouds.

Gramp's truck is gone, and Kay thinks he's getting something in town or maybe picking up Emmeline. We go inside to check. A pungent, familiar aroma increases in strength as the four of us head upstairs. "Oh, looks like John's here anyway." Kandy laughs, rapping gently on the first door at the top of the landing.

"Come on in," calls a muffled, even-toned voice. As we step into the almost bare room, the sharp odor of freshly smoked marijuana engulfs us.

216

"Oh, sorry to disturb you," someone says as he rouses himself from his lotus position in a corner.

"That's all right. Really glad to see you." He nods, benevolently peering at us. From my briefing last night, I know this is one of Gramp's tenants, most likely the theology student between divinity schools, retreating.

We continue our tour of the house: the upstairs room where Kandy will be spending the summer, writing her script for *Watership Down* (her senior project in her drama program at the university), the downstairs bedroom where Grandma Eunice died, the living room with its worn couches and easy chairs clustered around a stone fireplace. Clutter has been ordered into neat piles, and there's no sign of the carbon dioxide canister.

The photographs on the mantel grab my attention, especially one of Grandma Eunice. She's in her fifties in the picture, her wind-blown hair growing white, face tanned and smooth, shining. There are those prominent, high cheekbones that all the Metcalfs seem to have, a feature faintly Indian. "Actually, we think there's Indian blood somewhere on Daddy's side, the Metcalf side, not Mother's," Kay says in answer to my question. "The Grannis side of the family is pretty well all old English-American stock. They emigrated from England way back in the seventeenth century. The Metcalfs didn't come over until the mid-nineteenth century."

My grandmother's eyes are laughing in the picture, and her lips are open, showing strong, perfect teeth. But the detail that leaps out at me is the prominent dimple in her chin. So that's where it came from. It skipped Kay but came out in Kandy and me and then in Derek. "Mama was a Scorpio too," Kay says, picking up the photo. "That makes four of us: Mama, me, you, and Keeva."

Kandy asks me if I'd like to go down to the barn with her and see how the new calves are doing. Kay and Keeva say they'll set things up in the kitchen and join us in a few minutes. Down at the barn, Kandy and I lean over the fence, studying the gentle-eyed young animals in the pen. My camera strap weighs heavily on my shoulder, and I try to shake off the feeling of city-kid tourist.

Kandy asks, "Well, how do you like the place?"

"It's so beautiful! I'm just remembering our place in Ukiah. It was sort of a mini-farm, within a small town. But it wasn't quite like this. That gorgeous water down there! And the mountain, and all the land! Do you feel like this is home?"

"Yeah, I spent a lot of time in the summers and on weekends here, growing up. I really connect with this place down deep."

Kay and Keeva stroll down the hill to meet us. I watch them, marveling at Kay, so neat, trim, and exotically dressed in these rural surroundings, with her loosely cut batik top and her dangling, handmade earrings. So graceful she is, stepping through the weedy field with Gramp's weathered old house behind her. This jarring contrast intensifies when she says, "Hi! I'll just be a minute. I have to go check the worms."

"The worms?" Kay and her younger sister Ev dreamed up the worm farm idea, she explains, as a way to help Gramp pay the taxes on the land. They grow the creatures in bins, harvest them, and sell them. "Eventually we hope to turn the operation over to Daddy," Kay says, "but I don't think he's too keen on the worms."

Inside the barn is the familiar mingled scent of hay and manure. Chickens cluck from somewhere, and swallows, their nests mud-cemented onto the rafters, dart around the upper reaches. Sunlight slants in through long cracks between the old boards, catching dust and flecks of hay in its beams. Kay steps purposefully over to several large, covered table bins. I watch my elegant mother don a pair of dirt-encrusted gardening gloves and plunge her hands into the crawling black earth of the first bin.

"I'm just turning them over," she explains helpfully, with an enthusiastic lilt in her voice like Julia Child demonstrating a culinary maneuver. "They're really the easiest creatures to take care of. They'll eat absolutely anything and turn it into gorgeous soil. Harvesting's the hard part, though. That takes hours with a wire mesh."

The weekly turning job finished, the four of us begin heading back up to the house when we see a figure striding down the hill to meet us.

There he is! Kay breaks out into a big smile and calls out, "Well, at last! We were wondering where in the world you were!"

He doesn't respond verbally, doesn't break his stride, but raises his right hand in silent greeting and continues his unhurried pace. Eighty years old, and looking fifteen years younger, he carries his still handsome body easily, with no hint of arthritis or other ailments of old age. As he nears us, I can see his smooth, tanned, quite unwrinkled skin, his strong jaw, lustrous white hair, his crinkly light blue eyes, and half-suppressed smile.

"Daddy, this is Pat."

He grasps my hand warmly without taking his eyes from mine.

"Welcome," he says simply, studying me closely with curiosity and affection in his startlingly blue eyes.

"I'm so glad to meet you," I say. "When I started all this, I never dreamed that I'd find my grandfather too."

He chuckles appreciatively and pats my hand, still not taking his eyes from mine. "Well yes, I'm still around," he says slowly and a little nasally, as if chewing his words. "And always happy to have another granddaughter."

The five of us climb back up the slope to the house. Under the flowering apple tree near the kitchen door, Gramp stops to show me the new chicks, several balls of yellow fluff jerkily negotiating the tall grass behind their sleek, rust-brown mother. He kneels down, cradles a peeping chick in his hand, and offers it to me to hold. I suddenly feel an odd sense of dislocation, as if I'm in a movie of someone else's life, and Gramp's simple gesture, with our hands meeting around the chick, is being shot in brilliant Technicolor.

Inside the kitchen, a roomful of relatives are milling around, waiting to meet me. Kay smiles encouragingly and squeezes my arm. There are Lou and Earl, who seem like old familiar faces now. There are two of their daughters, cousins Donna and Bev, both dark-haired and attractive, and Donna's husband. Then there are the unrelated ones, present out of curiosity or friendship: Bev's boyfriend Larry, and Gramp's two roomers, Brian and John (still looking slightly dazed from his meditations). Standing by the big wood stove, almost hopping up and down to control her agitation, is Emmeline.

They all greet me warmly, one by one. Emmeline grasps my hand power-fully in her two small ones, and, her sharp little blue eyes never leaving mine, declares, "It's a beautiful thing that you've done, and we're all surely glad." Her small, thin body vibrates, her voice is staccato, her movements are quick and bird-like. Someone asks about her "condition," and her attention switches instantly from me to the speaker as she discusses her doctors' diagnoses and recommendations, rapidly and seriously. Not once does she mention the (to me) screamingly odd fact that her doctors are disembodied spirits.

Emmeline's chatter reminds me that probably most of the people in this room, over half of whom I am related to by blood, are deeply into New Age spiritual phenomena, having varying degrees of interest in reincar-nation, channeling, UFOs, spirit guides, automatic writing, tarot cards, psychokinesis, and out-of-body experiences. Many have "expanded their consciousness" through drugs, including my mother and that unlikely-looking old couple now standing together amiably in front of the shelf of colorful fruit preserves, Gramp and Emmeline.

Lunch commences. We pick up plates of food and settle into the couches and chairs placed around the living room. The seat of honor, the couch opposite the stone fireplace, is reserved for Gramp in the center, with Kay and me on either side. I feel like I'm floating now, buoyed by the welcoming, celebratory feeling in the room.

Balancing our plates on our laps, our conversation covers a lot of ground. In answer to Lou's question, I deliver the detective-story summary of how I managed to find Kay. Bev tells us how she's going off to Findhorn, in Scotland, at the end of the summer, which will be a practical and spiritual trip. The family is starting to plan the best use for their land and discuss several ideas about building a conference center or a new kind of school. Absent family members are described to me, particularly a relative in Los Angeles, one of the few family members who also possesses the "true Metcalf nose," but alas, she had it fixed. I ask Gramp how he managed to support a family of five kids during the Depression, and he tells me "how rich we were — always had food on the table and clothes on our backs" because they lived off the sea and the land, catching, growing, and picking all their own food. "We'll take a walk down on the beach later on," he says between bites of meatloaf. "I'll show you where the old cabin was, where your Mama grew up." "Your Mama" — my skin tingles; it sounds good, but it jars a little too.

Kay peers around Gramp, smiling at me. "You fit in so well with this group — do you feel it too?" she asks. "I keep looking over to Kandy and Keeva and you, and I just feel this strong similarity again." Others pick up on the theme, mentioning physical resemblances but concentrating on this feeling that I "belong," that they know me well, have met me before, but can't remember where.

Just as last evening at Kay's apartment, I am conscious of more than one level in this conversation. There's the warm friendliness of the group. I feel accepted by them, as I probably would feel in any group of friendly, kind people. Then there's the level of blood ties, which Mom called with dread, "the bosom of the family," the fact that for the very first time in my life I'm surrounded by people to whom I am related by blood. I haven't felt an instant connection with everyone in the room because we're related, but I do feel a very strong bond with Kay, Kandy, and Keeva, and an exploratory closeness with Gramp too.

The third level I sense in the conversation still throws me. When they say they have known me before but can't remember where, I sense the flow of past shared lives and reincarnation in their minds.

Suddenly a tall, good-looking, middle-aged, slightly wind-blown person strides confidently into the room, bestowing greetings all around. "Well, Jack! This is nice!" Kay says. "We thought you couldn't make it for lunch."

"I can't. I've got to get on down to the house but just thought I'd drop in for a minute and say hello."

So this is Uncle Jack, Kay's younger brother, Washington State senator for the past twenty-five years. His manner is oddly at variance with the others in the room. Do I really detect a small twinge of discomfort behind Jack's ready smile and appraising look when Kay introduces us, or is it only my imagination?

"Hello!" he booms. "Nice to see you. Quite a resemblance!"

I am getting totally different "vibes" from this uncle. When the others greeted me, even the ones unrelated by blood, I had the sense that they were connecting with me, even touching my soul somehow. But with Uncle Jack, it feels more like he is keeping a little distance and mentally reaching out to pat me on the head. I suspect that his well-practiced political skills have automatically come into play in these few moments. Yet his manner feels in no way alien to me. If anything, Jack's friendly but reined-in interest and his politeness remind me a little of my parents, especially my dad, and their social milieu.

Someone asks about his house, and Jack launches into a description of the current project. Then, with a wave of his hand, and "We'll see you all later down at the house!" he leaves the room as quickly as he'd entered.

As the others resume the threads of interrupted conversation, I wonder about this uncle. It may just be that Jack's lifestyle, his religious beliefs (which Kay told me were more fundamentalist than New Age), and especially his long years in politics simply make him act differently from the other relatives I'm meeting. Perhaps he too, in his own way, accepts me and my entrance into "the bosom of the family" with warmth and curiosity. Nevertheless, for the first time since arriving in Seattle, I ponder the fact that I am Kay's illegitimate baby, now an adult, and consider how my appearance might affect the family's feelings about Kay. None of them knew she was pregnant at the time. Although Kandy, Keeva, and Keith learned about me at the time of the divorce, all the others, including Gramp, found out just a month ago. Is there any feeling at all of blame in them toward Kay, underneath their warm acceptance of me? No, no, I think, scanning the faces in the room. There's a lovely low-key sense of celebration here. But Jack? And perhaps his wife Norma?

Breaking into my thoughts, Gramp asks, "Do you do much reading?"

"Oh yes, I read a lot," I answer confidently.

"What sorts of things do you read?"

"I'm mainly interested in fiction, nineteenth and twentieth centuries," I say, hoping I'm not about to sound pompous, "but I enjoy reading on most subjects."

"Well, I don't mean fiction — just some author's imaginings of what life is like.... No, I mean real books, about truth and philosophy. Have you read *Life After Life* by Raymond Moody?"

"No, I haven't."

"Ah, you should read it," Gramp says, smiling at me as if he has a secret up his sleeve, as if he could pull a golden egg out from behind my ear any time he chose. "It will open your mind up to something very important. John, could you go upstairs and hunt around for a copy? I know I have two." John soon returns with a red and white paperback, which Gramp hands to me, smiling.

The phone rings, and Gramp leaves the room for what turns out to be a lengthy conversation. This serves as a signal, and the group begins to break up. Dishes are carried away, and a few women begin putting the kitchen back in order. Kandy, Keeva, John, and Brian cluster around me, suggesting a walk in the woods, ostensibly to check the progress of the marijuana seedlings. I suddenly realize that part of my giddy high might be due to the fact that I haven't had a cigarette for three hours. I set off with them gladly.

* * *

Once we are in the cool, ferny forest, John lights up a joint while I rummage in my purse for my cigarettes. The five of us talk easily, and as I begin to relax, I realize how taut I was during lunch. I tell the group I've been experiencing some sensory overload from the roomful of relatives.

"Oh, they're a great bunch really, despite a few kinks here and there," Keeva says. "We were all just so excited about you coming to visit. I can feel them all being natural and trying not to overwhelm you."

"What about Uncle Jack?" I venture. "Do you think he feels as good about this as everyone else? The vibrations from him seemed a bit different."

"Oh, that's just Jack," says Kandy. "He's a bit more closed about his feelings than most of the rest of us. But he's been very interested in your story since you first phoned. He is different, though. He's had a very different kind of life than the rest of us."

"Do you think he feels at all shocked at Kay for what happened?" I ask, pressing further.

"Oh gosh no!" my two half-sisters reply, almost in unison. "Uncle Jack's a big family man," Keeva continues. "Very close to his wife and kids. And he just loves Mom! I'm sure he'd never blame her for anything she ever did in her life. That's just her own affair, 'scuse the pun!"

We come upon a ravaged clearing among the tall trees, where the signs of logging are painful to view. The marijuana seedlings are nestled in little nooks among the stumps and fallen trees, some thriving in the natural mulch of decaying bark, others wilted and yellowing, in need of attention.

Kandy and I say we'll continue on walking through the woods, and we leave Keeva, John, and Brian pacing around the clearing, peering down at the ground. For an hour or more, Kandy and I walk and talk with hardly a pause. We talk about growing up with and without that blood tie, which Kandy took for granted and I never knew. When I tell Kandy how surprised I was by Kay's physical beauty, she tells me there's a "good line of genes backing us up," that most Metcalfs live a long time and keep their health and looks to the end. She tells me about one of the most difficult periods in her life, when Kay and Carl were going through the divorce. She feels that losing her father when she was a young teenager has influenced her "bad choices in men." My life with my parents, in comparison, she says almost wistfully, sounds so smooth and secure.

"What does your brother Rick think about you finding Mom?" Kandy asks at one point as we trudge along the forest path, so deep in conversation that we hardly register the lush ferns and towering firs around us. "Does he want to find his parents too?"

"Well, you probably won't believe this, but he doesn't know yet."

"What? What do you mean?" Kandy turns to look at me with shock written all over her open face.

I explain to her that Mom asked me not to tell him yet, that she was worried about how this news could affect him since his marriage recently broke up and his emotional life is kind of precarious now.

Kandy lets out her breath. "Wow, I don't want to sound critical, but it sounds like she's trying to do his thinking for him, not just letting things happen and giving him the chance to make his own decisions! Well, it's different, I guess. We were all always told to make our own decisions in life. Even though there was a lot of disagreement between Mom and Dad, they did agree on that — that we kids should learn to be independent and lead our own lives."

"No kidding?" I smile, remembering that last phone call between Kay and me and how she got my back up when she said, "I have always made my children's decisions for them. Now you just leave this up to me."

Wishes, reflections, regrets. Kandy wishes she could have had the stable family life I've had. I'm fascinated by Kay, and yet I'm grateful Mom and Dad are my parents. I imagine that if Kay had kept me, my scars might have been deeper than Kandy's, being Kay's child only, not Carl's too. I can't imagine growing up without Rick. All those shared years make us close in a way that Kandy and I may never be. I look over at Kandy as we step up our pace a little, aware that we might be late for coffee at Jack's, and I wish that somehow we could have grown up together too. Then, as well as beginning this adult friendship, we could also look back on a long, shared past. I wish she was really my sister, not just by blood.

* * *

"The house that Jack built" rises into view as we cross the field next to Gramp's place. It's a large log structure close to the beach, with a tall tower at one end. All the logs that went into building it, Kandy tells me, were either hand-hewn from the property or found washed up on the beach. Inside, the family is packed in tightly around a large, irregular table, also found material, an enormous root slice polished like shining stone.

"Hi!" Kay says. "You just made it. We were just debating who should eat the last two cinnamon rolls."

Jack's wife, Norma, a compact, gracious, simply dressed woman with short brown hair, pours us each a cup of coffee and we take our plates and cups over to the stairs to join Keeva. I look at Kay, who has turned her chair slightly so that she can easily take in the three of us. Next to Kay is Gramp, leaning back on a kitchen chair, hands folded in his lap, the patriarch serenely surveying his family. That secret, pleased little smile still plays around his lips.

Jack leads the conversation much of the time, and half of it has little meaning for me. I have the fleeting impression that the grown-ups are comfortably ensconced at the table, while we three girls munch away at the kids' table. This impression is heightened by the way most of them, especially Kay, keep looking affectionately over at us. But the conversation soon turns.

Cousin Bev says to Emmeline, "You know, you really should do a numerology chart of Pat, too, Emmeline, to see if there are any similarities."

"Already have done that, yes, yes! Just as soon as Kay gave me the facts," replies the bird-woman, peering over at me with her bright eyes. "Very interesting indeed!" I have to listen closely because she speaks so rapidly, in sparkling little bursts of phrases.

"How do you go about making a numerology chart?" I ask Emmeline.

"Oh, my!" She laughs. "There are whole books written on it! Main idea is you take all the facts — full name, date of birth, time of birth, and so on — plug them into formulas and come up with a life number. Very important, the life number. Characteristics of the person matching the astrology."

This is all an amusing fiction to me, but I want to know what she has come up with, in order to see how she places me in relation to the family.

"Well, how did I come out?" I ask, swallowing a bite of Norma's cinnamon roll.

"Oh, my dear! Your life number turns out to be thirteen! Strongest number there is! Thirteen means great willpower, determination, independence, fine qualities of mind. Anything you set yourself toward, you will accomplish. And your goals are always high."

"Well, I don't know about that...." I actually feel myself blushing.

"Oh yes, oh yes! According to the chart, this year is a most important one for you. You'll grow and accomplish much, and you'll recognize it too, that's sure. Now, the very interesting thing about your chart," and here she turns to Gramp, smiling brightly, while he's looking more than ever like the cat who swallowed the canary, "is that John's life number is also thirteen. Only duplication of life number in this family!" Gramp and I look at each other conspiratorially.

"And until you came, he had twelve granddaughters. Now he has thirteen!"

"How about that!" I say but seize the chance to deflect the topic from mystical numbers to progeny. "You must have quite a few great-grand-children by now too, Gramp."

"I had eleven before you came," he says slowly, as if chewing and savoring each word, "but with your little ones, now I have thirteen."

The hairs on my forearms begin to stand up. There are murmurings around the table. Kay says how strange it was, too, that I began looking for her in early February, just around the time she told Ev and Lou about me for the first time. This information is also received enthusiastically, although I can't quite read Jack's expression.

We all get up from our seats at the table and on the stairs and wander over into the living room. A large bay window, its beams formed by two arching ten-foot long driftwood logs, provides a spectacular view of Puget Sound and Mt. Baker. The large fireplace is hand-laid stone. Near it stands a gleaming brown baby grand piano.

"Pat, could you play something, please?" Kay is suddenly at my side, gesturing at the instrument. "I'd love to hear you play the piano."

My hands begin to sweat. "Oh, Kay, I'm so out of practice." But it's not the idea of sitting down and playing this piano that's bothering me, really. It's the fear of not being able to get through any piece of music without tears and embarrassing myself and everyone else. For as I stand beside Kay, the memories of all those years of playing the piano to my imaginary "real mother" wash over me. The moment is becoming too charged for me to hold.

"Oh, yes, please Pat," chime in some of the others, and before I can back out gracefully, they've all expectantly settled into the chairs and couches. I slide down onto the piano bench.

I confidently begin the haunting melody of Chopin's "Raindrop" prelude, though my hands are trembling a little. It's an achingly beautiful theme, a melody of longing underpinned by building bass chords that always get to me deep in my bones. I want them all to feel the power of this music too, especially my very real "real mother," now sitting in a wing chair, her hands folded in her lap, gazing out over the sound, listening.

I play to her. I play the pain she suffered at twenty-three, I play my need to find her once my courage won out, and the bond growing between us now. I remember the phantom mother of my childhood, that pale blond creature of my imagination who crept nervously into a seat at the back of the auditorium, and I compare that wraith to this vibrant woman who is looking over at me now and smiling. All those nightmares of my birth mother, and look who I've found!

The music, just play the music. This is a musical family, remember. Gramp's father, old Frank Metcalf, was a violin maker, and many of them play instruments, dance, and sing. It runs in the blood, this music, those genes, that blood tie, it runs, plays, sings, in me too.

I take my hands off the keys and my feet off the pedals. There's silence in the room for several seconds. Gramp is looking at me intently from his place on the couch, smiling quietly. Kandy smiles too, nodding. Kay seems withdrawn and absorbed into herself now. Perhaps she rouses herself to make some appreciative remark along with the others, but I'm concentrating so hard on the inner channel between us that I can't hear. I'm trying to read her face, hoping I didn't choose the wrong kind of piece or distort it out of all recognition because of what I was trying to convey. Yet mainly, as I rise from the piano bench and mingle with them again, I feel exultation. At last! At last I've lived what I only played out in fantasy before! My heart overflows.

* * *

We walk down the beach in a scattered line, our bare feet sinking into the warm sand: Gramp, Kay, me, Kandy, Keeva, and Gramp's housemate, Brian. Gramp wants to show me where the old cabin used to be. As we walk, I take in the immense scenery: the great long stretch of sandy beach, the gradations of blues in Puget Sound, and directly opposite us across the Sound, Mt. Baker, the colors of which have changed subtly since the morning when Kandy and I stood looking at it from the barn. Now, the snowy peak rises right out of the forest below, no longer buoyed up by a misty layer of cloud. My thoughts turn to Grandpa Boyd, Mom's father, whose home was in Washington and had also loved these mountains. I remember him speaking often about Mt. Rainier and Mt. Baker when I was a child.

The grandfather beside me strolls with his hands clasped behind his back, looking out over the scenery with as much interest as I am showing, even though he's lived in it for most of his eighty years. "This beach land was a favorite camping ground of the Indians from many generations ago, the Snohomish, Skagit, and Tulalip people," he tells me. "They called it 'Slalowas,' which meant 'resting place' in their language."

As we near the site of the old cabin, he begins talking more animatedly. "Built it myself, a tight little log cabin, and we moved it over from Marysville on a raft." He points out across the Sound to a small community, which he can see clearly, but I can't. "The only time it got uncomfortable was during a very rough storm. Then the water would flood into the house under the door, and we'd be faced with a lot of cleaning up."

"That's the reason we never had a piano," Kay says, "and I remember we kids wanted one so badly."

"Well, you had a lot of other things, which I hope made up for it," Gramp says in his slow, deliberate way.

"Oh, sure we did," Kay smiles, reminiscing as we walk. "It was a protected life. We mostly had just each other to play with as kids, and our cousins. It was a very hard life for Mama and Daddy, though. We kids didn't really appreciate that at the time — we were so busy exploring the

229

woods, playing in the sand, swimming out there almost every day, right in front of our cabin. The family was very close. And Mama and Daddy were quite strict."

"Oh, but only with words and rules," Gramp says. "You know, we never had to spank our kids," he explains to me. "We always tried to raise them reasonably, with a lot of love. I remember just one time when I found out Eunice had spanked one of the boys, I was angry with her about it for days. It isn't necessary to punish kids physically. All it does is hurt the bond between you."

"Just makes them end up hating you," Kay agrees, smiling up at her father. Taking all of this in, I'm comparing it to how I was raised: with love, certainly, but with spankings too. I wonder what Kay and Gramp would say to that. Yet I have no wish to put Mom in a bad light by contributing to this conversation.

"You know, I always tried not to have favorites among the children," Gramp continues, speaking to me. "Always tried to love and treat my five equally. But you know, your mama was such a darling, such a loving, good little child. Secretly I think she was my favorite."

I am moved by the interplay of tender words between these two, whom I have to remind myself are my mother and my grandfather. Through initiating me into the past, they are also expressing their affection for each other. Yesterday, Kay said that becoming pregnant before marriage was the one thing she feared would ruin her life. Now I am wondering whether doing that most feared thing was the most effective way that she, the good and darling child, could break away from this protected, loving environment and begin to make her own way in life. I also sense that today Kay is bringing the evidence of her ruinous mistake, me, back to the heart of her family, and experiencing the acceptance and forgiveness that she didn't dare ask for then. And it's as if with every careful, loving phrase, Gramp is saying to her that it's all right, that it always was all right.

When we reach the site of Kay's childhood home, Gramp kneels down and brushes away a layer of sand, exposing an outcrop of hard stone and cement. "See, all that's left of the old place are the stone foundations," he says. "The sand has washed up so much over the years that you'd hardly notice them any more."

Retracing our steps back along the beach now, Gramp is filled with a boyish eagerness to show me things and present things to me. He wades out into the water, turning over stones to show me the peculiar little fish that hide there and swim away quickly when exposed to the light. I mention that Derek has a shoebox collection of beach glass and shells, and by the time we begin climbing up the path back to Gramp's house, my pockets are bulging and grinding with the amber onyx stones and sturdy little shells that Gramp has been slipping into them.

It's almost five o'clock when we reach the house, and time to leave if we're to make the ferry. I say goodbye to Gramp, kissing him on his soft, dry cheek, wondering whether I will see him again.

Kay and Gramp hug each other, and, with his arm still around her, he says, "Well, little sister, I hope this isn't too hard on you. We would have loved to have had another little one around here to raise. But I hope you're not feeling badly about what you decided then."

"Thanks, Daddy. No, I'm fine."

* * *

Back in Seattle, the four of us flop in Kay's living room with iced teas. Now that I have met the people I've heard about, I have even more questions. I'm basking in the familiarity growing between us and feel slightly dislocated when we rise a few minutes before 8:00 p.m. to drive me over to Joe and Elaine's. My self-protective mechanisms had set this situation up to ensure there would be "spaces in our togetherness," time to step back from the intensity of our meeting, but now I find I'm thriving on that intensity. I do want to spend time with Elaine, but I also know I'll miss Kay, Kandy, and Keeva tomorrow. Since Kay has to work at the shop tomorrow, Monday, Elaine is taking me on an all-day excursion to Mt. Rainier, and later "the family" will gather together again for the evening. "Have a nice day tomorrow," Kay says as we step outside of the car and hug goodnight. "I'll be thinking of you, up there on the mountain." I hug Kandy and Keeva too and wave goodbye as I hurry up the steps to Elaine's apartment.

Before I sit down to dinner with Elaine, Joe, and Charlie, I make a quick phone call to Harald, and in answer to his probing questions, I try to reassure him I'm not "getting overwhelmed" or "losing my head." I'm suddenly missing the children, who have just gone to bed, Harald reports. I am both relieved and a little disappointed to learn that they have been doing just fine in my absence, visiting Mom and Dad in Monterey and following their daily routines in the Valley.

Impressive large platters and bowls have appeared on the table while I've been telephoning. Joe has spent the hot afternoon preparing an Italian dinner, the "graduation menu" from the gourmet Italian cooking course that was a Christmas present from Elaine last year. Charlie, who unlike Derek is not in bed at this hour, sits at the table on a stack of telephone books, sucking in long worms of spaghetti and joining in on the conversation as a miniature, three-year-old adult.

Later, after Charlie and Joe are in bed, Elaine and I stay up talking again. Finally I take a long, relaxing bath to wind down, and then lie in bed trying to get into the book Gramp gave me. But my own adventures of the past two days are so much more fascinating to me than whatever adventures there may be after death and have left me so pleasantly and deliriously exhausted that I put the book down and immediately fall asleep.

PATRICIA MOFFAT

Kandy, me, & Keeva on my last morning in
Seattle of that first reunion

Kandy, Keeva, Kay and Kay's "gentleman friend," Henry,
before our dinner on the space needle

CHAPTER 20

It's a glorious day again, unusually warm and sunny for Seattle. There's excitement and expectation among Elaine, Charlie, and Joe's sister Corinne as we set off in Elaine's car. I'm curious about Corinne, a stout, gray-haired single woman whose intelligence and high spirits are evident whenever she opens her mouth. Yet I am mentally dragging my heels, too, fighting an emotional torpor that is beginning to settle over me. For irrationally, as we drive through the city, with an amusing running commentary from Corinne and Elaine, and out into the dark green countryside on the way to Mt. Rainier, I am feeling wrenched away from Kay, Kandy, and Keeva, even though this day trip was planned weeks ago. I hadn't anticipated the strong pull I'd feel to my new family, and the psychological energy it would take to turn away from them and concentrate on something else for a while, even something as magical as this trip.

And it *is* magical. As we ascend the mountain, flowering dogwoods appear along the twisting roadside, with their graceful reddish branches and large, abundant creamy flowers. Everywhere are variations of green: the chartreuse of young fern shoots, the mellow spring green of the hardwoods coming into leaf, the deep royal tones of evergreens, and the occasional powder blue-green of spruce. Wildflowers burst into colorful patches along the road, water trickles out of tall rock faces, and once in a while we come upon an unexpected, splashing waterfall. As the summit of Mt. Rainier rears up suddenly around a bend in the road or through a gap up the steep slopes, "There it is! There's the mountain!" pipes up the high-pitched voice in the back seat.

We stop for a picnic halfway up, and nearer the summit we stop for a romp in the June snow. While Charlie and Elaine fling snowballs at each other, Corinne and I walk along the edge of a frozen lake and gaze off over the peaks of the volcanic mountain chain in the distance. "That's Mt. Hood over there," Corinne says, pointing, "and off on the horizon you can just see Mt. Adams." As she names the distant giants with such comfortable familiarity, I wonder whether I will feel something similar about this mountain after we descend. I'm remembering Mt. Baker from Gramp's farm: how majestically remote it had seemed, the tall white cone jutting up across the blue water of the sound. "Corinne, which direction is Seattle down there, and where is Whidbey Island?"

I came to Seattle to find one woman, to take in the features of one face among millions, to hear the story of one life, and my connection to it, out of all the lives in that city down below in the shimmering distance. All my life she has been anonymous, a faceless figure "out there," a woman vitally part of me, whom I would never know. I would continue to try to forget, I would continue concentrating only on the here and now, on the relationships that currently fill my life, and maybe I would almost block out her existence. I would die without knowing who my mother was.

But now, down in that faraway city, one woman among many goes about her day, living out this very moment perhaps no differently than on any other day. She chats with customers, sews her dresses at the table behind the counter, sips her herbal tea, listens to classical music on the radio, perhaps meets a friend for lunch. But the difference is: I know her now! I know the features of her beautiful and strangely familiar face. I know her soft voice, her musical laughter, her manner of choosing words and phrases. I know the outlines of her life, which is now, again, finally, entwining with mine.

Elaine, Charlie, Corinne and I drive, and then walk, as near to the summit as we can, and then begin our descent. The wonders rush by in reverse now: the waterfalls, trickling rocks, green forests, creamy dogwoods. The day has been glorious, but now I keep checking my watch. Will we make it in time? Five thirty at the shop, Kay had said. She wants to give me a batik to wear tonight for dinner on the Space Needle with her long-time "gentleman friend," Henry.

At 5:35 we pull into the parking lot at Pioneer Square, pile onto the escalator, and exit into the batiks, jewelry, and incense. There they are! "Hi!" Kay waves. "Hope you didn't have to hurry too much. Did you have a good trip?"

Kay, Keeva, and Kandy gather round to greet us and Kay and I grasp each other's hands. As always a glowing advertisement for her shop, Kay is wearing a batik dress, this time in deep reds and browns. Her hair is recently combed, and she's fresh-looking and attractively intact. As I turn to introduce Corinne to Kay and my sisters, I see what a contrast we must make, the four of us bursting wind-blown and disheveled into the quiet shop. We chat for a few moments, I thank Elaine and Corinne again for the trip, and they leave, with Charlie bouncing between them.

Now Kay, pressed for time, takes me on a rapid inspection of the racks of long dresses and skirts, all handcrafted Indonesian batiks, most of them sewn by her. My attention is drawn to some loose-fitting long summer dresses, but Kay has other ideas. "Oh, they're lovely to wear, but don't you think Harald would like to see your waistline? Men usually go for contours."

"Well, um, I don't think he much cares. He likes big designs and bright colors, though." The hell with this! It's my dress, not Harald's! I don't like big designs and bold colors. I like all these subtle shades and intricate patterns of the batiks.

But Kay seems not to have heard what Harald likes anyway. She's pulling out several long skirts, and I'm so delighted to be receiving one that I decide to let her go ahead and pick it out, since they all appeal to me.

She whips out a black, scoop-necked jersey for me to try on with the skirts, and even though the shop is now closed, I curtain myself with the clothes into the small dressing cubicle. Odd, this modesty in front of my mother and sisters! I'd never shut the door at home to try on clothes with Mom. My mild embarrassment provokes another wave of that feeling of dislocation, which now seems like a normal part of my Seattle experience.

Modeling the clothes for them, I'm partial to a turquoise-and-black skirt, but Kay thinks the silvery-white and black one suits me better. It's more "regal and elegant," she says. Does that mean she thinks *I'm* regal and elegant? I stand back with her, surveying myself in the full-length mirror, feeling a little foolish, like a fussed-over manikin. I'm also succumbing to that familiar dizziness yet again, that sense of things being askew, for memories of shopping trips with Mom in Ukiah and Monterey are flashing through my mind, superimposing themselves upon this new and tentative mother-daughter scene unfolding before me in the mirror. Taking a deep breath to steady myself, I tell Kay the skirt is gorgeous and thank her for it profusely.

The clothing settled, Kay's attention turns to jewelry. "Kandy, you're going to wear your cameo tonight, aren't you? I was going to wear Keeva's, but I'd like Pat to wear it. Don't you think that would be a nice idea?"

I'm feeling a little out of my depth and glance over at Kandy and Keeva for help. I heard about the cameos in passing the other night, hand-painted enamel portraits of my half-sisters. Keeva steps right in. "Oh, c'mon, Mom, don't you think that's a bit much?" And I'm relieved to know she must be thinking what I'm thinking: that Kay is trying to make up for lost time. With a wave of her magic wand, my fairy birth mother is turning me into her third grown-up daughter, Carol, for this one special night. But I'm not Carol, I'm Pat. I don't want to go to dinner tonight wearing an effigy of Keeva around my neck.

"Oh, maybe you're right," Kay says, her voice melting into that now familiar tinkling girlish laughter. "There are lots of necklaces over there at the counter. Why don't you pick out one that you like?"

* * *

Dinner on the Space Needle. Henry and his bevy of batiked ladies. We must make quite a sight, all four of us in our long, flowing batik skirts. Henry is a handsome, tweedy man Kay's age, with graying hair and boyish features. He's parked his Irish wool hat on the back of his chair, and a polished pipe stem curls out of his shirt pocket. The conversation is easy and unflagging. I like Henry's quiet, droll wit, his amusingly self-deprecating style, and the way he looks over at Kay frequently, as if checking in. We talk about mountains. Henry is planning to hike up to the top of Mt. Rainier again in August and wants to take on the Andes sometime. We talk about Holland, Australia, Uganda, Ethiopia, Japan, Indonesia, and other places we have been. We talk about politics. Henry is conservative but not stridently so. We talk about the water, the hills and the other landmarks down below, as the lavender and peach tones of the sky darken and the lights of Seattle begin to come on, delineating new patterns of streets and neighborhoods. All through dinner, though, my senses are having trouble adjusting to the slow revolutions of the restaurant pod. It seems a fitting end to my three days here, during which I have felt off balance much of the time.

Back at the apartment, Henry declines Kay's invitation to come in for tea. Though I appreciate his generosity in taking us all out to dinner and have enjoyed his company, I'm glad it's just the four of us again, kicking off our shoes and settling in for this last evening together.

There's a catch in my throat as I look around the room, which is beginning to feel like our center. It's warm and dark and comfortable, with the jungle of plants at the windows, the dark batik on the wall, and Keith's haunting painting looking down on us. We've all settled into our usual places, still in our long skirts. Kay is in the rocker by the plants with her long fingers resting lightly on the arms of the chair, Keeva with her golden curly hair is sitting tall in the straight-backed kitchen chair, while Kandy and I sit on the couch with our legs tucked up under our skirts.

I'm feeling calm on this last night and also sad that I have to leave so soon, for I don't know when we can be together again. Having found Kay and reclaimed a relationship that was severed thirty-one years ago,

I don't want to separate again. I felt a bond with all three of them from the moment we set eyes on each other, and over the past three days that sense of immediate connection has mellowed into something closer than friendship.

There is a sense of family in this room that is very different from the family I grew up with. There is very little intrusion of generational distance. It's as if the four of us are sisters, as if we are all equals. Can this be for real? Do the three of them act this way with each other all the time? This is so different from Mom and me, where I cannot seem to grow up in the relationship, or perhaps she cannot let me. Almost always, I'm the daughter and she's the wiser mother dispensing advice. Maybe that's one reason that my search for Kay has upset Mom so much. The habitual imbalance of power in our relationship has shifted. She has lost control over me.

"It's hard to face leaving tomorrow," I finally say. "I feel so close to you all in such a short time."

"Oh, we all feel it too, so strongly!" Kay says immediately. "I feel like we've known each other for years, not just a few days. It's more than just having caught up on lots of experiences from the past. It's like somehow you've been here with us, and we've been with you always."

Our conversation tonight is even more personal than before. They want to know more about my now mostly agnostic spiritual beliefs, while I learn that Keeva is "pretty much on board" with Kay's New Age agenda and Kandy is intrigued but more skeptical.

"Well, who's to say what the truth is?" Kay sums up, looking directly at me. "I really respond to this idea of creating your own reality. Maybe what you believe will be true for you, and what I believe will be true for me." I ponder this uneasily — the idea that I could be slowly disintegrating six feet under, while Kay could be expanding her consciousness and planning her next incarnation. But we move on to other topics.

Kay wants to know more about Harald, and as I try to describe him, she is reminded of Carl's negative qualities: the way he used to pick on her, the way he focused on things that she considered trivial and made life so much more difficult than it had to be. Kay ponders whether there might be something to "the German character" after all. This is a subject I don't want to pursue, as I always worry whether it verges on racism. Besides, how are Kandy and Keeva feeling about this criticism of their father? Their expressions are unreadable.

"Harald sounds like a pretty powerful person — I'd really like to meet him, and your kids," Keeva says, deftly veering the subject. "It's easy to forget that you have your own family down there, that you have a husband and you're a *mother*, when just the four of us are sitting around talking as if we didn't have any other responsibilities."

We talk about when we can get together again. We hold on to the moment by trying to make plans for it to happen again. I tell them that I unfortunately probably won't be able to detour up to Seattle with Harald and the kids on the way back to Toronto because it's just too expensive. But then Kay says she's been thinking about whether she could take a few days off from the shop and come down to visit us in California before we leave. "Do you think it would be all right?" she asks. "If you feel it would upset your mother, I wouldn't want to intrude." She's asking tentatively, almost apologetically, while my heart is leaping and my melancholy about leaving tomorrow is suddenly lifting.

"Oh, Kay! Could you really?" The words tumble out of my mouth. "Mom seemed to be coping better when I left. I'm sure if she can work this through, she will really like you. I'll just have to feel it out when I get home and we talk about my trip. Of course you could come down without her knowing about it." Misgivings begin piling up inside before I've even finished the sentence.

"Oh, no! I wouldn't feel right about that," Kay replies. "I wouldn't want to sneak down. I'd really like to meet both your parents, and Rick, but if they couldn't accept it quite that far, I'd understand, and I'd just be happy to have a chance to be with you again and get to meet Harald and the children."

The children! Uh-oh. I can see more hurt there for Mom, even though she might have accepted my relationship with Kay by then. What would

Kay's attitude be toward Derek and Tessa? She is their biological grand-mother, but Mom is their "Nana."

"I guess it isn't as easy as I thought at first," I say. "All I was thinking was how much I wanted you to come. I guess it is sort of complicated. I really hope it will work out, but I'll just have to see over the next few weeks when I get home, and I'll let you know if it feels right."

I ask Kandy and Keeva if there's a chance of seeing them again soon too. Kandy says she's going to be tied up this summer, working and finishing her school project. Keeva's time is a little more flexible, but they both say, "Mom deserves the first trip," and that they'll look after the shop for her if it works out that she can come.

The feeling of calm completion I had at the beginning of this evening has flared up into euphoria. I'm hanging on to the idea of Kay's trip to California to lessen the pain of flying away tomorrow. It's all right, I'll see her again before we leave for Toronto. We're not going to be separated again. Nobody is going to be left or abandoned. From now on, departures will be balanced by arrivals, and absences will be temporary. I'll be careful in bringing the idea up with Mom, but deep down I feel certain that Kay will come. I am going to make room in my life for Kay and Kandy and Keeva and someday Keith too, and the rest of my Seattle family, come what may.

It's almost eleven o'clock, and my suitcase is still at Elaine's. I phone her sheepishly. Elaine says she'll be up for a while and to come whenever we're ready. This is the third night and time for our compromise that I'll stay at Kay's place.

"Hey, you two look gorgeous!" Elaine greets us as Kay and I get out of the car still in our dinner ensembles. After a few minutes of chit-chat, we say goodbye. "How do you thank somebody for such a thing," I say as we hug each other, "helping you find your mother?"

"Don't worry Patty, I take more than half the credit!" Elaine laughs, breaking up the emotion of the moment.

When we return to Kay's apartment, Kandy and Keeva have unrolled their sleeping bags on the floor and are lying on them in their cotton nightgowns. They're propped up on their elbows, talking, as if a slumber party is commencing.

"We thought it would be nice if we all could be together on your last night and see you off in the morning," Kandy announces from the floor.

"I'm so glad you can stay!"

"Don't worry, you don't have to sleep on the floor," Kay says. "You and I can sleep in my room like civilized people."

I say goodnight to Kandy and Keeva and then go into the bedroom first to change, feeling that jarring sense of modesty again. I put out the light and crawl into one of the twin beds pushed together. I hear murmurings in the living room, and soon Kay comes into the darkened bedroom, closing the door softly behind her.

"You must be very tired after all of this," she says as she unhooks her clothing and slips on a nightgown. She settles in beside me in the other twin bed.

"My body's tired, all right. I'll catch up on my sleep when I get home. But my mind's still wide awake."

The moon is full tonight. Blue moonlight shines in through the diaphanous curtains and highlights the bones of her face, her bare shoulder, the pattern of the lace gown on her chest. She's half reclining, leaning her weight on her right elbow, her long fingers cradling her cheek, looking down at me.

Now she relaxes and lies down on her back, her head on the pillow. We watch the shadow play of branches on the ceiling and the walls. "Is there anything else you'd like to know about your birth?" she asks. "Or anything at all? Have all your questions been answered?"

I'm quickly in the misty past again, facing the nonrelationship from which I sprang. There's Kay in her early twenties, breathtakingly lovely, plunging into a brief affair with my handsome but faceless father for no good reason at all. Certainly not for love. I feel her confusion, shock, and numbness at learning she is pregnant, and I feel almost as close to that young woman as I do to the mature woman lying beside me.

"No, I don't think there's anything else." I've been so much in the present this evening that I've almost forgotten the past, taken it for granted. Of course there must be more, but there's lots of time left, many years to cover that ground.

But wait! Why have I not thought to ask such an obvious thing before? "Well, maybe just one question. It's sort of personal..."

"That's all right. We can talk about anything you want to."

"Okay, then. How is it you got pregnant with me in the first place? I mean, weren't you using anything?"

"Oh, dear!" She's laughing now. "You wouldn't believe how naive I was in those days. There was no pill then, of course. I guess diaphragms were available, but I didn't even know what a diaphragm was. I'd just had so little experience with sex, it never would have occurred to me to have planned for it. I did begin to get nervous, I remember, by the time Bobby and I were in bed, and I asked him something like, 'Shouldn't we be careful?' And he said, 'Don't worry, I'll take care of it,' and so we just went ahead. Of course he didn't do anything to 'take care of it,' but I just sort of imagined, totally ignorant, that because he'd said that, it was okay."

Ohhhhhh. I'm smiling with her too, at the delicious irony of it: he "took care of it" all right, and here I am! Bobby Z----, who are you? Where are you, at this very minute? What would you say if you could tune in on this scene? Those words she clearly remembers you having spoken, echoing in her mind down the years from a room somewhere here in this city — in Seattle, in February or March of 1945, it would have been — were, "Don't worry, I'll take care of it." Maybe you meant to withdraw at the last moment, and then, forgetting yourself, about to sail off in your ship anyhow, so who cares? ("What does this moment matter when I might be dead next week?"), you just let it happen and left a seed behind. How many others are there, I wonder? How many half-brothers and sisters will I never meet?

Or maybe it wasn't like that at all. Did you know she didn't love you? Did you sense it, even as she surrendered her naive body to you? And sensing it, did you maybe hope deep down, as I hoped when Paul and I did the very same thing, that she would become pregnant? You might have thought that you could claim her then, that she wouldn't, couldn't say no, that she could be yours. You did look her up in San Francisco later, after all....

"You've said you didn't love him. Was there anyone else you did love?"

She breathes in deeply. "Yes, there was someone. Before I met your father there was a young army captain. I have never felt such a deep, sure feeling for anyone else, not even in my marriage and in the affairs I've had since then. There was nothing physical between us. We kissed goodbye and that was all. He was a musician. One night we stayed in the restaurant after it closed, and he sat down and played the piano for me, something he had composed. I remember standing there, leaning on the piano, watching him as he played, feeling every note of the music like I was part of it. I was the music, I was him.

"He wasn't even very handsome, certainly not as handsome as Bobby. There was just this powerful feeling I had for him. It's strange how often I've thought of him over the years. I've wondered how different my life might have been if he'd stayed, if the times had been different. We wrote a few letters after he shipped out, but they stopped suddenly. I have no idea whatever happened to him. He may have been killed."

The bedroom wall is dancing wildly with shadows as the wind picks up outside. I'm fighting back tears. I feel quite certain that this is the closest my mother has ever come to love, this unconsummated, wistful wartime dream.

"Sometimes I wonder whether that experience has somehow prevented me from loving other men as fully as I could," she continues, her words weaving in tandem with my thoughts, "because I knew that deeper feeling is possible. But I've also grown a lot since the divorce. I find sex fulfilling now. Maybe that memory has helped me too, helped me give in to sexual feelings."

Have her fantasies of the musical captain helped her through sex with other men, helped her through all her years of marriage? Is that really what she means? We lie for several moments without saying anything.

Now she props herself up on her elbow again and turns to me. "Has it really been all you'd hoped it would be?" she asks. "Are you even a little disappointed with us, with me?"

I reach over and grasp her hand. "Kay, how can you think that? You're so wonderful! I still can't quite believe you're my mother! I feel so incredibly lucky to have found you!"

"Come here and let me hold you, my little baby I never got to cuddle."

She slips one arm under my neck and wraps the other around my back in a warm, comforting embrace, while I am too stunned for words. Oh my God, what is *happening*? Mom and I have never hugged each other like this.

Seduced by the baby-oil-innocent smell of her skin, her hair soft as a kitten on my cheek, I begin losing myself in her, and I hug her back. As Kay gently rocks me like a baby, my life careens through my mind in jumbled visions: Mom and Dad and Rick down all the years, scenes from Ukiah and Monterey, good times and sad, their faces changing, growing older, myself changing, growing up, and accompanied always, everywhere, by the blurred vision of my birth mother — just out of sight on a San Francisco street, slipping away as the piano chords fade, emanations of love shining in on my life often, and those later, witch-like nightmares that I now know were so untrue. I'm so caught between the past and this astonishing present that I'm fighting dizziness, breathing her in, holding on to the moonlight playing in her hair.

"I love you, darling," her voice murmurs in my ear. Luminous Kay, I love you too. Inside Pat, cradled in her mother's arms, Carol hums with joy.

* * *

Seven o'clock in the morning. Rush hour, have to go. Just orange juice and coffee. A few last-minute snapshots on the balcony in the morning sun. I hug each of my sisters for a long time and cry, wondering when we'll be together again.

The airport is the usual fumbling procedures of lines, crowds, tickets, and baggage, but Kay and I have a few moments together before I have to board. Content, sitting quietly in the plastic chairs of the terminal, and talking of inconsequential things, to passersby we must appear to be any ordinary mother and daughter in transit.

Our farewell is tearless and our hugs are tight, not tentative anymore. I can't afford to think we might not be together again soon in California, or I would dissolve into tears. As I walk into the "passengers only" corridor, I turn and wave to her one last time. She's smiling and blowing kisses — radiant and serene.

As the plane roars its ascent over Seattle and begins to level off, it tilts downward on my side for a few moments. From my window seat I am suddenly looking down on a dazzling mountain. Its sharp, snow-covered cap rises up through a bed of gray clouds, sparkling in the sun.

My geography is hazy. This could be Mt. Rainier, the slopes of which, alive with dogwoods and waterfalls, I visited yesterday with Elaine, Charlie, and Corinne. It could be Mt. Baker, which the day before stood like an elemental witness to the family reunion on Whidbey Island. It could be Mt. Hood, Mt. Adams, or any other of the tall young peaks of the Cascades that Corinne spoke of with such familiarity.

My quest for Kay and for my beginnings has been my own mountain to climb. When I began, the quest at times seemed too arduous, success unattainable. But I have conquered the mountain! Dizzy from the heights and the sudden turnings along the way, I've held on tightly to the familiar stranger I sought and viewed life from the summit. I know that this journey will continue for the rest of my life.

My adoptive parents, Kate & George

Kay at ferry dock

One of Kay's modeling photos

PART IV:
TWO MOTHERS

BEST IN SHOW was Mrs. George Dietterle's original embroidery wall hanging, depicting the scene from one of the windows of her home.

Mom and her stitchery wall hanging

Rick in High school

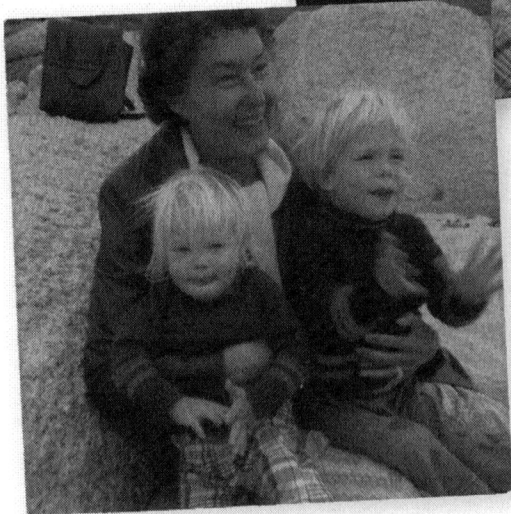

Kay meeting Derek and
Tessa for the first time
during her visit to
Carmel

CHAPTER 21

reentered my California life trailing clouds of euphoria. But when I tried to describe those few days in Seattle to friends and family, I couldn't seem to break it all down into manageable parts to narrate, for those few days were like a seamless flow of emotions. Gradually, I managed to convey most of the experience to Harald: specifics of what we did, my impressions of the different members of the family, the strong currents connecting Kay and me, especially that odd combination of exciting discovery and secure familiarity with which we approached each other.

It was much harder to talk about my trip with Mom and Dad. The worry that I might hurt Mom even more in the telling filtered and censured my words. The day after I returned from Seattle, she and I talked on the phone. She wanted to know about my trip, but her tone told me she was resisting it too. I was surprised to notice a gentle sort of detachment within myself. *She has chosen to feel hurt and threatened,* I found myself thinking. *That is how she has decided to experience this. I'll just stand by while she works it through.*

Then there was Rick. He had moved back to Monterey from Chico during that time, and at Mom's insistence he was still ignorant of my search. At the end of June, Mom and Dad took a short trip, and one

251

evening while they were away, Rick joined us in Carmel Valley for dinner. We had hardly gotten the kids to bed and sat down at the big oak table when Rick said, "I've noticed Mom's been acting really edgy lately, and I can't figure out what's up. It's just not like her. I asked her about it, and she said she'd been kind of jittery; she'd even been snapping at Dad lately. I tried to get her to talk about it, but she just clammed up. Have either of you noticed it? Do you have any idea what's wrong?"

Harald and I exchanged a quick glance. The promise that Mom had extracted from me weighed heavily, but much stronger was the desire to stop the lies of omission to Rick.

"Yeah, I'm pretty sure why she's upset," I answered. "Remember that talk we had back at Christmas about our biological parents?"

As I began describing the events of the previous five months, Rick listened silently, tensely, his hands folded tightly above his untouched plate. Then he exploded.

"Pat! How could you have done that? How could you have hurt them like that! Why?"

I steadied myself by tracing the Indian patterns in the thick cotton placemat with the handle of my knife. "Well, I finally decided that my need to know who and where I came from was more important than their right to keep it hidden."

"Your mother gave you up when you were a baby!" he said hotly. "Mom and Dad are your only parents! It's ungrateful!"

"Look, Rick, back in 1946, Mom and Daddy needed a child probably as much as I needed parents," I began again, trying to enunciate carefully my new thoughts about closed adoption. "It's always been a two-way street. We all owe each other a lot of love. But I'm grown up now. I needed to know."

"Why? What difference could it possibly make? Personally, I feel absolutely no connection to my biological parents. I owe everything that I am to Mom and Dad — everything!"

I glanced at Harald, who was the only one eating his salmon, asparagus, and mashed potatoes. Though he was watching us closely, he uncharacteristically stayed out of the conversation. "Well, now that I've met my biological family," I continued, "I think that heredity has a lot more to do with who we are than I ever thought before. Besides, think about this, Rick. If you had children, wouldn't you want to know what your genetic heritage was, if only for your kids' sakes?"

Rick pondered all of this, unconvinced, sipping his wine and studying me over the glass. "But why did you have to tell them?" he asked quietly, setting his glass down on the table. "Couldn't you have kept it to yourself and not hurt them?"

"Oh, Rick, that would have been lying. It would have been so out of keeping with what our relationship has been. I felt that if I didn't tell them about this, there would always be a barrier between us. I wanted them to be able to share it with me. I thought we all could gain from it."

"Well, has that come about?" He swirled his wine glass on the table, his fingers tense on the base. The evening had darkened, and the candlelight brought out the golden highlights in his shoulder-length hair, the copper sparkles in his beard.

"Not yet. It's still too fresh. But I hope it will."

"I don't know, Pat." He sighed. "You're really an idealist."

As we continued talking, Rick finally began to relax. He asked questions about Kay and the Seattle family, and out came the pictures I had recently had developed. His initial reaction never quite disappeared — his worry for Mom and Dad, his hurt for Mom's hurt — but by the end of the evening he had softened. What I didn't detect in Rick at all was what Mom had feared: a sense that he was being supplanted by my new siblings. "You know," he said toward the end of the evening, after we had moved into the living room, "I feel that in a strange sort of way I've gained too by what you've done. I'd really like to meet Kay and Kandy and Keeva. Funny, but I feel like they're part of my family too."

Later that summer, after Rick had met Kay and Keeva (to whom he joked, "You know, you're really lucky, Keeva — you have Pat for a sister, but you didn't have to grow up with her!"), he said to me one evening, "Your experience has really started me thinking. For the first time in my life, I realize that there are at least two people somewhere out there that I'm related to. I've always thought of Mom and Dad, and nobody else, as my parents. Now I just can't help wondering. It makes me feel strange, like I don't know who I am any more."

"I really understand how you feel, Rick," was all I could bring myself to say, for a complex feeling was suddenly sweeping through me, making me hold my tongue. I saw that we had been living our shared twenty-six years as if on the edge of a precipice. I had just jumped over and landed softly among a clan of biological family who had welcomed me. What if Rick jumped too? Who and what would he find? All those fears I had had at the beginning of my search surfaced again for him.

I decided that if Rick did want to search someday and asked for my help, I would help him as much as I could. But I didn't want to persuade him to do it.

* * *

A couple of weeks after my return from Seattle, while Mom and I prepared lunch in her kitchen and Derek and Tessa busied themselves hauling all the toys out of the big wooden chest in the dining room, I broached the subject of Kay's possible trip to Carmel. Mom seemed taken aback and immediately asked if Kay would want to meet her and Daddy.

"I think she would," I replied, attempting to act casual as I sliced up the carrot and celery sticks, "but it isn't necessary. She'd probably be able to leave the shop for just a few days, and...."

Kay had made it clear, again, in a recent letter that she didn't want to sneak down to California without Mom and Dad knowing, and also that she didn't want to come if it would make them uncomfortable. I saw no hope of Mom being comfortable about Kay's visit, but I was determined that Kay would come — so that we could enjoy a few more days together and she would be able to meet the children and Harald — so I tried to suggest to Mom the least uncomfortable alternative: Kay could visit Harald and me, but Mom and Dad needn't feel pressured to meet her.

"No, no, of course we would want to meet her!" Mom insisted, halting her sandwich-making activities at the cutting board on the other side of the kitchen. "It would be very awkward if we didn't."

"You don't have to do anything that would make you uneasy," I tried to reassure her.

"Well, it would be a difficult thing for me, that's for sure," Mom said, "if you can imagine how it would feel to meet your own daughter's mother!"

But Mom, out of the need to prove to herself that she could handle the situation, out of loyalty to me, or out of sheer curiosity, over the next several days became adamant about meeting Kay. She suggested that Kay and I come over and have coffee with her and Dad one morning. My mind boggling and knees weakening at the proposed scene, but relieved and full of foolish hope, I said that would be fine.

* * *

On the afternoon of July 5, 1977, Harald, Derek, Tessa, and I hung over the railing of the observation deck at the Monterey Peninsula Airport, waiting for Kay's plane. It's a small, personal kind of airport. You stand on the windy deck, covering your ears when the jets come roaring in, then rush downstairs to the gate to greet the passengers as they walk across the runway and into the terminal.

I spotted her as soon as we stationed ourselves at the runway level. Holding her batik skirt up slightly with one hand and carrying a round overnight case in the other, she descended the steps and walked across the pavement toward us. It was different this time. My legs weren't shaking, my heart wasn't bursting. There was a warm, bubbling feeling of welcome in me, and also a flushed sense of pride. In a little moment of role reversal, I felt proud of her, so pleased to be introducing Harald to my lovely birth mother, as if she were my creation and not the other way around.

Kay and I hugged each other. Harald pecked his second mother-in-law on the cheek. Then Kay kissed each of the children, bending down to embrace three-year-old Derek at his level and taking Tessa from Harald's arms for a moment to hug her, as easily as if she were seeing them not for the first time, but only after a short absence.

"Well, let's go get your suitcase," Harald said, ready to plunge into the crowd around the baggage claim.

"Oh, this is all I brought," Kay said with an apologetic little laugh. "I'm practicing traveling light for my trip to Indonesia. Henry thought it was disgraceful of me to come with just this...this hatbox. He wanted me to borrow his set of matching luggage. But I said, 'I'm sure I don't have to try to impress them with all that!'"

"You're quite right," said Harald, nodding meaningfully at me, thoroughly approving of Kay's attitude. I laughed, remembering the suitcase *and* overnight case I had lugged up to Seattle for less time than Kay would be with us.

By the time Kay visited us, we had moved from the rambling Carmel Valley house into a magnificent old three-story Carmel home with twenty-foot beamed ceilings, a massive stone fireplace, dark oak paneling, and antique furniture throughout. The house was not our usual style, but for Kay's visit I was glad we were there. The soaring height and openness of the house matched the celebration in my heart.

Kay's five days with us were as full as my three and a half days in Seattle: sightseeing trips with the children to Carmel, to the wharf in Monterey, the 17-Mile Drive, excursions to the beach, and investigations of the tide pools. Rick came over for dinner one evening, and there were a couple of low-key social meetings with close friends I especially wanted Kay to meet.

Yet with all the activity, the quality of the visit was different. Seattle had been a constant high for me, a flow of emotionally charged and often disorienting moments. Carmel was a quieter time. There was time to talk, and we talked wherever we were, even though the minutia of daily life made more demands than in Seattle. We pushed the shopping cart up and down the aisles at Safeway, with Derek hanging onto the front and Tessa in the child's seat. We prepared meals together, comparing notes on cooking. Kay helped with the housework, the laundry, the children.

Kay related to Derek and Tessa with ease and affection. There was nothing in her behavior toward them that was stereotypically grandmo-therly. She treated them as little people, hugging them whenever they climbed into her lap but not lavishing attention on them when they were busy with other things. She read to them, played games with them, and treated them with loving respect. While Mom related to the children in a more take-charge kind of way, finding interesting things that would occupy them and organizing their activities, Kay's stance was more one of sitting back, observing, and relating to them more quietly.

From the beginning, they called her "Kay." Rather, Derek called her "Kay," while Tessa, at seventeen months, called her "Kay-Kay," because she doubled up all of our names: Dada, Mama, Kaka (Derek), Nana, Apa. I had suggested the children call her "Kay" out of concern for Mom. We agreed that when they were old enough to understand, I would tell them who she was, but for the moment it was enough that they accepted her as a special friend or family member and called her "Kay."

Harald asked Kay whether she felt that Derek and Tessa were "really" her grandchildren. She said that she felt the same toward them as she felt toward Keith's six-year old son, Aaron. But she didn't often talk about Derek and Tessa as her grandchildren. What she talked about mostly in the context of our little family was seeing herself as a mother again in me and experiencing many flashbacks to those years when my three half-siblings were the same ages as Derek and Tessa. She told me many anecdotes about Keith, Kandy, and Keeva when they were little and recalled her feelings as a mother of young children. While I was very interested in these reminiscences, I also felt a jarring sense of emotional distance, similar to the afternoon when we had perused her photo albums in Seattle — for I, Carol, Pat, also her child, was not part of her life history in that way, not part of her memories. While she was mothering my half-brother and sisters, I was growing up in our two-acre paradise in Ukiah as Mom and Daddy's daughter and Ricky's big sister. As Kay talked, I watched these two films playing simultaneously in my mind's eye with more curiosity than sadness.

Kay also shared with me, with even more conviction than she had before, her sense that Harald and her ex-husband, Carl, were similar. When Harald made picky, critical comments or "suggestions" to me, as he often did, Kay would tell me privately that she was experiencing a sense of *déjà vu*, since that was exactly how Carl had treated her. When Harald acted inflexible or irritable, as he often did, Kay was again reminded of her difficult married life, and as she had in Seattle, she wondered whether there was anything to the idea of the German character. The implication was obvious, and chilling to me: since Kay had ultimately divorced Carl, perhaps I might consider similarly freeing myself someday.

Yet most evenings after Derek and Tessa were in bed, Harald, Kay, and I sat amicably together in the spacious, cathedral-ceilinged living room. Once Kay and I got out sketch pads and did contour drawings of each other and objects in the room. But most evenings we just talked. Since my trip to Seattle, I had done some reading on reincarnation (Kay was surprised to discover that Harald had too), and we talked about regression hypnosis, Western mysticism, the nature of reality, life purposes, the afterlife, thought waves, and we shared tales of vivid dreams we'd had and moments of intuition. More than once during those evenings it struck me that Mom and I never discussed such topics, except possibly as tossed-off comments in passing. Kay and I also talked a lot about the wonder of meeting each other, about how our lives had been influenced by each other even before we had met, and about the powerful combination of newness and familiarity that we felt for each other.

We also began trying to define our relationship: when and why it felt like "friends" or "sisters" and whether it was a "mother-daughter" relationship in any sense beyond biology. I knew I loved her, and I was still fascinated by her. But what roles were we playing in each other's lives, and would we play in the future? I felt the difficulties in defining our relationship most strongly when I had to introduce Kay to someone. If the meeting was with a close friend who knew our story, no explanations were necessary. But the first time we ran into a casual acquaintance together, I was at a loss. I couldn't say, "This is my mother," because Betty knew

Mom. Saying, "This is my good friend from Seattle" seemed stupidly inadequate. And I wasn't quite brave enough for the jaw-dropper: "This is my birth mother whom I just met last month." So the first time it happened, I didn't introduce Kay at all and apologized as soon as we were alone again. After that it was easier. I introduced Kay as my birth mother or my natural mother. Inevitably, an excited conversation would ensue, and we just took the time for it.

One morning after breakfast, Kay and I were having a second cup of coffee at the cluttered dining room table, with the sun streaming in through the gabled windows. Harald had gone upstairs to his desk, and Derek and Tessa were playing at our feet under the table. They were putting on a tea party for all their dolls and stuffed animals, which necessitated many trips into the kitchen and playroom to bring in supplies. There were animated discussions under the table, conducted mainly by Derek, about who should sit next to whom, and what would be served. Kay and I had been watching the children and talking about nothing very profound.

Then, suddenly, she began to cry. I mistook her tears for sadness or regret. Concerned, I reached out to comfort her. But she turned to me, smiling, with tears running down her cheeks, and said, "I just can't tell you what a feeling of joy and relief it is to know you at last!" I got up, knelt beside her chair, and we held each tightly. While Derek and Tessa carried on with their tea party, Kay and I allowed ourselves to cry together for the first time. "I love you," we said at the same time.

* * *

The night before the morning coffee with Mom and Dad, Kay asked what sort of a meeting we thought it would be. Harald and I were in complete agreement: Mom and Dad would be uptight but gracious and friendly and would see that the conversation stayed on pleasant, unemotional topics. I said it was possible that we could spend two hours there without the subject of *who Kay was* ever coming up.

"Oh, do you really think so?" Kay asked, incredulous. "I honestly don't know whether I'll be able to *not* say anything about it, because I feel so much for them. From what you've told me about your mother's reaction, this may be the only time we'll ever meet. If I don't convey some of my feelings to them, I'll feel very badly, like the meeting was meaningless, like I'd missed the chance."

"You should do whatever feels right to you," I told her. Yet I couldn't help feeling some trepidation. What was I afraid of? That Mom, when finally confronted with this beautiful apparition, my birth mother, would become even more jealous, and then close off and reject me? That she wouldn't be able to help herself and would sprinkle her clever wit through the conversation tomorrow, hurting Kay's feelings? After all, in 1945 Kay had been the "fallen woman," and Mom and Dad had swept in to my rescue as the ideal adoptive parents who had passed all the social workers' tests with flying colors. Or was I afraid that Kay might be too forthcoming and push Mom and Dad into an emotional direction with which they were very uncomfortable? Or was I just irrationally afraid that somehow, something would go horribly wrong in the morning, something I hadn't even thought about, and as punishment for being so over-reaching as to attempt to have two mothers in my life, I might lose them both? As I fell asleep that night, I tried to put my worries to bed too, so that I could appear and truly feel calm in the morning. I concentrated on how interesting and unique each of my mothers was and imagined them warming to each other, liking each other....

Shortly before ten the next morning, Kay and I pulled up at the top of the hill in front of Mom and Dad's house. We had dropped Derek off at his nursery school on the way in to Monterey, and we had left Tessa at home with Harald, much to Harald's chagrin, because he had wanted so much to be a fly on the wall. At the sound of the Datsun motor, Mom and Dad both came out into the front courtyard. As Kay and I walked down the slope to meet them, somewhat proudly, like a personal tour guide, I explained to her how Mom and Dad had made the large cement squares of the patio and walkway themselves using pebbles they'd collected from the Carmel River, and how Mom had designed and Daddy now tended the beautifully landscaped courtyard. Today it was brilliant with the colors and subtle scents of the large rhododendron bushes, camellias, and jasmine climbing on trellises, and pots of orchids and azaleas.

As we stepped through the redwood gate, Mom came forward, extending her hand, and said, "Hello, Kay, it's good to meet you," with what my antennae picked up as genuine warmth.

Daddy beamed. "Hello, Kay!"

Kay took Mom's hand and then Dad's, and said, "Hello, Kate. George. I feel as if I know you already."

"Really?" Mom said half-humorously, as if caught a little off balance. Watching the three of them together, I began feeling faint and realized I'd forgotten to breathe.

We were all smiles as Dad led Kay into the house and Mom and I followed a few steps behind. "Well, how are you doing, Patty?" Mom asked.

"Me? Oh, I'm fine," I said, though my heart was still fluttering wildly. "The main thing is, how are you?"

"Don't you worry," she said, squeezing my arm. "Your Dad and I are managing just fine." We linked arms as we walked up the front steps.

"What a lovely house! And that view!" Kay exclaimed as soon as we walked into the living room with its high ceiling, used-brick fireplace, tall built-in bookcases, and floor-to-ceiling windows looking out through the pine trees to Monterey Bay. I was pleased that Kay noticed the large hanging above the fireplace right away, the Monterey woodland scene in stitchery that Mom had designed and sewn herself, with deer, raccoons, squirrels, blue jays, and monarch butterflies made from fabric remnants, all playing among the pine trees and wildflowers. I suddenly realized that both of my mothers were talented at crafts. Kay made her living by sewing clothes and making jewelry to sell in her shop, while Mom, in addition to her more high-powered volunteer work such as chairing the municipal committee on civic appearance and serving as president of the local art museum, was also active in local fundraising projects that involved designing, making, and sewing Christmas ornaments and gifts. A large corner of the rec room downstairs was jammed to the ceiling with boxes containing shells, beach glass, beads, pine cones, ribbons, sequins, fabric, and seed pods of all kinds.

"You all make yourselves comfortable at the table, and I'll bring in the coffee," Mom said, declining my offer of help and setting off into the kitchen. I noticed that she'd taken some care in dressing this morning. Instead of the solid-color jogging suits I was used to seeing her wear around the house, today she wore soft gray, tailored wool pants, a cream-colored cashmere sweater, and the necklace of gray and red intricately painted wooden beads from West Africa that Dad had given her for Christmas. Her fine, wavy, almost white hair contrasted with her tanned and freckled skin, which was wrinkled with frown lines between her eyebrows and smile lines at the corners of her mouth and green eyes.

Aside from a common interest in crafts, my two mothers were so different, I reflected, watching Kay as Daddy motioned for her to sit in the chair with the best view. As usual, she was dressed in batik — a delicately patterned skirt in browns and blues that came just below her knees — with a short-sleeved jersey top, also cream-colored. Her necklace was one she'd made herself: iridescent mussel shells macraméd together, interspersed with small glass beads. While Mom exuded her usual confidence and competence, Kay looked gentler and more vulnerable. In contrast to Mom's full-of-character face, Kay's skin was unlined and glowing, and her clear blue eyes were highlighted by subtle eye shadow. I was a little disappointed that she'd dyed her hair since I'd been to Seattle. The silver temples were gone, and her hair was henna-colored throughout. The effect did, however, make her appear even younger.

Mom soon returned with a tray of cups, silver coffee pot, and warm coffee cake. It was a role I had seldom seen her in, and I began feeling oddly like a guest.

"Have you been to the peninsula before, Kay?" Daddy said as an opener as Mom poured the coffee and cut up the cake.

"Yes, but more as a tourist," Kay replied. "One spring break when Keith was at Stanford, we all drove down here for a couple of days." If this comment rattled Mom and Dad, as it did me somewhat, neither showed it. How odd that unbeknownst to each other, my brother and I had both gone to Stanford, missing each other by just a few months. Keith and I had so much in common, I thought. Keith painted, played classical music, had also learned German. Yet sitting there around the table smiling politely, none of my three parents commented on this obvious coincidence.

But with that bit of personal history, the conversation was launched, and the topics flew along surprisingly easily: the varied beauties of the Monterey Peninsula, the character of Seattle (a city Mom and Dad also knew fairly well), the Gouda Canal trip in Holland, and places in Australia that the three of them had visited. They touched on topics of more personal interest: Daddy's postretirement teaching positions, Mom's community work, Kay's business. They even brushed the main point without getting snared by it: the interesting differences between raising three children close together in age and two children far apart, and summaries of the activities of those children who were absent at this table: Rick, Keith, Kandy, and Keeva.

At one point during their discussions of children, Mom spoke of my single-mindedness in setting about a task, ostensibly describing my attention to my schoolwork but also alluding to my attitude during my search. "Must be heredity," she said jokingly. "Probably is environment," Kay countered immediately, smiling.

"I'll bet you're really enjoying having your grandchildren so close to home," Kay commented a little later.

"We certainly are, Kay," Mom replied, hardly flicking an eyelash. "The kids seem so far away in Toronto. This year has been very special."

"I know what you mean. I still picture my grandson, Aaron, as a three-year-old. But he's six now, and I've missed watching him grow while Keith and Elenna have been in Holland."

Wait, wait, what is happening, I wondered as Mom refilled our cups from the silver pot. Surely Kay was making a distinction between "her" grandchild and Mom's grandchildren in order to be tactful? Or did she really not yet feel that she was Derek and Tessa's grandmother?

None of my three parents wanted to offend in any way. Every word seemed chosen with care. I participated now and then, tossing a few remarks into the conversation, but mainly it was their show. Four ordinary people having coffee on a sunny morning. The best cups clinked on their saucers, and the coffee cake was nibbled politely. Many topics were pleasantly discussed, while the main one was skirted assiduously. My two mothers sat on either side of me, studying each other quite openly as their words met. Daddy, opposite me at the table, prevented lulls from developing in the conversation, catching my eye and smiling reassuringly.

Finally, it was eleven thirty. Derek had to be picked up at nursery school at noon. As we all rose from the table, a little wave of emptiness rolled through me. The words had been friendly, but I had hoped that the powerful undercurrents of the morning would have been tapped, would have been even tentatively acknowledged and expressed, to provide some small release from this controlled pleasantness.

Kay was quiet as we all moved slowly across the living room to the front door. Then, in front of the fireplace, she stopped. She turned to Mom and touched her arm. "Kate, I just can't walk away from you without saying what's in my heart. I want to thank you and George. You've been such loving, wonderful parents to Pat, and I...."

She had begun bravely and confidently, but her voice caught before she could finish, and tears filled her eyes as she looked at Mom.

"Kay, you hardly need to *thank* us," Mom objected, stepping away slightly.

"Please don't misunderstand me," Kay continued, her hand now gripping Mom's arm. "All those years, not knowing where she was, or what sort of parents she had, and now, meeting you and hearing about Pat's life from her, I just feel very thankful and relieved. It makes me feel more sure that I did make the right decision for her back then, and I do feel thankfulness to you both, very deeply."

She's strong, I thought, *because she's in touch with her feelings and acts on them. Thank goodness someone has broken this too-pleasant spell.*

Mom, rarely at a loss for words, was speechless. Then, as if in slow motion, she reached out to Kay and put both arms around her. My vision shimmered as I watched my two mothers embrace. I clutched Daddy's arm, and as he turned to put his arm around me, I saw that he was tearing up too, a sight I had witnessed only once or twice in my life.

Now, with the tears, the truthful words flowed more easily. We all stepped out into the fragrant courtyard. Mom and Kay walked on ahead to the car, chatting, while Dad and I trailed quietly behind, picking up bits of their conversation, his arm still around my shoulder.

"You know, George and I have always joked that we never could have produced two such beautiful children ourselves—"

"San Francisco has always been a haunted city to me. I dreaded going there, always searched faces in the crowds. Now it'll be totally different—"

"It wasn't difficult for her growing up adopted. Adoption was quite common in Ukiah. She didn't suffer from it—"

"It's wonderful, isn't it, that she looks so much like you. Whether it was just chance or growing together all those years—"

"Funny thing is, my parents came from Washington. There was a Metcalf on my mother's side—"

"Really? Is that right? Who knows, maybe we're all...!"

When we reached the car, as Kay and Daddy were saying goodbye, Mom and I gave each other a hug. Conspiratorially, she lowered her voice to a whisper. "Well, what do you think? Did I pull it off okay?"

"Mom!" I laughed, startled. I stepped back and saw the tears and the smile mingling in her eyes. Did she really mean that this morning was some sort of performance, or endurance test, or pretense? Giving her another little hug and playing along, I whispered into her ear, "You were terrific, Mom!"

* * *

The leave-taking at the Monterey airport was much different from the tearless, confident farewell in Seattle. Harald and the children and I were returning to Toronto in six weeks. Kay and I knew we would get together again, but we had no idea when that might be. Although I had managed to see Mom, Dad, and Rick at least once a year since moving to Toronto, to Kay and me, saying goodbye that day in Monterey, the distance between Seattle and Toronto seemed enormous.

This time we didn't even try to fight the tears. I believe they were delayed tears: delayed from our parting in Seattle, probably even delayed from our first parting more than thirty years before. I felt a wrenching in my heart when she finally turned to walk to the plane.

PATRICIA MOFFAT

CHAPTER 22

Harald, Derek, Tessa, and I moved out of the Carmel house at the end of July and stayed with Mom and Dad until we flew back to Toronto on September 1st. During those busy weeks, it sometimes seemed to me as if the search, Seattle, and Kay's visit had all been a dream, for, just as during the search, the subject rarely came up unless I introduced it.

My hopes of working the search into my relationship with my parents before we left California had been ridiculously idealistic after all, as Rick had suggested. True, I had found Kay well before our sabbatical was over, but her visit to California was probably still too fresh for any resolution before we left for Toronto. I discovered, by little comments dropped, by pauses, by all those nonverbal signs we can read in those we know well, that Mom had indeed "pulled something off" at that morning coffee. It had been an ordeal for her; she had gotten through it, but her hurt and her feeling that our relationship was threatened hadn't changed much. Perhaps those feelings had even intensified.

A few days before Harald and the kids and I returned to Toronto, Mom took me out to lunch at one of her and Dad's favorite restaurants on Cannery Row. As we settled into the red velvet upholstered booth at the picture window overlooking the old fish canning factories and the bay,

I wondered whether this mother-daughter lunch would be any different from earlier ones, at other peninsula restaurants. To observers, we surely appeared as just an ordinary mother and her grown-up daughter lunching together. We even looked somewhat alike. Though my hair was long and braided and my pierced earrings were hand-wrought silver, both holdovers from the sixties, my style was still closer to Mom's than to Kay's. Both of us wore no-nonsense, casual California clothes, Mom a two-piece jersey skirt and top and I a cotton shirtwaist dress. The scene was similar to previous occasions, I thought, but the players were changing — living through internal shifts. I knew this was my chance to try to make peace with Mom and move forward. I hoped I wouldn't blow it, and I hoped she would meet me halfway.

Through the grilled scallops and crab salad, we talked mostly about how to survive the Canadian winter after being spoiled by nine months in the sun. Mom had been thinking about how we could adapt our Toronto house to make it more livable during the winter. She suggested renovation ideas that were fun to talk about but way beyond our means. Finally, when the waitress brought our chocolate mousse and coffee, I changed the subject.

"Mom, how do you feel about my search and about Kay now?"

The eagerness on her face faded, and she set her dessert spoon back on her plate. "Well, I still don't really understand why you had to do it, but you had to, I guess," she replied. "Whenever you decide on something, there's no stopping you. I think you were very fortunate in finding a woman who was so welcoming. You really could have suffered a blow if she'd been different, or if the circumstances of her life had been different."

"Yes, I know I've been lucky," I said. This wasn't too bad so far, I thought. But I wanted to push further, to try to get at the heart of it. "But Mom, have you been able to understand yet why I needed to find her?"

Across the table, Mom sipped her coffee and looked at me closely. Finally, she put the cup down firmly in its saucer and said, "I think my personal philosophy is quite different from yours, Pat. Maybe I've learned this about you through this thing. To me, certain basic things about life are givens. You accept your life, you accept your lot, and do the best you can within the boundaries you have been given."

I looked up at her uncertainly. This was getting harder. I needed to lever in with a softer approach. "Well, I guess part of my lot in life was knowing that somebody had given me away when I was born, and always wondering why, and who she was, and where I had come from."

"To me that's one of your 'givens,' that's all," Mom said flatly. "You move forward from there, not back."

"Well, there came a point where I didn't seem to be moving forward very well, Mom. That's why I needed to go back, to answer those questions."

Now we paused, at an impasse. I turned from her and gazed out the window. From this high point, the cannery roofs formed geometrical patterns in rusty grays. Tiny white triangles of sailboats dotted the indigo bay. Pastel-clad tourists moved in and out of shops holding ice cream cones, pulling balky children by the hand. That afternoon in Cannery Row, I was still so steeped in guilt at having hurt my mother that it never occurred to me to point out to her that she hadn't accepted her "givens" and her "lot" in life any more than I had. The Old Maid card of infertility had been dealt to her as one of her "givens," yet she had refused to accept it. She had bucked fate by becoming a mother, while I had done the same by finding one.

I had felt Mom's eyes on me while I was watching the scene below. Now she took an audible gulp of her coffee and said, "You know, I've been wondering through all of this whether it might have been better if we hadn't told you that you were adopted."

"Oh, no, Mom! What if I'd found out later? I think most adopted children who aren't told sense things and eventually find out. How would I, how would we all have felt then?"

"Maybe you would have found out, maybe not," she continued. "But at least you might have felt more secure, wouldn't have needed to go off on this search."

"But that would have been a false security — my life built upon a lie."

She sighed and wiped the corners of her mouth with her white linen napkin. "Well, there was never any doubt in our minds, then, that we should tell you," she continued. "We just never saw this coming — never, ever picked up on it. Looking back on your life, the only sign your Dad and I have recognized, in retrospect, is your overachieving and perfectionism. You just never seemed to be an insecure child."

"Yes, I knew nonadopted children who seemed much more insecure than I was," I agreed. "But the overachieving was an attempt to make you and Daddy proud of me and to prove my own worth to myself. I don't think that at the time I thought it had anything to do with my being adopted."

"Maybe it didn't at all," Mom replied quickly. "Maybe this is all just interpretation in hindsight. Still, it might have been a signal we didn't pick up on, because your adoption was always so far from our minds."

"Yes, I know.... But Mom, I think we're both falling into the trap here of assuming there must be something wrong in a person's childhood that leads them to want to find their birth parents — that there are lacks, that the child is insecure or something — when really it's a very natural thing to wonder what your heritage is, to want to know who you are and where you came from." I was warming to the subject now, hoping I was carrying her with me, leaning forward on my elbows over my half-eaten chocolate mousse. "You've probably never given this two minutes' thought," I continued, "because you always knew your background and took it for granted. Anyway, adopted people from very different backgrounds are searching."

"Not all, Pat, not all. I've done a little casual checking around among friends, and of those cases of adoptions I know well, you are the only one — the only one! — who has done this." Mom's green eyes flashed in a little moment of perverse triumph.

"Really? That surprises me," I responded lamely. "I wonder if they will someday, or if they already have and just haven't said anything." Who was she talking about anyway? I wondered. Our cousins in D.C.? Or Faith and Fred, our neighborhood friends in Ukiah? I didn't care to know, didn't want the conversation to get deflected off into other people's lives. This chance to mend fences wasn't going very well. I felt her growing hostility across the table. There was another pause in the conversation, a long couple of minutes as we both sipped our cool coffee. The waitress came and removed our dessert plates. As she refilled our coffee cups, I again sought comfort in the geometrical shapes of the cannery roofs. The waitress left. I looked at Mom and tried once more.

"Mom, I still hope that someday we'll see my search as a positive thing for all of us. I'd hoped so much that it would be good for you and me. Sometimes I think it has been already. How do you see it?"

"Well, I'll have to be honest, Pat. I feel that our relationship has changed. It just feels different."

"Different how?" But of course she was right, I admitted to myself; it *was* different. For one thing, we had never had to talk about "our relationship" before.

"I don't think I can describe it very well," Mom said, and now she was the one turning her head away, searching for words and gazing out the window while I searched her face intently. "It's just a feeling that things aren't the same and never will be."

I began feeling cold, and alone, and a little scared. "Mom, do you really think I'll ever feel that Kay is my *mom*, the way you are?"

"No, I don't suppose so," she replied. "It's too late for that, I guess. But it's simply *knowing* that she's there. Another woman, another *mother* is there, in your life now," she continued, her voice rising so that I began to worry whether the elderly couple in the next booth could overhear us. "It doesn't matter exactly what your relationship to her is, it's just that her presence affects our relationship. I have to share you now. And that takes some getting used to."

I shivered. I still wasn't sure, myself, what role Kay would come to play in my life, or how Mom and I would continue relating to each other in the future. However, I made a stab at definition. "Mom, I'm quite sure that if I had a serious problem, I'd come to you," I said. "I really don't think I'd go to Kay with it."

"No, I'm sure you wouldn't. *Quite* sure you wouldn't," she repeated with emphasis, now looking at me with outright anger. "I think that your relationship with Kay is something other — that you'd want to spare her the details, that you'd want to keep your relationship with her higher, untarnished...."

Stop! I hadn't meant to charge into that battlefield. I had intended my remark generously, as an offer of appeasement. But even as I'd said it, I had doubted its truth. At this stage, so soon after finding Kay, I sometimes saw my two mothers as archetypal opposites: one ethereal, beautiful, spiritual, the other earthy, practical, and real. But over time that could change. I doubted that I'd ever feel that old need so strongly again to go running to Mom with every little problem. I sensed that by finding Kay I had finally cut some apron strings that should have been cut many years before. Maybe this is what Mom meant by saying our relationship felt "different" now. Besides, as Kay and I got to know each other better and developed our own history, we likely would share our problems with each other. Automatically, I had slipped back into the confessional with Mom. I needed to put that attitude aside and move on.

"Have you felt like pulling away from me lately?" I asked her.

"Yes, to be honest I have, Pat," she said with a deep sigh. "It's a matter of self-protection, I guess. Wanting to move back so it won't hurt as much. Not being so involved with you for a while."

Now the anxiety rose in me again. Was it possible that she could simply walk away? That if my mother and I weren't in fact biologically related, and I had broken her rules, could she just turn her back and walk away? "But that would change our relationship, and maybe not in a good way," I began babbling, trying to push down my worry. "I think you and I have been able to be very honest with each other through this experience, Mom, and have opened up to each other more than ever before. At least, I've learned a lot about your feelings and your experiences since I started my search. We can build on that, can really know and appreciate each other better as people, as adults—"

"But no longer quite as mother and daughter?" she cut in.

"No, Mom, I didn't—"

"Let me finish, and let me say something I may live to regret," she said, firing her words rapidly at me, "but in all our new-found honesty, here it is: if in 1946 I had known what I know now, I would not have adopted you."

Her green eyes flashed with renewed anger. I stared at her. It felt like her words had blasted out a hole in the earth right under my feet.

"Or at least I would have thought long and seriously about it before I did," she added, perhaps in an attempt to soften her words; she must have registered the shock on my face.

I was silent for a few moments. What was she really saying? Had she ever loved me for myself, unconditionally, just for who I was, or had she loved me only as *her* child, as an extension of herself, a possession, a mirror to reflect her own successes? If she had truly loved me, surely she would have understood why I had needed to search for my birth mother and genetic roots and would have supported me in the effort. Maybe I had been right all along, overachieving through my childhood and teens because I knew I had to earn her love, because it wasn't freely given.

"Mom, is a child a possession?" I finally asked.

"Back when we adopted you, the whole feeling, the whole climate of adoption was different," Mom said, leaning back against the red velvet of the booth and deftly skirting my question. "This child was yours, period. Not to be reclaimed by the parents who gave it up, not to be shared, but yours, as rightfully as if you had given birth yourself. Maybe we were wrong then, and shortsighted, all of us — the birth parents, the adoptive parents, the agencies. Maybe we were living in a dream world, but we lived it all our lives with you, and it became reality. Until now. Maybe parents who adopt today feel differently. Maybe they can love less completely, maybe they can be content to raise someone else's child, not make it their own."

Her speech ended. My head was spinning. "'Make it their own'?" I repeated. Although I couldn't help responding to the simplicity and eloquence of Mom's words, the possessive attitude embedded within them nagged at me. There was indeed an implication that the child given up for adoption was just a thing, not a person, exchanged between parents through a middleman. There was no hint of any concern for the wishes and needs of the child in Mom's little speech — no empathy with the child's natural questions, desires, sense of loss, or yearning for roots and the true independence that that knowledge can bring, not even when the "child" grew up to become an adult.

"You know, I honestly don't think I feel that way about Derek and Tessa," I said. "Their lives are their own. They're dependent on me now, but I hope they'll be less and less so as they grow up. They'll love other people too, and I'm glad for that. That's the way it should be, if they're to be independent, to become themselves."

"But you'll never have to share them with another mother," Mom said, looking at me directly. "You'll never have to face that. It's quite a different thing from just 'loving other people.'"

"No, of course I won't. But I really feel that in all relationships, one love doesn't subtract from another," I explained.

Now I was surprised to notice that the anxiety, even fear, I'd felt in the face of her rejection hadn't made me cave in after all. Perhaps it was only the calm in the eye of the storm, but that afternoon I began feeling grown up in the presence of my mother for the very first time. I felt that I was drawing on an inner reserve of strength that I had forgotten about. I began feeling a strange but not unpleasant electric sensation all over my skin. "I do love Kay," I continued, meeting Mom's eyes, "but the feeling is very different from the love I have for you, and it doesn't take one little bit of love away from you. Don't you see that, Mom?"

"Well, maybe it doesn't take away," she replied, a hint of resignation now replacing the anger that had been driving her voice, "but it does *change*. And when you're right up against it, it's hard to grasp the distinction."

* * *

That afternoon Mom did the one thing that all my life I must have subconsciously feared she could do. It was what all my striving to be the good and perfect daughter had been designed to prevent. In effect, she rejected me. Giving in to her anger, she abandoned me emotionally as my birth mother had abandoned me physically so long before. She said that if she had it to do over again, she would not have adopted me.

It took me many years to even be able to wonder why I did not react with anger to match Mom's that day in Cannery Row. In fact, it was Tessa, now grown up and reading a draft of this book, whose question made me face what hadn't even occurred to me at the time. *Mom!* she wrote in red pen in the margin of my draft. *Why didn't you get angry at Nana? She was acting so selfish and mean!*

Anger is a difficult emotion for most families to deal with. But perhaps it was especially so in our case, because we were a family created through adoption, a family that, in Betty Jean Lifton's words, had to behave "as if" we were a normal, biological family unit. Perhaps anger is more threatening in adoptive families than in biological ones because the ties that bind us are more fragile, composed not of blood and sinew but of need and hope.

In our family, anger was habitually avoided, tamped down, and denied. We presented the smiling faces of the happy family to the world and also to each other. The only anger allowed expression when we were growing up was Mom's anger at Rick's and my occasional bad behavior. Then she would spank us, send us to our rooms, or deny us an anticipated treat. (Dad never once spanked us or meted out harsh psychological punishments.)

Similarly, that afternoon in Cannery Row, by habitual, unspoken agreement, the only anger allowed expression was Mom's. Yet I honestly did not feel any anger at my mother that day in Cannery Row — only disappointment, anxiety, and fear. What I wondered, discussing that mother-daughter lunch so many years later with Tessa, was whether I truly had not been angry at my mother, or whether anger had simply been drummed down deep inside so effectively in my childhood that I no longer even recognized that emotion, at least in relation to my parents.

I remember only one incident in my childhood when I gave in to open, hostile anger, indeed rage. I was very little, perhaps only three. Here is the fragment of memory, like a glass shard piercing the picture of my happy childhood.

My parents and I are sitting at the dining table in our small, second-story living area. They are in their usual places, and I am on my stack of yellow telephone books on a dining room chair. I begin crying and yelling at my mother and scramble down from my seat to stamp my feet on the wooden floor like an enraged little Rumpelstiltskin. I'm so small that my head barely clears the tabletop. In my anger, my whole body feels hot. I scream at her, holding my fists in tight balls, and hurl at her a version of the epithet that every adoptive mother dreads: "You're so mean! I hate you! You're just like Cinderella's wicked old stepmother!"

My mother, whose head I can just see over the top of the table, sits shocked and still, not saying or doing anything. I am screaming, sobbing, gasping for breath. I run into the bedroom and flop face down on my parents' bed. And then, as my howls shake the bed, my burning anger begins slipping into bottomless grief. A heavy sadness presses me down, immobilizing my small body and squeezing wails of grief and fear from my lungs. It seems to me that my parents are strangers, and I am all alone in the world. I feel like I am falling through a vast, dark, and empty space.

After a while, my father comes into the bedroom and sits on the edge of the bed beside me. As my body shudders in the aftermath of my tears, he pats my back and says gently, "You've been a bad girl, Patty, you have hurt Mama's feelings. You must go and tell her you're sorry."

I never became that angry again during my childhood. In comparison, my punching my friend in the mouth over the toy donkeys was more a corrective action than rage. Something may have been said or implied that evening when I was so young, or another evening, something to make me fear the withdrawal of love. Or perhaps my inner shift from anger to grief and that frightening sense of aloneness had been enough to do the trick. For over time, my rage got stuffed down into two boxes labeled "guilt" and "fear," which have been on hand to substitute for anger when it was called for.

I used to say with admiration that my parents never fought, never even argued in Rick's and my presence. But that was also bewildering, for it meant that I have found it very difficult to get angry with someone I loved and then make up. It took several years of my rocky relationship with Harald, and some fierce verbal battles, for me to learn how to release honest anger without sending the house up in flames.

A decade before the mother-daughter lunch in Cannery Row, a Peace Corps psychiatrist thought he spotted the anger lurking within me. All of us had several interviews with a psychiatrist during training, in addition to the personality tests we had to take. Unlike Paul, I didn't get "deselected" from the program, but I did get a shock during my final interview, when the psychiatrist assigned to me summarized his opinions. At the time, I was convinced that he must have been talking about someone else. He told me that I was highly antiauthoritarian, that I was angry and resentful toward my parents, and that I scored abnormally high in defensiveness for an American — 85 percent as opposed to 50 to 60 percent. (But that was no great obstacle to my teaching in Uganda, he assured me, since most Ugandans also scored around 85 percent in defensiveness.)

During those days of the Vietnam War, peace marches, and draft card burning, I wasn't displeased to hear that I was "antiauthoritarian." It made me feel like a member of the right crowd. I wasn't sure what "defensiveness" meant to a psychiatrist, but the term didn't bother me much, and I shrugged it off. But I was deeply shocked by his suggestion that I was angry and resentful toward my parents. I summoned all my reserves of defensive eloquence to try to convince the psychiatrist that his conclusion was totally erroneous. I protested that I loved my parents, had always been close to them, particularly my mother. I insisted that my childhood had been wonderful; I couldn't even remember my parents arguing. They had loved and supported me, given me all the understanding, material things, and opportunities I had ever needed or wanted. I said there must have been a mistake in the testing. All the while, the psychiatrist peered over the top of his reading glasses, watching me and smiling patiently.

His assessment bothered me for months afterward. I rolled it around in my mind, toying with the idea that okay, maybe I did have some anger or resentment toward my parents. How close *was* I to Mom, really, I asked myself. Although I talked to her about my hopes, plans, disappointments, successes, and boyfriends until my words trailed off into mindless repetitions, I recognized that there were things closer to my heart that I kept private, such as my spiritual leanings and my childhood thoughts about my birth mother. And how much did I know, really, about my mother's inner life? So little, I realized, that I had long ago concluded that she lived entirely in the here and now, the day to day.

So my relationship with my parents was something of a facade. So what? We were still a lot closer than some of my friends and their parents, who couldn't even talk about politics without setting off fireworks at the dinner table.

No, I thought, maybe it was my own dependency upon them, especially Mom, that I might resent. I could hardly make a decision without going over every little pro and con with Mom and Dad. Since leaving home, I had written long, detailed letters to my parents. If more than a week went by without my writing Mom and Daddy a letter, I began feeling that the disparate threads of myself were tangling beyond control. I needed to organize my jumbled features again into that intelligent, balanced, humorous, socially concerned, superficially philosophical, and somewhat emotionally self-centered person they recognized as their daughter.

But was I angry with my *parents* for my own hypocrisy and the double image I had created? By the end of Peace Corps training, having mulled it all over, I answered this question with a resounding "No." I reverted to my original opinion in the psychiatrist's office: somehow, the tests and his assessment were all wrong.

During that time, I did consider the possibility that some portion of my supposed buried anger might have been directed not at Mom and Daddy at all but instead at my anonymous birth parents, especially my mother. In dark moments, I believed that they had begun my life in an irresponsible manner and had then blithely given me away. They had acted selfishly, having their fun, and must have felt relieved to so easily toss me into the convenient wastebasket of closed adoption.

But during Peace Corps training in 1967, I did not allow myself to feel openly angry with my unknown birth mother, either. Instead, and characteristically, I was uneasy and guilty about having such dark and unfair thoughts about any of my parents, either my "real," everyday, adoptive parents, or my imaginary, biological, shadow parents.

* * *

On the day of our lunch in Cannery Row, any currents of resentment toward my parents, anger at my own dependence on them, possible suppressed anger at my birth mother for what she'd done so long ago, or anger at Mom's inability to budge, to understand me and my search, must have flowed far below the surprisingly calm surface of my consciousness. What shot to the surface like a leaping fish was my fear. The Peace Corps psychiatrist might have labeled it disguised anger, but to me it felt only like fear.

I feared pushing Mom over the brink and losing her love and our closeness. It was inconceivable to me that she and I could become estranged! She was my mom! Whatever Kay was in my life, I still wasn't sure, and we would probably be discovering the answer together for years. But even as Mom's eyes flashed with anger at me that day in Cannery Row, I knew for certain that I had only one mom. I needed to continue to try to mend fences.

I hoped that she would come to see, even years later, that she was still my "mom" and that no one else had taken that place. I hoped that her jealousy and possessiveness would someday give way to a more generous kind of love. But I doubted that could really happen. The best outcome, I believed in the aftermath of our conversation, was that over time Mom would become mollified, and our relationship would eventually fall back into its comfortable grooves. So in the few days we had left together, I didn't talk about Kay and Seattle. I tried to enter fully into those last trips to the beach with the children and Mom and Dad, the last trips to the park, the shopping excursions to load up on children' clothes and linens, items that always seemed to be less expensive in California than in Ontario. And Mom and I achieved a tentative, unspoken detente.

But inside, as my fear gradually subsided, I recognized how changed I was. I felt stronger psychically and emotionally than when we had arrived in California nine months before. I realized that soon I would be looking back on this time from far away, from Toronto and my life there. This present turmoil would then have receded, I hoped, yet the significance of what had happened over the past several months would remain clear.

As our time in California wound down, I felt more and more certain that I had been right to search for Kay. No matter what Mom said or did, no matter how much of her hurt I sucked up, I believed strongly, and still do, that it is cruel and unnatural to deprive any person of the knowledge of their biological parents and heritage. The closed adoption contract had only been between the parents, both natural and adoptive; it did not consider the adopted person in their own right, and it should have! Even though my actions had obviously hurt my mother, I did not feel I had anything to apologize for.

I also looked forward to many years in the future of learning more of Kay and becoming closer to her, having her become part of our lives. If I did harbor any buried anger, resentment, or other negative feelings toward her, I was willing to let those feelings surface in the future, whenever they were ready. But during those last days in California, whenever I thought about Kay, I was simply overcome by joy.

PATRICIA MOFFAT

CHAPTER 23

M onths later, back in Toronto, I dream that Harald, the children, and I are living in another rented house on another hill in Carmel Valley, a modern house made of wood, glass, and exposed brick. The main part of the house is one huge room, with a round stone fireplace in the living room and an open kitchen with handsome island work units at the other end. It's a grand house, with an Asian feel to the interior and the furnishings.

It's early evening. Mom, Dad, and Rick are with us, and so are some close friends or relatives: a handsome older woman with several companions about my age. We had planned to drive down to the Village to a Chinese restaurant for dinner, but for some reason none of the cars are working and it's too far and too dark to walk. There's a pleasant feeling of being stranded together on this hilltop. I decide to make do with whatever is in the kitchen for dinner.

"Pat, there's not enough food. All these people! You can't possibly do it," Mom says. The two of us are in the kitchen taking stock, while everyone else is in the living room chatting, calmly and confidently waiting for dinner. I lift the lids of a few red lacquer soup bowls and find that the only food in the house is about a quarter pound of hamburger, a few spoonfuls of leftover rice, some cashews, and a handful of bean sprouts.

"This is fine," I say. "I'll whip something up."

A little later, I call them all to the table and dish up good-sized portions of an interestingly spiced, stir-fried concoction to everyone.

As they are beginning their meal, I slip off into the bedroom wing carrying another plate of food. I walk down a long, bright, sky-lighted corridor, my bare feet sinking into the thick, pale blue carpet. I stop at one of the closed bedroom doors and open it slowly. The colors and fabrics in the room are deep and rich: reds and maroons with gold brocade. Seated in the lotus position on the rumpled white sheets of the bed is an arresting, almost absurd figure: a pink, plump, white-haired Buddha of a man, wearing an open dark red silk jacket with a golden sash. For all the oddness of his appearance, there is something reassuring and peaceful about him. He smiles at me as I enter the room, his young blue eyes twinkling in his old face, and he raises his right hand in greeting, with the first two fingers held up. I place the food before him like an offering on the bed and bow slightly out of respect. As I prepare to leave, he chuckles and widens his fingers, still upraised, to form a V.

I woke up from this dream feeling recharged. I'd had many dreams of Kay, members of the Seattle family, and Mom and Dad in the year or two after we left California, no doubt attempts by my subconscious to work out the meaning of my search and the experience of now having two families. But this dream was especially vivid.

For me, preparing food has always been more than putting physical sustenance on the table. It's an enjoyable, everyday expression of creativity and a way of giving love. And in the dream, above Mom's protestations that there wasn't enough food (enough love?) to go around, I had made enough. Somehow, the odd bits and pieces increased, in miraculous loaves-and-fishes fashion, and everyone received a goodly portion, all the close family I have: husband, children, parents, brother, and veiled birth mother, sisters, brother, grandfather.

The details of the dream suggested the spiritual orientation of my new Seattle family and also my own excursions into Eastern religions, first undertaken mostly out of curiosity to understand these relatives better, but then, increasingly, out of my own interest. And behind the scenes in the dream, meditating, detached from the action and yet fully aware of it, was the patriarch guru, Gramp — a little laughable in his Eastern garb, but also sympathetic, benevolent, and wise. Yet I felt the figure was larger than Gramp too, that somehow he/it embodied a Buddha-like spirit of balance, love, wisdom, and humor. And in his whimsical parting gesture, he conveyed something positive to me: that the scene out there in the main room was a victory. There was sharing and an abundance of love.

Or was my dream of the loaves and fishes and the "expanded circle of love" merely wish-fulfillment? Certainly, in the early months and years following my search, it seemed very unlikely that my two families would ever sit down together and enjoy a meal. What Mom most wanted, I realized not long after we returned to Toronto, was to go back in time, to pretend as if my search had not happened and Kay did not exist. After a few weeks of mild withdrawal from me after we left California, she seemed ready to resume our relationship on the phone and in letters as if nothing important had intervened. While I appreciated that was probably the most she could offer in the way of reconciliation, I did occasionally inject news of Kay into our conversations. I felt it was important to live the reality of having two mothers now, although I was still struggling to define what that meant.

After we returned to Canada, Kay and I continued to write long, frequent letters, talk on the phone occasionally, and exchange visits. We shared our thoughts, feelings, and dreams, and we sought to define our relationship. *I can feel you pulling back whenever the tone of our relationship becomes mother-daughterish,* Kay once wrote. And in a letter right after her first visit to Toronto, she recounted a dream: *I dreamt that you and Harald were out, and I was in the house with the children asleep upstairs. The doorbell rang. It was the mailman delivering a package. I went all over the house, trying to decide where to put the package. I opened all the cupboards and closets, and everything seemed to be nicely organized; everything was in its proper place, and I just couldn't decide where to put this thing. Finally I left it out in plain sight on the table, so you could decide where to put it yourself.*

Kay went on to say that she felt the package was herself, or perhaps our relationship, and that she didn't know yet quite how to fit into my life. Our relationship seemed so outside of our nicely set-up lives, where relationships were already defined (and, the meaning was implicit, where I already had a mother). After meditating on this a little while, I wrote back and told her that we should consider that I was building another room onto my house. She would not have to be squeezed into cupboards and closets that were already filled; rather, a new space was being created for her.

Even though I continued the long-distance balancing act with Mom, I did feel more and more at peace within myself over the months after I'd found Kay because of the rich communication between us. I felt more grounded now that I was able to see the roots of my life. I felt more confident and secure now that the monstrous old fears about who and where I'd come from had been put to rest. I felt lighter, happier, freer now that I knew my birth mother. I looked forward to a lifetime of discovery and increasing closeness.

* * *

For at least one other member of the family, having both Mom and Kay in our lives was not at all problematic.

A week or so after Kay's first visit to Toronto, Derek was playing in the bathtub while I sat cross-legged on the bath mat, watching him. He was four years old now, no longer a toddler. He lay back on his elbows in the tub, teasing the yellow rubber ducky with his toes. His cheeks were flushed pink from the warm water and steam, and his straight, white-gold hair floated on the water. He looked relaxed and thoughtful.

"Mommy, I was in your tummy before I was born, right?"

"Yes, you were. Do you remember it?"

"Remember it! No, I don't think so. Do you?"

"Sure I do. You moved around a lot. Sometimes you even kicked me."

He laughed and then looked up at me with concern in his long-lashed eyes. "I didn't hurt you, did I?"

"Not much. You were very little then."

Sighing, he abandoned the rubber duck and rolled over to float on his stomach, bracing himself with his elbows on the bottom of the tub. "Mommy, Tessa was in your tummy too, right?"

"Yes, she was."

"But not at the same time as me?"

"No, you're older. You were born first."

He paused before the next question and blew a little volley of bubbles on the surface of the water. "Well, was Daddy in your tummy too?"

I chuckled. "No, Derek. I'm not Daddy's mommy. I'm his wife."

"Well, whose tummy was Daddy in then?" More bubbles.

"He was in Omi's tummy. Omi in Germany. She's his mother."

"Oh... You weren't in Omi's tummy too, were you?"

"Nope. That would mean Daddy and I were brother and sister, like you and Tessa."

"Oh. Well, whose tummy were you in, then?"

I paused. I watched him floating in the water, his head expectantly turned to look up at me. I hadn't meant to tell the children so soon, but I just couldn't make up stories in answer to his questions. I knew, too, that my bright, sensitive son had been teasing me. This was the question Derek really wanted answered.

"I was in Kay's tummy," I said.

"*Kay's* tummy! You were?" Now Derek suddenly sat up straight in the tub, the water splashing lavishly around his little body. He looked at me intently. "Is Kay your mommy then?"

"Well, I'm lucky, Sweetie. I have two mothers. Nana is my mommy because I grew up with her. And Kay is my mother too, because I grew inside of her before I was born."

"But you didn't grow up with her?"

"No, I met her for the first time last year when we were in California."

"Well, why didn't you grow up with her?" he persisted, his forehead furrowing into a frown.

"Because she wasn't married when I was born. Back when I was a baby, there had to be a mommy and a daddy living together to make a family."

"Brian's daddy doesn't live with him. David and Anne's daddy doesn't either."

"No, they don't. Things are different now."

He was quiet for a few moments. Finally he asked, "If Kay is your mommy too, then I have three grandmas, don't I?"

I looked at him in astonishment. Somehow I hadn't expected this deduction so soon.

"Yes, you do."

Derek sank back into the water, splashing the rubber ducky again with his toes. A smile spread across his face. "That's nice," he said. "I like that."

PATRICIA MOFFAT

Me & Kay when Kay visited in the fall during Canadian Thanksgiving

Me, Mom, & Derek, Monterey

CHAPTER 24

I am the daughter of two mothers. Both were impressive, intelligent, interesting, warm, and loving mothers and mentors to me. I recognize aspects of myself that are like Mom and aspects that are like Kay. Both had their faults — Mom an irritating need to control, and Kay an occasional perplexing self-centeredness — but I never doubted that they loved me. I loved them both and still miss them today.

Kay became an important part of our lives soon after I found her. She visited us in Toronto every year, usually at Canadian Thanksgiving in October. She was part of Derek and Tessa's lives for twenty-one years. We probably saw more of Kay than of Mom and Dad over the years, because she made that commitment of regular visits.

Finding Kay was the watershed event in my life. It is very difficult to imagine what my life would be like now if I had not undertaken that quest. Finding my birth mother and my biological relatives, connecting with the roots of my life, had a huge influence on the course of my life.

I sometimes can't help playing the "what if?" game: if I had not found my birth mother, would I have changed my career? My life partner?

Writing a first draft of this book soon after the events took place led me directly into journalism. I never returned to high school teaching but worked as a magazine writer for twenty-five years, beginning with articles in science and medicine and then moving into business stories, women's issues, and mental and spiritual health. If I had not written about my search and discovered how much I liked to write, I'm quite sure I would have returned to high school teaching when Tessa started school. And then I would not have written an article in 1982 for a Canadian news magazine about John Moffat, a University of Toronto physicist whose theory of gravitation was challenging Einstein. We have been together ever since.

In the spiritual realm, Kay's beliefs were definitely "far out" compared to my conventional Presbyterian background and my state of numbed agnosticism when I met her. Kay told me that she had started receiving "automatic writing" from her mother four years after Eunice died. Kay said she'd felt an overwhelming need one evening to sit down at her desk with pen and paper. When she did, her arm seemed to move independently of her, and slowly, these words appeared in large, shaky writing on the page: *I love you. Mother.* Practice helped her to become a better, clearer receptor, she explained, and soon she was receiving automatic writing regularly not only from her dead mother, but also from her two spirit guides, "Nan" and "Neen." Kay filled notebooks with these messages, most of them consisting of advice on how to lead her life or answering her questions about the afterlife and life's purposes.

Kay read tarot cards and would often do readings for me. She meditated regularly and taught me to meditate. The first time she visited Toronto, she said that while meditating on our living room couch one morning (the same orange couch Harald had been sitting on when he suggested I search for my birth mother), she became aware of a group of our spirit guides gathered together up near one corner of the ceiling. She said she was aware of her two guides, and mine, and Tessa's, and they were talking happily, as if getting together again after a long absence. "See, there are reunions taking place here on more than one level!" she declared.

Kay talked to her plants, believed in and tried to train herself to become sensitive to communications from the devas, or spirits, of the plants in her garden and her larger environment. Kay was tantalized by UFO-ology, intrigued by the idea that more evolved beings from other planets, or from other levels of reality, could be helping humankind to evolve. (I know only one person who has ever seen a UFO, and it is not any of my New Age relatives, but my skeptical scientist husband, John.) Kay was interested in her past lives, but not obsessively so. She tried to understand the hints she received about them through dreams and meditation in order to help herself move forward better in this life. To Kay, life was a fascinating adventure. She approached it with love and trust, and a spirit of inquiry and fun, and had no fear of death.

Throughout our twenty-one years together, Kay constantly passed books on to me, books that would show me The Way, that would open me up to larger inner worlds, that would help me see the importance of living in tune with one's own Higher Self, of receiving guidance, of discovering one's own life plan, of trusting the universe. She often talked to me about such subjects when she came for a visit.

And sometimes I found it all extremely annoying! I see myself now, feeling harassed, struggling to make my magazine deadline so I can relax while she's here. We're in the kitchen. I'm cooking dinner for the five of us. The kids have homework to do and need to eat on time, and John will be walking in the door any minute. Kay, meanwhile, is sitting at the round pine kitchen table, her graceful fingers curled around a mug of herbal tea, oblivious to my stress, and she's talking, talking, talking to me about her kooky New Age ideas while I'm trying to concentrate on what vegetables to toss in the pot and what kind of salad dressing to make.

Kay was genuinely concerned about the progress of my soul. She was perhaps even more concerned about Keith's soul, because he wasn't just a science writer like me, but a real live scientist, a person who apparently believed only in a reality that can be checked out by the five senses and their extensions such as microscopes, telescopes, and accelerators. While I was occasionally irritated by Kay's attempts to convert me, my gentle half-brother could become quietly furious. Once, when Keith visited

John and me in Toronto, I mentioned what I felt were some positive aspects of Kay's philosophy. Keith became so agitated that he jumped up from the table and had to pace several times around the dining room before resuming the conversation and his breakfast.

Of course, Kay's relentless and charming pressure had an effect on me, just as water dripping on granite will carve out a hole eventually. And after all, my heart was not made of stone. Lurking not too far below the surface of my rational intellect was that awe-filled, religious child who had once prayed for and found a kitten and had watched three angels chatting on a sunny afternoon.

In the beginning of our relationship, I read about all the ideas that Kay threw at me. I tried to keep my skeptic's thinking cap in place, but I couldn't deny that these new ideas were exhilarating. I was especially attracted to Buddhism and to the idea of reincarnation. Over the years, I read more selectively, talked with people who were deeply involved in various spiritual and psychic phenomena, and eventually I researched and wrote magazine articles about near-death experiences, meditation, creative visualization, chakra energy centers, Therapeutic Touch, mind-body healing, and other subjects that I once would have considered downright weird. I learned to touch and influence the human energy field (which feels a lot like static electricity). Once, I was able to see it. I meditate regularly. I remain open to guidance and most frequently receive it in dreams or as flashes of intuition. I have experienced such flashes and dreams all my life but never paid much attention to them until I knew Kay. I have wandered in and out of different groups — from the Quakers to Buddhist meditation centers — but mostly, my explorations have been private.

Helping me to attune to spirituality again was Kay's greatest gift to me. I now understand that my search for my birth mother was not only an emotional search to answer questions about my origins — it turned out to have been a quest for spiritual renewal as well.

* * *

If finding Kay was the watershed event in my life, Mom was its bedrock. It is difficult to even imagine parents more positive, encouraging, and trustworthy than my adoptive parents, George and Kate.

Mom was a living example of her own "do all" and "be all" philosophy. I have written about her M.A. in psychology, her self-made profession as a landscape architect, and her vast amounts of energy for community service. Mom loved life in a very immediate way. She didn't spend much time pondering the meaning of it the way Kay did, but she loved people and related easily to people from all walks of life. She loved animals, too, and always had at least one "furry friend" nearby, whether a dog, cat, or horse. Unlike Kay, who had difficulty with men and was often critical of even the most unassuming members of the male sex, Mom related well to men and always had a few among her closest friends. Mom had a down-to-earth, no-nonsense approach to life, a throaty laugh, and a salty sense of humor, which she used often to ease social situations and lighten even the darkest moments of life. In August of 1994, when I phoned her at the hospital soon after she woke up after the surgery that had removed most of her pancreas and large parts of an alarming number of other organs, she announced, "I'm sure glad I'm gonna be around a while longer to heckle you all!" (Sadly, the massive surgery did nothing to prolong her life but only made her last few months more uncomfortable.)

One of my last memories of Mom, just weeks before she died, is pushing her wheelchair through the gardens at La Mirada in Monterey, a historical adobe house owned by the Monterey Museum of Art, to which she had devoted so much of her time and talents. Ostensibly, as we stroll along the paths, she is discussing the progress and future of the various garden beds with the head gardener. But really she is saying goodbye to this kind man she'd become so fond of over the years, patting his hand and conversing with him in Spanish, while tears roll down his wrinkled bronze cheeks.

Mom never did come to understand why I had to search for Kay, but she did get over the pain and intense jealousy she had felt during my search and for months afterward. Over the years, she came to feel certain, as I knew she would, that only she was my "real" mother. Contrary to what

Mom had feared the most during my search, it was Kay and I who became good, close friends, but it was Mom who always remained my "Mom." In the final years of her life, Mom often confided in me, using me as a sounding board, asking for my advice — reversing the mother-daughter roles we had played out for decades — because there was too much pain to handle on her own through Dad's decline into Alzheimer's. We became closer than ever during her final three years.

Though Mom was never capable of joining the post-reunion "widened circle of love" that Mary Ramos had spoken so glowingly about, she did ask about Kay from time to time, and I always kept her up to date with news from my Seattle family. Mom told me that Kay wrote a very kind letter to her after Daddy's death. But they never met again after that morning coffee in Monterey.

* * *

Over the years, I have thought many times about that searing conversation Mom and I had in Cannery Row four months after I found Kay. And I have understood that I never did have any anger toward Mom that day, despite my attempts to dig it out. Even at the time, I understood that her cutting words came from a place of deep pain, and so I only felt sad and sorry for Mom, and scared, too, that our relationship might fly off the rails. But I did not feel angry at her about that conversation either at the time or since.

Anger is an important issue for many adopted people. And so I still keep trying to root it out of all possible hiding places, to test whether I've only been repressing it or denying it. I've said I felt irritation sometimes at Kay's proselytizing. Is irritation the emergent tip of buried anger? If I didn't, after all, feel angry with Mom for her jealousy and her possessive attitude toward me, did I ever feel angry at Kay for having given me away in the first place?

Unlike Mom, Kay was not easily given to jealousy or anger. Her deep places of pain put forth other emotions, other smokescreens to hide the pain, to put off facing and feeling it. I realized quite early on, during my first visit to Seattle in fact, that Kay had a habit of hiding her head in the sand, particularly of not facing up to emotional pain. This included — and might actually have begun with — the pain of giving her baby up for adoption. The fact that she had never connected her work at the Children's Home Society (when she had transported homeless infants from hospitals to foster homes) with my adoption was the first hint. So many of her comments to me in those early days told of her avoidance of pain: she reminded herself of Scarlett O'Hara, who would "think about it tomorrow"; right after my birth she "turned her head away"; she never let herself really cry, was "just the stoic, going on." The modeling pictures we looked through that first afternoon on the couch in Seattle showed my slim young mother with a twenty-one-inch waistline again, just six weeks after I was born — as if her illegitimate pregnancy, and I, and her pain, distress, and panic had never occurred.

Here is how the avoidance of pain looks close up:

At last, Kay has come for a visit in November, our birthday month. She thought it would be fun to celebrate our birthdays together, she'd said, hers on the twelfth and mine on the nineteenth. Tonight, it's the Saturday between our birthdays, and this is the special dinner. We've had the roast chicken and braised carrots and salad and have been sitting and talking at the dining room table in the candlelight: John at one end of the table, Derek, fifteen years old now, at the other, Kay in the back so that she has the best view of a favorite abstract painting of John's, while Tessa, now thirteen, and I sit together opposite Kay and nearest to the kitchen.

"Run upstairs and get Kay's present," I whisper to Tessa in the kitchen as the kids help me clear the table. When they're both seated in the dining room again, I walk in slowly carrying the chocolate marble cake with its burning candles.

"Happy birthday!" we all sing. "Happy birthday, dear Kay, happy birthday to you!"

She looks around at all of us, smiles and laughs, surprised, says "thank you" as I place the cake in front of her, and then blows out all the candles.

As I cut the cake and pass the pieces around, Kay opens our present to her, a book. She says "thank you" again and smiles.

But there is something wooden in her manner. Her lovely face glowing in the candlelight appears blank. I wait for her to say "happy birthday" to me too, or to produce a card or a small present. I wait. A lump forms in my throat.

During the remaining days of that visit, I came to understand that Kay did not intend to be cruel at the birthday dinner. She was simply frozen. After thirty-one years of trying to forget about my birthday, and after almost a decade of marking the event from a distance, with a card, she was incapable now of opening that old wound she had kept so tightly closed. That evening, I saw the iron will in my birth mother's thin body holding her emotions down. Metaphorically, I saw her quickly turn her head away, as she'd done the day I was born. But I did not feel even a twinge of anger toward her, merely sadness.

Mom, too, was well practiced at bottling up pain. Just as Kay was "the stoic going on" after she signed the relinquishment paper, so Mom was able to put the pain of her infertility firmly behind her after adopting Rick and me and to "obliterate" the fact that we weren't her children by birth. When I first told my parents about my decision to search for my birth mother, Mom denied that she was at all disturbed by this news. My search was "something we can handle," she asserted. Only several months later did her buried feelings of anger and jealousy erupt.

It may be that the system of closed adoption itself encouraged everyone involved to bury pain. It was (and often still is) the fairy-tale solution to three very painful life situations: the childless couple can become parents, the unmarried pregnant young woman gets her problem solved, and the orphan gets a home. Everyone is happy — as long as the pain remains securely locked away.

Today in adoption there is more openness around emotions; there is often counseling for both sets of parents, helping birth parents to grieve the loss of their child and adoptive parents to grieve the loss of the idea of their biological child. There is even completely open adoption, where birth parents remain part of their relinquished children's lives, part of the extended family as the children grow up. But back in the 1940s when I was adopted, the "guaranteed" secrecy of closed adoption fostered the denial of pain.

It may also be that both of my mothers shared the attitude of locking pain away and soldiering on because, only six years apart in age, they were of the same generation. They were children and teenagers during the Depression, and young women during World War II. And in those challenging times, hard work, bravery, self-sacrifice, and fortitude were the virtues that enabled individuals as well as society to survive and thrive. Ignoring personal pain, or at least moving on quickly from it, was the "stiff upper lip" necessary for survival. To give in to pain, even to cry it all out, was weakness.

I was born two months after the end of World War II and was thus in the vanguard of the Baby Boomer generation. In the world of relative peace and prosperity that we grew up in, our parents' values now seemed old-fashioned, even unnecessary. Boomers (as everyone knows and is sick of hearing about, especially our Gen-X children) grew up in an atmosphere that encouraged creativity and self-actualization. We were "into" encounter groups, new therapies, communes, sexual and psychotropic drug experimentation, and changing society. We tried hard *not* to bury personal pain; rather, we "worked it through." Out with self-sacrifice and in with self-actualization!

In this context, my search for my birth mother was an essential part of Boomer self-realization. How can one know oneself without knowing one's biological heritage? Such a question was irrelevant to the previous generation: my adoptive Mom simply did not think in terms of "knowing herself," she derided "naval gazing," and rarely thought about her heritage. I wonder whether the search-and-reunion phenomenon could even have taken off any sooner than the mid 1970s, which was when the early Boomer adoptees, having recently experienced the sixties, hit their twenties and early thirties with that one question still burning: How can I ever know who I am if I don't even know where I came from?

Yet despite generational differences, my search did not crack only me open emotionally and spiritually and set my life on a truer course. I know that it also helped both of my mothers to release locked-up pain and find some peace. For Mom, the months of my search and the first several months after I'd found Kay were very painful. She shed many tears as she was taken back to her twenty-five-year-old self and grieved anew the loss of her fertility. Shedding the illusion that I was her child in all senses, that she possessed me somehow, that our relationship and our family were a fortress, safe from incursions by "that other mother," was extremely difficult for her.

Kay began releasing her bottled-up pain from my birth fairly soon after I found her. She cried on the phone before we met in person; we cried together when she visited in Carmel; and one of her finest moments in my memory was that morning in Monterey when she stood in my parents' living room and thanked them, wept, and then clarified her feelings to make sure they understood.

The final release of Kay's pain came as she lay dying. In a letter not long after I'd found her, and before we met in person, she had written: *I promise I won't be overcome with remorse or guilt if I decide I did the wrong thing, because for that time and at that time it was the only decision I could have made.* Yet a few weeks before she died, she broke that old promise. Kandy, Keeva, and I had been taking turns sitting with her after she'd stopped eating and drinking and lay waiting for death. On this particular night, it was my turn. I was sitting beside her bed, knitting, and thought she was asleep.

The light on the nightstand across the bed shines warmly behind Kay, outlining her profile in translucent pink. I wish I had a pad of paper. I would love to draw her face in this light.

Suddenly, her left hand forms a fist. She strikes it hard against the sheet again and again, while her features distort into a rigid frown and tears squeeze out of her eyes.

"I'm a terrible person!" she suddenly cries out. Her eyes open, startled, and stare at the ceiling. "I did such an awful thing! I gave my baby away! My own baby! How could I have done such a terrible thing?"

Between her sobs, she says she's been having disturbing dreams that have shown her what a bad person she is. She's feeling such remorse, she says, for having given me up and then marrying Carl just six weeks later without

even loving him, just to try to make herself settle down and be respectable.
She cries harder, hitting her fist with ever greater force on the bed.

I am alarmed; I'm afraid she could hurt herself. I have never seen such
anguish in her before, or in anyone, in fact. Even though I sense she needs to
walk through this grief before she can die peacefully, I'm shocked to witness
it. So close to death, I fear she might cross over in this self-hating state.

Her cries string out into a long, high-pitched keening. Her eyes are tightly
closed again, leaking tears. Trembling, I place my knitting on the floor and
gently hold her left fist in mine, stopping its piston-like pounding. I smooth
her fingers out and talk soothingly to her, using whatever words come to
mind. They are the old words, which we have used over the years to salve
that first wound of parting: "Kay, you mustn't say these things. You mustn't
think such bad things about yourself. You did the very best thing you could
have at the time. I don't blame you at all. I can't imagine my life without
Mom and Dad as my parents, and I'm so grateful that you and I have had
all these years to be close. Try to relax now. Everything is fine. I love you."

Her cries weaken, but her tears still flow. She doesn't look at me yet. "No,"
she whispers, "you don't understand. It was a terrible thing that I did, the
worst thing in my whole life. How could I have thought I was a good person
all these years when I did such an awful thing?"

Kay's anguish that night was so powerful that it struck me it must
have been the first time she allowed herself to fully grieve giving up her
baby, an event now more than fifty years in the past. Understanding her
belief system as well as I did, I knew it would be important to her to die
having cleared out that hidden painful spot. Otherwise, the wheel of
karma would have to run in that same groove again and again, having
her repeat similar losses until she finally accepted responsibility for her
act and felt the anguish of it.

* * *

Loss. Kay lost me and I lost her. Even though we finally found each other
again, the old pain never entirely disappeared. This is the legacy of closed

adoption for me: loss and the fear of abandonment. Other adoptees may be angry and may lash out against "the system" or act out against their parents, adoptive or biological. But what stuck within me is a sadness that must have come from that first separation, and a fear of being abandoned again.

So many good things came out of my growing up in a loving adoptive home and from searching for and finding my birth mother. I love those moments when I suddenly realize, "Oh! This is like Kay!" or "This is like Mom!" Somewhere along the way, I lost my stage fright and, like Mom, I now enjoy chairing a meeting or speaking to a packed room. A new mini-passion is knitting socks, and sometimes in the evening as I sit knitting in rounds with five needles, I think how much fun Kay would have had with the textures and colors of the wools, how we would have enjoyed learning this skill together. When I plant my garden every spring, both of my mothers are in my head, giving advice on what to put where. Mom's influence I feel on large projects, whether writing or community work, helping me to be efficient in organizing my thoughts and my time. Kay's influence I feel in deciding what projects to undertake in the first place, by getting in touch with and then following the desires of my heart. I'm glad I soaked up Mom's wit and balanced, humorous outlook on the problems of everyday life. And when I look in the mirror these days, getting older, I'm glad to see Kay's familiar mouth and jawline emerging. I'm often startled to catch a glimpse of her beautiful profile, high brow, and cheekbones in Tessa.

Though there are constant reminders of how rich my life has been with my two mothers, I believe that my core sadness, sense of loss, and fear of being left alone will never disappear. Deep inside of me even today remains that stunned newborn, whisked away from her mother, whose lovely face was turned aside; inside is the sobbing three-year-old floating alone in a dark void and the perfectionist child working feverishly throughout her childhood and adolescence to earn and keep her parents' love.

My search, my reunion with Kay and my biological family, all the life since then, and the processing of my emotions have helped me to see these core issues. Meditation helps to handle them. I've learned that the important thing is not to bury the painful demons, but rather to allow the feelings of sadness or loss or fear to surface when they need to. Then they will pass away for a while, and the waves of wonder and gratitude will return.

Derek & Tessa
almost grown up

Brother Keith Kroll

John & Dad,
Monterey Wharf

Our last vist to Kay, March 1998.
Derek, Marie, Keeva, Kay, and me.

EPILOGUE

It is now forty years after the events in this story took place. What has happened to everyone, and what did it all mean?

Easiest to talk about are the life changes that have occurred. First, some important people in my life have died.

Gramp died in his sleep in 1989 at age ninety-two. Despite his dismissive remark about fiction at our family reunion lunch, Gramp spent decades researching and writing a powerful historical novel about the native people of the Pacific Northwest titled *Kayhut*, which Kay published after his death.

Dad developed Alzheimer's in the late 1980s and had to be hospitalized for his own protection, and Mom's, during the final year of his life. He died at age seventy-nine in December of 1993.

Mom lived less than a year after Dad died. Worn out from his lengthy illness, she died of pancreatic cancer in November 1994, only three months after her diagnosis and surgery. She died at home in Monterey, with her many friends visiting daily, Derek and Tessa phoning frequently, and Rick and me caring for her. She was eighty years old.

My birth brother, Keith, was one of the gentlest, kindest people I ever knew. As a scientist, a heart physiologist at the University of Washington, and a lover of art and classical music, he had much in common with my husband John, a physicist and also a painter. Keith died of stomach cancer in July of 1997 at the age of forty-eight.

Only ten months later, Kay died. When her ovarian cancer was diagnosed in November 1997, she refused medical treatment and prepared for her death. She insisted on one last trip to visit us: Kay, Kandy, Keeva, and Tessa joined John and me for a week in Florida in February 1998. Derek visited her with me a month later on Whidbey Island. That May, at seventy-six, Kay died a pain-free death at home without any medication and with her family close by.

Uncle Jack went on from Washington State senator to three terms in the U.S. House of Representatives, beginning in 1994. He was one of the Republican congressmen who voted for every article of impeachment against President Clinton. He died in 2007 of Alzheimer's.

There have been other changes.

Rick searched for his birth parents several years after I did. He found both and developed a closer relationship with his birth father than his birth mother. His birth family, like mine, has roots in Washington State, where his birth father still lives. During Rick's search, Mom and Dad were more supportive than they had been with me. Rick is divorced and is retired from elementary school teaching. Tragically, in November of 2018, he lost his home and a lifetime of memories in the Camp Fire in northern California.

As I believe Kay always knew I would, I left Harald in 1981, when Derek was seven years old and Tessa was five. We had joint custody of our children for the rest of their years of growing up. It wasn't an easy childhood for them being shuttled back and forth between two houses all the way through high school, but they did grow up with both of their parents and knew how much we both loved them. Harald still lives in Toronto, in the house we shared when our children were small. He has not remarried.

In 1982, I met and fell in love with my husband, John, and we married in 1986.

Paul and I are still in contact. He is retired from teaching and lecturing. In his late sixties he did what he once thought he would never do: he married a bouncy, warm Australian named Georgia, and they live together with their two dogs on the Oregon coast.

Derek and Tessa are in their early forties now. Tessa is managing director of the Canadian operations of a global digital media company and a divorced single mom of our littlest grandchild, Georgia. Derek, too, is divorced. He is working in England as a consultant in a wealth management firm and is father to identical twin sons, Jasper and Nathan, and their sister Clara.

Since Kay's death, Kandy and Keeva and I try to get together every year and keep in touch by email. It feels to me like they have always been my sisters. Kandy lives in Seattle surrounded by her beautiful garden, and Keeva lives near the old family property on Whidbey Island.

I stopped smoking in 1985.

* * *

My birth father has been a shadowy figure in this memoir, as indeed he has been in my life. Soon after becoming a mother myself, I became driven to find my birth mother, not so much my father. I needed to know why she had given me up because I could not imagine ever giving up my children. Thinking about my birth father was always a more abstract exercise, particularly after Kay told me he had not even known she was pregnant.

But now, aware of the end of my life gradually approaching, I think about finding closure regarding my father, too. Though it is unlikely he is still alive, perhaps I could find descendants of his, and relatives of mine, through commercial genetic testing. I would like to learn who he was, what his life was like, and what he may have passed on to me, my children, and grandchildren.

George and Kate

Kay

ACKNOWLEDGMENTS

There are people to thank who helped me find my birth mother and family back in 1977, and there are people who encouraged and helped me in the writing and now publishing of this book over many years.

The people who helped in my search all appear in this memoir. My relationship with my ex-husband was difficult, but I will always be grateful to Harald for nudging me into searching in the first place. Elaine Durham, my friend in Seattle, was essential to my search. I can't imagine having success without her help, especially back in those days before computers and the Internet. Elaine has remained a good friend all these years. Mary Ramos of ALMA provided, as she said, the "permission" for me to search, and valuable advice along the way. Two pioneers whom I did not meet in person, but whose books I devoured during my search, were Betty Jean Lifton (*Twice Born*) and Jean Paton (*Orphan Voyage*).

Loving thanks to my birth family — members both living and now dead — for welcoming me so warmly forty years ago. Special thanks to my sisters, Kandy and Keeva Kroll, for being close all these years and for reading and commenting on a long draft of this book, giving me encouragement every step of the way.

Loving thanks also to my adoptive family. Rick and I are still close, talk often on the phone, and visit when we can. Thanks to him, too, for reading a draft of this book and being so engaged in it and positive. My cousins, Jeff Dietterle and Sue Ellen Dietterle, who are also adopted, have generously shared their experiences of search and reunion with me. No two experiences are the same.

As for this memoir, I am grateful to my two New York agents, Kate Somers in the late 1970s and Joelle Delbourgo in the early 2000s, for having had faith in the book. It appears, though, that now is the time for publishing this memoir, not back then. One feels a groundswell of interest in biological relatedness and family connections building today, with the millions of people who are involved in genetic testing and searching for relatives through companies such as Ancestry.com and 23andMe. I think that though the process may be different now, and certainly faster, the emotional impact of these quests is quite similar to what I and others experienced from the 1970s on in breaking through the secrets of the closed adoption system. Finding family is an emotional journey, whether it is done entirely through old-fashioned detective work or aided by DNA testing.

Thank you to my Toronto editor and publisher, Alex Wall, for his enthusiasm for this book and his willingness to take it on — and his interest in my dozens of family photos! — and to good friends Marty and Colleen Myers for bringing us together.

I have worked off and on (mostly off) on this memoir for over forty years, writing the first draft of it only a few months after the events took place, with my detailed journals in hand, in the fall and winter of 1977. I feel gratitude to Joyce Tyrrell for the early-morning peace and quiet of her boathouse at Georgian Bay where I started my first draft. Taking a Freefall writing course in 1993 from Barbara Turner-Vesselago spurred my interest in returning to this manuscript after almost two decades of neglect.

In the late 1990s and early 2000s, I belonged to a small writing group of fellow journalists wanting to move into memoir or fiction, or already published book authors. All of us were working on novels or memoirs and took turns reading aloud and getting feedback from the others in a supportive and trusting atmosphere. Many thanks to my Toronto writing group: Bev Biderman, Sarah Jane Growe, Kim Pittaway, and Barbara Turner-Vesselago.

Thanks, too, to a great many people in the magazine business in Canada and the United States who helped me hone my writing skills over twenty-five years of journalism, too many people to name, but including John Aitken, June Rogers, Tom Hopkins, Keitha McLean, Rona Maynard, Val Ross, Gail Adams....

Thanks to our adult children, Derek and Tessa, and Sandra and Tina, for their support and encouragement over the years. Finally, I can't imagine summoning up the courage to finish this very personal memoir and get it published without the constant love of my husband, John. He is my center, there for me every day.

Waterloo, Ontario
May 2020